Exodus

A Commentary for Children

Herein is Love
COMMENTARY SERIES

Exodus

A Commentary for Children

Nancy E. Ganz

© 2002 by Nancy E. Ganz

ISBN 0-9723046-1-4 (previously ISBN 0–9688830–2-8)

Shepherd Press
PO Box 24
Wapwallopen, PA 18660
www.shepherdpress.com
(800) 338-1445

Graphic Layout & Design: Tobias' Outerwear for Books (www.tobiasdesign.com)
Production: Andrew MacBride

Cover Artwork: Nicora Gangi—www.machairastudio.com
Cover landscape is from her original pastel entitled "Isaiah 64". The prophet
prayed to the Lord, "Oh, that You would rend the heavens and come down,
that the mountains would tremble before You" (Isaiah 64:1).

Unless otherwise noted, Scripture is taken from the Holy Bible,
New International Version (NIV), © 1972, 1976, 1984 by the
International Bible Society.

Manufactured in the United States of America

Dedication

To my daughter, Shoshannah

Acknowledgements

The many books by Jewish author and holocaust survivor, Elie Wiesel, have deeply affected me over the years. I thank him for his agonizing testimony and for sensitizing me to the persecution of his people. Please pray with me that the LORD, the God of Israel, would bless him and save him forever.

Once again I am indebted to Bible commentator Matthew Henry, whose works unfailingly instruct and inspire me in my study of God's Word.

I also want to thank the many pastors, elders and friends who have given me words of encouragement along the way, especially my own husband, Dr. Richard. L. Ganz, who has supported me in this work from its inception.

Finally, I offer my sincere thanks to two artists: Stas Jesionka, for his technical work on this book, and Nicora Gangi, for another landscape of splendour.

CONTENTS

INTRODUCTION

E xodus is the second book in The Gospel According to Moses, which continues the blessed proclamation of God's great LOVE and mercy and salvation for His people. The LORD of LOVE, "the Father of compassion and the God of all comfort" (II Corinthians 1:3), does not suddenly appear in the New Testament as some new god. No, the one and only God, who is the same yesterday, today and forever, was there from the beginning; He was there before the beginning, and He continues the revelation of Himself and His great LOVE in Exodus. In this book we see God raising up Moses as a deliverer for His people. In this Moses was a type of Christ, foreshadowing the Messiah, who would save His people from their sins and rescue them from the bondage of Satan, the power of death and the agony of hell. God's great deliverance in Exodus, which undoubtedly displays God's LOVE for His people, nonetheless points beyond itself to a greater deliverance in Jesus Christ. In Exodus we also see the mercy of God in establishing Moses as the mediator between Himself and the people. In this Moses was again a type of Christ, foreshadowing the "one mediator between God and man, the man Christ Jesus" (I Timothy 2:5). Moses, mediator of the Old Covenant in Exodus, points to Jesus, the Son of God, "the mediator of the New Covenant . . . the mediator of a better covenant, which is established upon better promises" (Hebrews 9:15;8:6). In Exodus we also see God's LOVE in appointing a high priest to represent the people and by establishing the entire system of sacrificial worship by which the people might receive cleansing from their sins, but the ministry of Aaron pointed to the future, to a greater High Priest, a greater sacrifice, and the demonstration of a greater LOVE. "Herein is LOVE: not that we loved God, but that He loved us and sent His Son as an atoning sacrifice for our sins" (I John 4:10). Through the entire book of Exodus we see the LOVE of God shining forth in splendour. We see it in the burning bush, as God calls Moses to rescue His people; we see it in the wilderness in the pillar of fire, as God leads His people on their journey; we see it on the top of Mount Sinai, as God gives His people the Ten Commandments; we see it within the tabernacle, as God condescends to dwell in the midst of His people. In Exodus God's LOVE is demonstrated again and again for His people—as He rescues them from Egypt, as He baptizes them in the Red Sea, as He provides for them in the wilderness bread from heaven and water from the rock, as He bestows upon them His holy Law, as He establishes His covenant with them, as He sets up His tabernacle among them. Exodus is filled with the LOVE of God for us, and so for us it is a book which fills us with hope and faith and joy in the LORD. It is a book which fills us with praise for our God.

THE JEWISH PROBLEM

- Exodus 1
- Psalm 83:1–4
- I Peter 2:9, 10
- Revelation 12

Long ago God spoke to Abraham and promised, "I will make you into a great nation and I will bless you" (Genesis 12:2). God also promised to give Abraham the whole land of Canaan; He said, "Lift up your eyes from where you are and look . . . All the land that you see I will give to you and your offspring forever. And I will make your offspring like the dust of the earth, so that if anyone could count the dust, then your offspring could be counted" (Genesis 13:14–16). Again God spoke to Abraham and said, "Look up at the heavens and count the stars—if indeed you can count them. So shall your offspring be" (Genesis 15:5). Another time God said, "I will surely bless you and make your descendants as numerous as the stars in the sky and the sand on the seashore" (Genesis 22:17). God repeated this promise when He spoke to his son, Isaac; God said, "I will bless you and will increase the number of your descendants" (Genesis 26:24). This promise was repeated to his son, Jacob; God said, "I will give you and your descendants the land . . . Your descendants will be like the dust of the earth, and you will spread out to the west and to the east, to the north and to the south" (Genesis 28:14). Again God spoke to Jacob and promised, "A nation and a multitude of nations will come from you . . . and I will give this land to your descendants after you" (Genesis 35:11, 12). God also promised Jacob, "Do not be afraid to go down to Egypt, for I will make you into a great nation there" (Genesis 46:3).

So Jacob and all his descendants went to Egypt. They were not yet like the dust of the earth or the stars in the sky or the sand on the seashore. At that time they could be counted easily; the descendants of Jacob numbered seventy. After a few years there, Jacob died in Egypt. His twelve sons also died in Egypt. Then that whole generation passed away. All the children who had been born in the promised land, all Jacob's grandchildren who had made the long journey from Canaan, they died in Egypt too. Soon, there was no one left alive who had even seen the land promised to their great-grandfathers, Abraham, Isaac and Jacob . . . but their descendants did not die out or disappear in the land of Egypt. No. God preserved them as a people, and they became known there as the Israelites. Egypt became the home and native land for this race of people, the Israelites, and for many years they lived peacefully and happily in Egypt. Except for Joseph's coffin that was awaiting burial in another land, the Israelites might have forgotten all about God's promise to surely bring them back to the land of Canaan, the land He had promised to give them.

People may forget God's promises, but God does not. God always fulfils His Word. He promised to make Israel into a great nation in Egypt, and that was exactly what God was doing! Although the old people were dying, new people were being born. The Bible records: *"The Israelites were fruitful and multiplied greatly and became exceedingly numerous, so that the land was filled with them"* (Exodus 1:7). God was forming a nation, "a great nation" for Himself. Why? God was making a nation to proclaim His praises. God was making a people for Himself to magnify and glorify His holy name (Isaiah 43:21). God's plan was to be worshipped on earth, just as He was in heaven. That was God's purpose . . . from the beginning! But God was not being worshipped anywhere upon the earth. There was not one nation whose God was the LORD. In every land in the whole world people were making idols and bowing down to false gods. Egypt was one of the worst places of all. It was a land filled with sorcery and idolatry. It was a kingdom that belonged wholeheartedly to Satan. But it was there, in Egypt, right in the heart of enemy territory, that God was forming a nation to worship Him.

That wonderful work of God would not go unnoticed or unchallenged.

The forces of darkness and wickedness, the spiritual forces of evil in the heavenly realms, would try to stop the growth of God's nation and the advance of God's kingdom on earth. Satan would try to destroy the people who were being prepared to proclaim God's praises. Satan would try to stop the Word of the LORD. Did God really say that He would make them into a great nation in Egypt? Satan declared that he would destroy the Israelites in Egypt! Did God really say he would make Abraham's descendants more numerous than the stars in the sky? Satan declared he would blot them out before they were born or swallow them whole the moment they arrived! Did God really say that the seed of the woman would crush the head of the serpent? That ancient serpent, who is the devil, cried, "Never! The Saviour will never come!" God had promised that the Saviour would come from Israel, so the dragon, who is the devil, stood in front of her waiting, "that he might devour her child the moment it was born" (Revelation 12:4). Yes, Satan would strike full force, focusing his attack upon the people of God's promise, the Israelites. Their days of peace in Egypt were coming to an end.

A new king came to power in Egypt. He did not know about Joseph or care about Jacob. He hated these Israelite "foreigners" who were in his land. They were too prosperous and too numerous. He saw God's blessing on these people, and his response was to hate them. Like many wicked rulers after him, this king began to spread lies (or propaganda) about the Jews. He told his people that they were a threat to national security. He said that the Jews were really enemies, seeking to destroy their country. "Look!" he said to his people. "The Israelites have become much too numerous for us. Come, we must deal shrewdly with them or they will become even more numerous and, if war breaks out, they will join our enemies and fight against us—and leave the country." Didn't Pharaoh want them to leave the country? Wouldn't that solve the Jewish problem? Why didn't he just send them out of Egypt and back to Canaan? Why? Because Pharaoh didn't want them to become a great nation somewhere else; he wanted to stop them from becoming a nation at all. His purpose was to exploit them and then destroy them. He was the first of many kings and countries after him to proclaim: "Let us go up and end their nation. The name of Israel shall be no more." The seed of the serpent hissed along with Satan's venomous threats. Men joined their voices with the hordes of hell to declare: "Let us go up and end their nation. The name of Israel shall be no more" (Psalm 83:4). So Pharaoh began to scheme and plot against the people of God.

The First Solution

Like many evil men after him (like Hitler in Germany in our own century) Pharaoh's first, shrewd, cruel step in solving the "Jewish problem" was to enslave the Israelites. He set slave masters over them to oppress them with forced labour. This would keep the Israelites from multiplying. They wouldn't have the heart or the strength to have children, if they were whipped and worked almost to death. Pharaoh knew that if he drove the Israelites hard enough and made them tired enough, their broken and beaten bodies couldn't make many more babies. If the Israelites were depleted of all strength and hope, they would cease to reproduce. Pharaoh would weaken and end their nation, while he strengthened and built his own nation. Whole cities in Egypt (and perhaps the famous pyramids too) were built for Pharaoh by the Israelites' slave labour.

However, something very strange happened: The more the Israelites were oppressed, the more they multiplied and spread. Neither the plots of hell nor the schemes of men could stop the promises of God! When the Egyptians saw this, they were terrified. They came to dread the Israelites, but they did not fear God. They did not bless those whom God had blessed. Instead, they tried even harder to curse them and crush them. Now the Egyptians worked their slaves ruthlessly, making their lives bitter with hard labour. Egypt became like a huge concentration camp, where the Jews were kept as prisoners to do the worst work in the nation. They did the sweat-pouring, back-breaking construction work, labouring with bricks and mortar to build the nation of Egypt and the kingdom of Pharaoh . . . but still they reproduced at an alarming rate, for God was making "living stones" and building them into His nation and His kingdom on earth. The more the Israelites were oppressed, the more they multiplied and spread. Thus Pharaoh's first solution to the Jewish problem failed.

The Second Solution

Pharaoh decided that, if he couldn't keep Jewish babies from being born, then he would eliminate them another way. He would kill them while they were being born. How? He had a very easy and evil solution. The king of Egypt ordered the Hebrew midwives to kill all the baby boys as they were being born. Pharaoh said to the midwives, "When you help the Hebrew women in childbirth . . . if it is a boy, kill him; but if it is a girl, let her live."

Why? Pharaoh's reason was to make sure that there would arise no young man in Israel, who could lead a rebellion against him, or any other young men, who could form an army against him. But the invisible angel, that despicable devil, who was standing in the unseen realms behind Pharaoh, had his own reason. Satan's reason was to devour the promised Son, by killing every male child, to make sure that there would arise no Saviour from Israel to crush him. Yes, the great dragon, that ancient serpent called the devil or Satan, "stood in front of the woman who was about to give birth, so that he might devour her child the moment it was born" (Revelation 12:4). That spirit of anti-Christ was at work in Pharaoh's heart too, as he did the deeds of his father the devil, who was a liar and a murderer from the beginning. To annihilate all of the sons of God—that was Pharaoh's plan; to annihilate the Son of God Himself—that was Satan's plan . . . but neither one could stop the promises of God. Not even the most powerful man on earth (like the king of Egypt), nor the most powerful demon in hell (like the devil himself), could stand in the way of the Word of God.

The LORD used two, humble, Hebrew women to thwart all their wicked designs. The LORD used two, simple, single women to defeat His enemies. The midwives' names were Shiphrah and Puah, names which are forever recorded among the righteous and courageous on earth. These two midwives feared God more than the king, more than death. They did not do what the king of Egypt had ordered them to do; they obeyed God, and they let all the baby boys live. They continued their blessed work, which was to help the children of Israel—all of them, both boys and girls—come safely into the world. These two Hebrew women, Shiphrah and Puah, risked their own lives by disobeying the king. It would only be a matter of time before Pharaoh found out, before it was reported that baby boys were arriving at the same alarming rate among the Israelites. The day the midwives dreaded came. Pharaoh summoned them and demanded an explanation. "Why have you done this? Why have you let the boys live?" the king raged. What could they say? The midwives answered that they were not to blame. They said, "Hebrew women are not like Egyptian women; they are vigorous and give birth before the midwives arrive." They said that the Hebrew women were so strong and their labours so fast, that the baby boys were already safely in the mothers' arms, before they made it to the birth. It was unlikely that Pharaoh would accept their excuse; he was such a hard, cold, proud, shrewd, cruel man. What would happen to them now? Nothing, because God was protecting His two faithful maidservants. God was kind to the midwives, and Pharaoh, against his own nature, let them go. Perhaps Pharaoh feared that what they said was true, that the Hebrew women really were strangely, almost supernaturally, strong, which accounted for their population growth. How God worked in Pharaoh's heart and mind, we do not know, but it was an amazing deliverance! The midwives walked away . . . alive. Because the midwives feared God, He gave them back their lives in another way too: God gave these two women families of their own. These women, who had been barren, the LORD now blessed with their own children. The LORD also blessed the Israelites. The people increased and became even more numerous. Pharaoh watched helplessly, as his second extermination policy failed. He had not been able to stop Israel from becoming a great nation. God's Word was being fulfilled.

The Final Solution

Satan persevered in his assaults against the people of God. So did Pharaoh. The king of Egypt had a new plan, a new solution to the Jewish problem. Pharaoh gave this order to all his people: "Every boy that is born to the Hebrews you must throw into the Nile, but let every girl live." Pharaoh plotted to drown all the baby boys like rats in a river. He had tried to stop these vermin from being born; he had tried to kill them during their births; now he would kill them after they were born. This time he would succeed. This time he would use his own people and his own soldiers, to carry out his plan. Pharaoh would send his S.S. men (Satan's Service men) to search the Hebrew homes. Any baby boy that was found by them would be seized from his parents and thrown into the Nile River. Any parents who hid their children would be severely punished; they would be put in prison or put to death. This was the new law of the land: *Every boy that is born to the Hebrews, you must throw into the Nile.* There would be severe consequences for any person, whether Hebrew or Egyptian, who disobeyed this law. This time Pharaoh's extermination policy did not depend on two Hebrew women; it would be carried out by the whole nation. This time Pharaoh's extermination policy would not fail . . . or would it?

"There is no wisdom, no insight, no plan that can succeed against the LORD" (Proverbs 21:30).

The teacher's guide for this lesson starts on page 194.

BY FAITH, THEY HID

Long long ago, in the days of Abraham, before he had any children at all, God made a covenant with him. As the sun was setting, Abraham fell into a deep sleep, and a thick and dreadful darkness came over him. Then the LORD said to him, "Know for certain that your descendants will be strangers in a country not their own, and they will be enslaved and mistreated four hundred years" (Genesis 15:12, 13). God does not lie. Those words came to pass. Those evil years of brutal bondage eventually came upon the descendants of Abraham in the land of Egypt. A cruel tyrant, filled with hatred and bloodshed, rose to power and ruled with terror. This Pharaoh oppressed the Israelites; he enslaved them treacherously and worked them ruthlessly. This king was so wicked that he forced the Israelites to throw out their newborn babies, so that they would die. By the king's order, all their baby boys were being drowned in the Nile River.

However, the time was drawing near for God to fulfil His Promise to Abraham to give his descendants the land of Canaan. The LORD also said to Abraham, "But I will punish the nation they serve as slaves, and afterwards they will come out . . ." The Exodus was promised by God. The LORD even told Abraham when the exodus would occur. He said that four hundred years would pass. He said, "In the fourth generation your descendants will come back . . ." (Genesis 15:14, 16). It was now the beginning of the fourth generation. Yes, the time of God's deliverance was drawing near.

The first generation of Israelites in Egypt had all died. Joseph and his brothers were gone. Preserved for us in the Scriptures (Exodus 6:13–27) is the genealogy of . . .

1. Levi, who was in the first generation. He had many sons and daughters and lived 137 years before he died. The name of his second son was

2. Kohath, who was in the second generation. He also had many sons and daughters. He lived 133 years before he died. The name of his firstborn son was

3. Amram, who was in the third generation. Amram had sons and daughters also. Amram lived 137 years. The names of three of his children were

4. Aaron, Miriam and Moses, who were in the fourth generation of Israelites in Egypt. God promised to deliver His people out of Egypt in the fourth generation.

Yes, the day of God's deliverance was drawing near, but what a dreadful darkness had descended upon the Israelites, as Satan escalated his assaults upon them in an attempt to stop the Word of God. What could be worse than what was happening to them now? Their boys were being killed and their blood was being spilled. Either they threw their babies into the Nile River or whole families were slaughtered by the swords of Pharaoh's soldiers. Life in Egypt was not only bitter; it had become a horror. Egypt had become a land of bondage, terror, torture and murder. Now, by the king's command, innocent Israeli blood tainted the waters of the Nile. That river, which had been God's gift to Egypt and a source of life and hope for them, had now become a river of grief and guilt as the bodies of drowned Hebrew babies floated downstream to become food for the hungry crocodiles. Yet into this time of terror and land of horror, came the grace and LOVE of

Almighty God. He had not forgotten His people or His promise. In the very midst of death and defeat, God would bring forth life and victory. In the midst of man's wickedness, God would display His justice and His righteousness for all the world to see.

This then is the story of the birth of Israel's saviour from that time of terror and that land of horror. It is one of the most wonderful stories in the whole world. It is also the story of a family, who lived by faith in the grace of God in the worst of circumstances. But most importantly, it is a story of God's LOVE, a story that shows the greatness of our God and the wonder of His works. It is a story that praises the LORD!

There was a man in the land of Egypt, named Amram, of the house of Levi of the people of Israel. Although he led a bitter life as a wretched slave, Amram married. He married a woman named Jochebed, who was also a descendant of Levi. After a time, this man and woman had children, at least one little boy and one little girl. It was sad for them to bring forth children into slavery, but they believed that these children were the LORD's good gift to them. They loved their children, who were a source of joy for them in their very hard lives. But the situation in Egypt grew steadily worse for the Israelites. The Pharaoh who ruled the land was an evil man. Eventually he issued a new command for the country: *every boy born to the Hebrews must be thrown into the Nile river.* Like every other Israelite family, Amram and his wife and children must have heard those words with great sorrow. They were already expecting another child. Another baby was already on the way . . . living and growing and moving within his mother's womb. In a few months Jochabed would give birth to another child. What would happen if it was a boy? Fear gripped the whole family. The parents wondered, "What will we do?" They must have prayed to the LORD to please send them another little girl. The children must have prayed earnestly for God to send them another sister, not a brother . . . please, not a brother!

The LORD always answers the prayers of His people, but not always the way they want. The LORD's Way is not our way. We have our plans, but God has His Plan. The LORD did not send the family of Amram a little girl. God sent them a little boy, a beautiful little boy, an extraordinary little boy. The moment the family saw him, they loved him. Every baby is a gift from God, but they could all see that this baby was a very special gift. There was something about him; he was not an ordinary child. This child was precious in the sight of the LORD—and in the sight of his parents. What were they going to do? Were they going to throw him away? Were they going to drown him in the river? Absolutely not! They knew now (now that their baby boy was cuddled in their arms) what they had to do. They had to live by faith, not by fear. By faith they had to hide their baby, not fearing the king's wrath, but trusting God's grace.

By faith these Hebrew parents hid their baby boy for three months. Each day they lived by faith, trusting God to protect them. Each night they lived by faith, trusting God to preserve them. For three months the newborn baby boy was cared for in his father's house, but always the family was in danger. Finally, his mother could hide him no longer. He had grown bigger and his cries had grown louder. He was no longer a tiny bundle, who slept or nursed quietly most of the time. He was getting harder and harder to hide. A wailing, kicking baby would surely attract the attention of a passing soldier with his killing sword. They must do something soon, before he was killed, before the whole family was killed. But what could they do?

The baby's mother decided it was time to obey the king's command and throw her baby into the river. She would obey the law . . . at least the letter of the law. She would put her baby boy in the Nile River, but not to kill him. No, she would put him there in a desperate attempt to save his life. The mother began to make a little boat for her baby. First she got a big papyrus basket with a tightly-fitting top. Then she coated the entire basket with tar and pitch to make it waterproof. Then she probably made a soft little bed in the bottom of it, nursed her baby to sleep, gently laid him in the basket, kissed his little cheek before she closed the lid, and then walked down to the Nile River, as if she were carrying a basket of laundry, hoping and praying with every step that a soldier would not stop her. Then, very gently she placed the little boat with its precious cargo among the reeds along the bank. Now it would be the waves of the river, not the arms of his mother, that would rock the little baby to sleep. How that poor mother must have wept as she let her baby go. How she must have prayed for God to guard him and guide him. She had put her beautiful baby into the river, but she had also put him into the hands of God to keep him, both now . . . and forever. Amen.

But what would happen to her beautiful baby boy, whom she loved so much? She had so many fears: Although she had placed the basket-boat among the reeds, perhaps it would drift free and float away, never to be seen again. Perhaps the little boat would sink and he would drown, right there in the shallow water. Perhaps a crocodile would discover him, rip open the basket and devour him. Perhaps a soldier would find him and kill him. Perhaps . . . perhaps . . . oh, she had so many fears, but she must live by faith. She could imagine many terrible deaths for her child, but she could not imagine how he would live or how God would save him. She just believed. In hope against hope, she believed that God would somehow rescue her baby. For three months she had hid her baby boy by faith. Now, by faith, she hid him in a basket-boat. By faith she placed him in the river . . . and into the hands of the mighty and merciful God.

The baby's mother could not stay to watch what would happen to her baby. It might attract some soldier's attention; it might put her baby in more danger. So she took one last look at the little basket-boat floating among the reeds by the river's edge, and then she left. However, she left her small daughter to watch over him. The little girl stood at a distance to see what would happen to her baby brother. Pharaoh's soldiers would not bother a little girl playing by the river and, although the baby was in the hands of God, perhaps God could use a pair of little girl's hands to help.

This was what happened: Pharaoh's daughter, the princess of Egypt, went down to the river to bathe. God was directing her footsteps to the right place. As her attendants were walking along the river bank, the princess noticed something floating among the reeds. It was a basket. The princess was curious to know what was in the basket, so she sent one of her slave girls into the water to get it. What could be inside it? The princess opened the lid, and there was a beautiful little baby. He began to cry, calling to her for help, and the princess felt sorry for him. "This is one of the Hebrew babies," she said. She knew that this little boy was supposed to die, and she felt very sad. She knew that her father had commanded these babies to be killed, drowned right here in the Nile River, but she did not want this one to be destroyed. Her father would give her what she wanted, and she wanted this baby to belong to her.

Then a little Hebrew girl bravely walked up to the princess of Egypt. She must have been frightened to speak to the wicked Pharaoh's daughter, but her mother had left her there to help her baby brother, and this was her chance. She suddenly knew how she could help. She asked the princess, "Shall I go and get one of the Hebrew women to nurse the baby for you?" Of course the baby was crying; he was hungry, and the princess could not nurse this baby herself. "Yes, go," answered Pharaoh's daughter. So the little girl ran straight home and brought the baby's mother. The princess of Egypt said, "Take this baby and nurse him for me, and I will pay you."

So the baby's mother took him, hardly believing what she had heard. Never had a mother so happily held her baby! Never had a mother so joyfully nursed her son! She had doubted whether he would live. It was beyond her hope that she would ever see him again. She had never dreamed that she would hold him again or nurse him again, and yet, here he was, nestled in her arms, happily and hungrily eating, as if nothing at all had happened. And now, for the first time in his whole life, he was safe. The family was safe too. He could cry . . . and they could laugh . . . without fear. This child belonged to Pharaoh's own daughter. No soldier could touch him, for he belonged to the royal family. He was protected by the king! He was safe . . . at last. God had rescued him beyond their deepest prayers and wildest dreams. God had brought that little boat with its precious cargo to the only port of safety in all the land of Egypt, the arms of Pharaoh's daughter. Had any other person found him, whether an Israelite or an Egyptian, he would not have been safe. Even if someone had dared to disobey Pharaoh in sparing his life, no one had the power to protect him. It was an amazing deliverance!

But what God did that day was more amazing than just rescuing one little baby. That was the beginning of God rescuing all of Israel. You see, when that baby grew older, his mother took him to Pharaoh's daughter, where he became her legal son by adoption. And the princess of Egypt named him Moses. One day God would use this same Moses to lead the people of Israel out of Egypt. And so, while Pharaoh's new extermination policy seemed to be working, it had in fact failed. It was the soldiers of Pharaoh who would be drowned; it was the people of Egypt who would be destroyed. The children of Israel would continue to multiply, filling the earth like the dust of the ground, like the stars of the sky, like the sand on the seashore, just as God had promised. And the deliverer of Israel was hiding in enemy territory. He was living as a prince right in Pharaoh's own palace!

The teacher's guide for this lesson starts on page 196.

BY FAITH, HE LEFT

- **Exodus 2:11–25**
- **Acts 7:21–29**
- **Hebrews 11:24–27**

M oses was born an Israelite. By God's grace his life was spared and by God's grace he spent the first few years of that life in his own home with his own family. During those few short years, Moses' father and mother must have taught him all they could about the LORD, the God of Israel, and the promises that He had given to His people long ago. They also must have told Moses about his own birth and the amazing way that God had delivered him from death. However, that precious time of loving and learning passed quickly. Too soon the day arrived when Moses' mother could no longer keep him. Once again he had grown too old; once again she had to let him go, entrusting him to the care of Almighty God. Yes, the sad day came when Moses' mother had to take her little boy to Pharaoh's daughter, and he would not come home again, for now Moses would be the son of an Egyptian princess. Perhaps Moses' new mother would allow him to have visits from his old Israelite nurse, but perhaps she wouldn't, and Moses' real mother might never see her little boy again. How sorrowfully she must have said "good-bye" to her small son, but thankfully, he was still alive! The other little Hebrew boys his age had all been killed. At least he was still alive, and he would be a prince, instead of a slave.

Moses began his life in his mother's arms and his father's house, but after he left his Jewish parents and Hebrew home, he was nurtured in another way of life. Pharaoh's daughter brought him up as her own son. Moses was born as an Israelite slave, but he was reared as an Egyptian prince. By birth he was a son of Abraham, but by adoption he was a son of Pharaoh. While the lives of the Israelites were made bitter by hard labour and cruel treatment, Moses' life was made pleasant by all the pleasures and treasures of Egypt. He was a prince now. While his people ate scraps and wore rags, Moses ate the finest foods and wore the finest clothes. While his people were worked and whipped as slaves, little prince Moses played with golden toys and sparkling jewels in the king's palace. As the young prince grew older, how easy it would be for him to just close his eyes to everything but the luxury all around him. Moses could simply forget about the lowliness and ugliness and bitterness of his people; he could forget his past, because what lay directly in front of him and all around him was a life filled with the pleasures and treasures of Egypt. Had they not been given to him?

Something else had been given to Moses: an education. He was educated in all the wisdom of Egypt, for even a prince must study. Even a young pharaoh must go to school to learn how to rule. Moses learned his leadership lessons well, becoming powerful in speech and action. One day Moses could lead the country. Perhaps one day Moses himself could be Pharaoh, the king of Egypt, the most powerful man in that part of the world. One day those magnificent monuments, those towering pyramids, might be built to honour him, so that when Moses' day had passed, his memory would not be forgotten. He too could be laid to rest, not with his fathers, but with the pharaohs. He too could be immortal in one of the "wonders of the world," the pyramids. There was nothing that Moses could not be—if he wanted it. All the wisdom and power, all the honour and glory, all the splendour of Egypt, lay before Moses. Had they not been given to him?

But Moses did not take them. For awhile he may have been attracted to these things; he even may have been delighted by them, but at a certain point in his life Moses rejected all that Egypt had to offer. When Moses had grown up to be a man, he refused to be known as the son of Pharaoh's daughter. Although this princess of Egypt had given Moses every wonderful thing this world had to offer, although she had given him everything—even his name, even his life—Moses refused to be known as her son. At a certain point in his life, Moses refused it all. He left the country and began a new life, a hard life. He lived as a wandering shepherd in a foreign land (just as his fore-fathers Abraham, Isaac and Jacob had done before him). The pleasures of Egypt—the fine foods, the strong wines, the elegant women, the beautiful music—were all forsaken by Moses. The treasures of Egypt—the gold and silver, the gems and jewels, the royal robes and fast chariots, the exquisite palaces—were all forsaken by Moses. For the next forty years Moses lived a very different life than he had lived for the first forty years. Now he lived in a tent, not a palace. Where he went, he walked. What he ate, he earned. He owned nothing, not even the sheep he tended. Now he wore the rough clothes of a shepherd and ate the plain food of a worker. The woman he married was not a princess, for he was no longer a prince. No one listened to Moses now. He may have been powerful in speech and action, but there was only a flock of sheep and a few shepherds to notice him. Moses was a nobody now, an insignificant man doing menial work in an obscure place. When he died, there would not even be a pebble—let alone a pyramid—to mark his grave. Who would care? Unlike the pharaohs' graves, no one would know where the body of Moses was buried.

So, why did Moses make that choice? Did he make a mistake? Why did he choose a hard life, instead of an easy one? Why did he choose a painful life instead of a pleasant one? Why did he choose a poor life, instead of a rich one? Why did he choose to be a lowly shepherd, instead of a mighty pharaoh? Why did he refuse all the pleasure and power and honour and splendour of Egypt? Wasn't it a bad choice? Wasn't it a foolish decision?

No, it was a very good choice, a very wise decision. Moses chose very care-fully, very deliberately—perhaps over many years. We read in the Bible that it was "by faith" that Moses refused to be known as the son of Pharaoh's daugh-ter. Was Moses simply choosing his natural mother, who had given him life, over his adoptive mother. No, for Pharaoh's daughter had also given him life. She had named him Moses, saying "I drew him out of the water." Many times Moses must have heard the story how Egypt's princess had rescued him, and he was grateful to her, but what Moses was choosing was to be a son of Abra-ham, rather than a son of Pharaoh. By faith he recognized that it was of much greater value. Moses believed in God and Moses believed in the Promises of God, and so he knew that his connection with Israel was worth far more than his connection with the royal family of Egypt. It was far better, richer and safer to be a simple servant in the house of God that to rule in the palaces of the wicked. Moses understood that the pleasures of sin and the treasures of this world are fleeting. How quickly they pass away, but the Word of the LORD endures forever. If Moses chose the pleasures of sin and the treasures of this world, he could enjoy them for only a short time (at the most, for his lifetime) and then he would receive the wages he had earned: eternal death! However, if he chose the Promises of God, including the greatest promise of all—the Messiah, the Saviour from sin and death—then Moses would have another reward: eternal life! Because Moses was looking ahead to that reward, he chose by faith to bear the disgrace of Christ and the distress of God's people. Moses reasoned that it was better to be mistreated with the people of God, it was better to be persecuted for the sake of Christ, than to die in one's sins. When the Messiah finally came to this world He said, "Blessed are you when men hate you, when they exclude you and insult you and reject your name as evil, because of the Son of Man. Rejoice in that day and leap for joy, because great is your reward in heaven" (Luke 6:22, 23). That was the blessing that Moses chose. That heavenly reward was what he had in mind when he made his choice. Moses understood that the *worst* of what God offers, (that is, distress and disgrace in this life,) is better by far than the *best* of what the world offers. Moses weighed accurately the temporal and the eternal, the short-term gain versus the long-term gain. Moses reasoned righteously that it was better to serve the God of Israel and live, than to serve the gods of Egypt (the gods called Ease and Affluence, Fame and Influence) and die. Moses understood that he was choosing between life and death, and he made the right choice. He chose life. Moses made a very hard, but very wise decision.

Eventually, Moses left Egypt "by faith." In his heart he left Egypt long before he left it with his feet, but finally he fled the country, not fearing the king's wrath, but trusting God's LOVE. Moses did not look back longing for all the beautiful, valuable, powerful things of Egypt. No, Moses pressed forward, by faith, fixing his eyes ahead on the One who cannot be seen. Moses persevered in his new hard life, because he was focused on the invisible God and His eternal reward. Yes, by faith, he left.

From the Palace to the Pasture

We do not know when Moses made that decision for God or when he first believed the promises of God. Perhaps as a little boy, before he was taken to Pharaoh's palace, his parents taught him diligently, day after day, about the LORD, the God of Israel.

Perhaps as a young prince in the palace Moses researched his roots, finding out all he could about the people of Israel. Perhaps as a young man he even viewed the coffin of Joseph and pondered the meaning of the ancient bones of his great, great–uncle awaiting burial in another land, a land promised by God to the Israelites, who were now slaves in Egypt. It was all very strange. And then there was the remarkable story of his own life. Both his Hebrew mother and his Egyptian mother told him how he had been saved. Moses must have wondered about this. God had rescued him when he was just a little baby floating in a basket in the Nile River. Then God had raised him from slavery to royalty. Why? Why had God spared his life? Why had God made him a prince? What did God want him to do? Could it be that God had raised him to this high position for the great purpose of leading the Israelites out of the land of slavery and back to that land of promise? Moses began to think that the answer was "yes"; God was going to use him to rescue his people. (See Acts 7:25.)

So Moses had a great secret that he carried in his heart. He was not whom he appeared to be. He looked like an Egyptian prince; he sounded like an Egyptian prince; he acted like an Egyptian prince, but really he was Israel's deliverer! The only problem was, Moses did not know how he could rescue the Israelites. So, year after year passed, hard cruel years for the slaves, while Moses remained as a prince in the palace with a secret in his heart, wondering what he could do for his people.

We do not know how long Moses envisioned himself as Israel's deliverer. We do know that one day, when he was a grown man, when he was forty years old, Moses decided to watch the Israelites at their hard work. It was a terrible sight. The slaves were treated ruthlessly, viciously. As Moses, the prince of Egypt stood watching, a cruel Egyptian master began brutally beating one of the poor Israelite slaves. (It was not an uncommon occurrence). Again and again the whip was cracked in his face and across his back. Moses heard the screams and saw the blood of a brother. This fellow Jew was going to be beaten to death right in front of his eyes! The moment had come for Moses to act. He couldn't just dream about rescuing the people of Israel someday in the future. He must act to save one Israelite right now! Moses looked around. There was no one else in sight, so Moses came to the defense of the Hebrew man. He killed the Egyptian and hid his body in the sand. How happy Moses must have been. At last, he had begun to rescue the people of Israel! It was not just a dream.

The next day Moses went out to watch his people again. Perhaps he could save another Israelite from death, but what Moses saw shocked him. Two Hebrews were fighting each other. Wasn't it bad enough that the Egyptians were beating them? Did they have to hurt each other too? Moses tried to reconcile the men. "You are brothers!" Moses said. "Why are you hitting your fellow Hebrew?" But the man who was mistreating the other shoved Moses aside and snarled, "Who made you ruler and judge over us?" Moses was stunned. He thought that the Israelites would know the answer to that question. Moses thought the Jews would realize that God was using him to rescue them, but they did not. His own people did not recognize him as their leader. They did not respect him as the one whom God had chosen to deliver them. His own people didn't realize that God had appointed him as a prince, so that he could save them. Instead they shoved him aside and snarled, "Who made you a ruler and judge over us?" How could they not know that it was God? Moses was stunned. How in the world would he ever be able to help these people?

But then something else was said which scared Moses. The man said, "Are you thinking of killing me as you killed the Egyptian yesterday?" Somehow what Moses had done had become known. Had the body been found in the sand? Had someone watched what had happened? Had the man he saved told others? The problem was, if this man knew, then other people knew too, and soon it would be reported to Pharaoh. Moses knew his life was in danger. Pharaoh would soon know Moses' secret, that although he had been raised as an Egyptian, he was still a Hebrew at heart. Pharaoh would know that, although Moses was a prince of Egypt, his love and his loyalty were for Israel. Pharaoh would know that an enemy was right in his palace, and Pharaoh would try to kill him.

What Moses feared came to pass. Pharaoh did find out, and Pharaoh did try to kill him. Once again Egyptian soldiers were searching for him, and this time he had no basket to hide him or float him to safety. However, the LORD was Moses' hiding place. In the shadow of the Almighty, under the wings of God, Moses would find a safe refuge. Moses was not captured; he was not caught off guard, for God had warned him through that Israelite man. Moses was ready and he fled. That was when Moses left Egypt. By faith, Moses left Egypt. By faith, he fled for his life, and by grace, God spared his life, again.

Moses went to live in the land of Midian. Now what would he do? He was no longer a prince of Egypt; that life had vanished. He was no longer the deliverer of Israel; that dream had disappeared. He was nothing now, but a fugitive in a foreign land, an ordinary man sitting by a well of water, wondering what he should do. As Moses sat there, seven sisters came to water their father's flock of sheep. Then some other shepherds came and drove the girls away. That was not right; the girls had been there first, so Moses got up and came to their rescue and watered their flock. The other shepherds would just have to wait their turn. When the girls went home, their father asked them, "Why have you returned so early today?" The girls answered, "An Egyptian rescued us from the shepherds. He even drew water for us and watered the flock." The father was surprised that they had just left the poor man sitting by the well. "Where is he?" he asked. "Why did you leave him? Invite him to have something to eat with us." So Moses went back to the man's tent. At least he would have some dinner and shelter for the night. Moses and the man talked, and one thing led to another. Soon Moses was working for the man, tending his sheep. Then Moses was marrying one of the daughters, a girl named Zipporah. After a time, Zipporah gave birth to a son, whom Moses named Gershom or Alien, because he said, "I have become an alien in a foreign land." Some time later, Zipporah gave birth to another son, whom Moses named Eliezer or My God Is Helper, for he said, "My father's God was my helper; He saved me from the sword of Pharaoh" (Exodus 18:3, 4).

So that was how Moses went from the palace to the pasture. After all those years of training to be a leader and a ruler, Moses now worked in the wilderness, walking from place to place, tending a flock of sheep. That was what Moses did for forty years. Did he ever recall the days when he was a prince in Egypt? Did he ever recall his dreams of delivering Israel? Yes, he probably did, but it was only a memory now of a long-ago life in a far-away place. Moses led another life now in the land of Midian with his wife and his children and his sheep. He still lived by faith. He still loved God and hoped in God's Promises and praised God for His goodness to him, but Moses was an old man of eighty years. He thought he would die in the land of Midian, never seeing God's Promises fulfilled.

But God had other plans for Moses.

The teacher's guide for this lesson starts on page 198.

THE ANGEL OF THE LORD IN FLAMES OF FIRE

• Exodus 2:23–3:10
• Acts 7:30–35
• Hebrews 12:18–29

B y faith Moses left Egypt and for many years he lived as a fugitive in a foreign land. He was no longer a prince; now he was a shepherd, who wandered in the wilderness, leading another man's sheep from one poor pasture to the next. Moses' life was hard, but at least he was free. He was a free man, free to walk in this world where he pleased, free to kneel before God when he pleased. It was not so for his people. The Israelites remained slaves in the land of Egypt. During that long period of time, the Pharaoh, who had wanted to kill Moses, died. Yes, that wicked king of Egypt went down to the grave and to hell (where he belonged), but this did not ease the suffering of the Hebrew slaves, because another king in Egypt, just as wicked, rose up to take his place. The Israelites groaned in their slavery; they groaned in agony because of their hard labours and harsh masters, but who cared? The Israelites cried in their misery; they cried for help because of their exhausting work and exacting lords, but who cared? On this earth there was no one who cared. No one in the whole world cared about these pitiful people who had been trapped as slaves for almost four hundred years.

However, there was someone in heaven who cared. God cared. He heard their groaning and their crying. God looked on the Israelites and saw all their suffering, and God was concerned about them. He loved them. Not the smallest sigh of sorrow, nor the tiniest tear of grief, escaped God's notice. Although the LORD had not spoken for nearly four hundred years, God had not forgotten His people, nor His promise to them. Long ago God had promised to give the land of Canaan to their forefathers. Long ago God had said, "Do not be afraid to go down to Egypt . . . I will go down to Egypt with you, and I will surely bring you back again" (Genesis 46:3, 4). Since God had spoken those words, hundreds of years had passed, but with the LORD a thousand years are like a day. God had not forgotten His promise, nor was He slow in keeping it. The events of this world are firmly fixed in the schedule of God. He does not forget what He has planned to do, nor is He rushed or stalled in fulfilling His plans. God remembered His covenant with Abraham, Isaac and Jacob, and, at exactly the right time, God would bring to pass the plan, which He had purposed before the foundation of the world. God had planned a great deliverance for his people, which would point to an even greater deliverance in the fullness of time. God's salvation would be displayed in the sight of every nation, to the praise of His glorious name!

For the past eighty years God had been preparing a deliverer for Israel. From before the world began, God had chosen Moses to rescue His people. From the moment of his birth, even Moses' parents could see that he was no ordinary child. From his earliest days God's hand had been upon Moses, guarding him and guiding him. It was no accident that Moses had spent the first forty years of his life in the palace of Pharaoh, learning all the wisdom and power of the Egyptians. Soon he would need that knowledge to do God's work. Nor was it a mistake that Moses had spent the last forty years of his life wandering in the wilderness, leading another man's flock of sheep. That was also an important part of God's leadership training for Moses. Soon he would be leading God's flock through that same wilderness (and for the same length of time). Moses knew nothing about God's Plan for him, but the LORD was about to reveal it to him in a most extraordinary way.

One day Moses led the flock of sheep, which he tended, to the far side of the desert, where he came to a mountain called Horeb. Horeb means "waste," because it was a desolate mountain in a wilderness region. A waste-land stretched for miles and miles all around Mount Waste, but it was here, on this lonely mountian in this isolated region, that "the Angel of the LORD appeared to Moses" (Exodus 3:2) to reveal to him God's Plan for his life and his people. This was what happened that day on that mountain:

As Moses tended the sheep beside the mountain he saw a very strange sight. A bush was on fire, but it did not burn up! There were actually flames of fire burning within the bush, but the leaves didn't shrivel and the branches didn't crackle. The fire burned, but the bush remained the same. Moses was amazed at the sight. Such a thing had never been seen by any man. Moses decided to take a closer look. He thought, "I will go over and see this strange sight, why the bush does not burn up." Then, as Moses moved closer, an even stranger thing happened. A voice, which knew his name, called to him from within the bush. "Moses! Moses!" called the voice. Moses answered, "Here I am." The voice said, "Take off your sandals, for the place where you are standing is holy ground." Moses obeyed the voice, without knowing for certain who was speaking.

Then the voice revealed to Moses who He was. He said, "I am the God of your father, the God of Abraham, the God of Isaac and the God of Ja-cob." At this, Moses hid his face, because he was afraid to look at God. "Moses trembled with fear and did not dare to look" (Acts 7:32) because it was the LORD Himself, who was appearing to him and speaking to him from the flames of fire in the burning bush. One day in the future, at this same mountain, God would say to Moses, "You cannot see My face, for no one may see Me and live . . . My face must not be seen" (Exodus 33:20, 23).

That was why Moses hid his face and was filled with fear. The LORD is holy, holy, holy, and we are unworthy, unworthy, unworthy even to look at God. Moses knew (and later would say to all Israel) that "God is a con-suming fire" (Deuteronomy 4:24). How could Moses look upon the LORD and live? Would he not be consumed in the flames of God's holiness? Moses hid his face, because he was a sinful creature standing before a Holy God. Even the ground where he was standing was holy, because God was there. What Moses did (taking off his shoes, hiding his face and trembling) and what Moses felt (fear and awe) were the right responses of a sinful creature before a Holy God.

Other men and women who were visited by God responded in the same way. For example, there was a husband and wife, who were talking to the angel of the LORD. They did not know He was God. They thought he was a prophet, a man of God who looked like an angel of God, very awesome. They made a sacrifice to the LORD on a rock. While the husband and wife watched, the LORD did an amazing thing: As the flame blazed up from the altar toward heaven, the angel of the LORD ascended in the flame. Now they knew who this awesome "man" was. It was God! It was the angel of the LORD, and they both fell with their faces to the ground. The man said to his wife, "We are doomed to die! We have seen God!" (See Judges 13.)

Who was this angel of the LORD who ascended in the flames? Who was this angel of the LORD who appeared to Moses in flames of fire within the burning bush? Throughout the Scriptures the angel of the LORD is equated with God Himself as a pre-incarnate appearance of the Son of God, who was with God in the beginning, who was God from all eternity. When the second person of the triune God humbled Himself and became a man, "taking the form of a servant and being made in human likeness" (Philippians 2:7), He was truly God and truly man. As a man, walking on this earth, the Son of God said, "I and the Father are one" (John 10:30). Another time Jesus Christ said, "I tell you the truth, before Abraham was born, I am" (John 8:58), clearly alluding to the fact that He was there, speaking to Moses from the burning bush. Who was this angel of the LORD? It was the Son of God. The voice from the burning bush said, "I am the God of your father, the God of Abraham, the God of Isaac and the God of Jacob."

The God of Israel had been silent all through those years of slavery. Through four centuries of Israel's suffering, God had not spoken. The last Word of God had been given to Jacob, when God promised to bring them out of Egypt and into the Promised Land. All through those bitter years the Israelites had to live by faith, not by sight, believing those ancient promises. It was the only hope these enslaved people had, that one day God would fulfil His promise to them. But as the years passed, they must have wondered: Had God forgotten? Had God been sleeping, while they were slaving? No, the LORD had been keeping watch over Israel and now the angel of the LORD came to Moses with some very exciting and comforting news. The LORD said, "I have indeed seen the misery of my people in Egypt. I have heard them crying out because of their slave drivers, and I am concerned about their suffering. So, I have come down to rescue them from the hand of the Egyptians and to bring them up out of that land into a good and spacious land, a land flowing with milk and honey . . ." It was wonderful news.

God had not forgotten nor forsaken them. God was going to fulfil His Promise and free His people!

The LORD said to Moses, "So now, go. I am sending you to Pharaoh to bring my people the Israelites out of Egypt." God also said, "I will be with you. And this will be the sign to you that it is I who have sent you: When you have brought the people out of Egypt, you will worship God on this mountain." This Waste Mountain in the wilderness, Mount Horeb, would be known now as the Mountain of God. It's name would be changed to Mount Sinai, which means the mountain that shines. The glory of the LORD had shone on this mountain this day. The angel of the LORD had appeared to Moses in flames of fire in the burning bush on that mountain. Soon the glory of the LORD would settle on Mount Sinai before all Israel. To the Israelites, the glory of the LORD looked like a consuming fire on top of the mountain. (See Exodus 24:15, 17.) The Israelites were not allowed to come up Mount Sinai; whoever even touched the foot of the mountain was put to death because the whole mountain was set apart as holy. It was holy because the God Who is holy, holy, holy, descended upon it in fire. It was not just the ground where Moses was standing near the burning bush that was holy; no, now the whole mountain was holy. One day all the people of Israel, would stand at the foot of Mount Horeb or Mount Sinai, "while it blazed with fire to the very heavens, with black clouds and deep darkness." Then the LORD would speak to them out of the fire. Then they would hear the sound of words, but they would see no form. There would only be a voice—and that voice would terrify them. They would tremble before the sound of that voice. They would plead for mercy: "This great fire will consume us, and we will die if we hear the voice of the LORD our God any longer." They would fear God on this mountain as Moses did, for God is a consuming fire. (See Deuteronomy 4:11 & 5:25.)

The teacher's guide for this lesson starts on page 200.

THE NAME OF GOD

• Exodus 3:7–15
• John 8:58, 59
• I Corinthians
  1:26–31

Two Questions, Two Answers

From the burning bush on the mountain of God, the LORD told Moses that He had seen and heard everything that was happening to His people in Egypt. The LORD of LOVE said, "I am concerned about their suffering." That was why God was visiting Moses. That was why God was appearing to him and speaking to him from the burning bush on that desolate mountain because God loved His people. "So, I have come down to rescue them . . ." said the LORD. God remembered His covenant. He was here to fulfil His promise, to bring His people out of the land of Egypt, the evil land of their slavery and poverty; God was here to bring them into the land of Canaan, a good and spacious land, a land flowing with milk and honey. God said, "The cry of the Israelites has reached Me, and I have seen the way the Egyptians are oppressing them." But how was God going effect this rescue? The LORD said to Moses, "So now, go, I am sending you to Pharaoh to bring My people the Israelites out of Egypt."

Question: Who Am I?

Moses was shocked. How could he possibly do such a thing? Long ago, when he was a prince in Egypt, in the prime of his life and the height of his power, he had wanted to rescue his people. He had even attempted to rescue them, but he had failed. If he had failed then, what could he do now? Forty years had passed. Now he was a weak old man, a poor shepherd who tended someone else's sheep, a nobody. He was less than nothing, for he was a fugitive in a foreign land who had spent the last forty years fleeing and hiding for his life. How could he go to Pharaoh or free his people? Who would listen to him now? Why would a poor old Jew, a lowly shepherd, even be allowed to speak to Pharaoh? The Egyptians despised such men. Why wouldn't he be captured as an escaped slave or executed as a wanted criminal? And his own people, if they had not listened to him when he was a prince, why would they listen to him now? God's plan was impossible. But the LORD said to Moses, "Go, I am sending you . . ." Moses answered God with a question, "Who am I, that I should go to Pharaoh and bring the Israelites out of Egypt?"

Answer: I Am With You!

Moses asked, "Who am I?" and God answered, "I am with you." It was an amazing answer. Without God, Moses could do nothing and Moses was nothing. All men are without hope, without strength and without life, if they are without God. But God was with Moses! God often chooses the foolish things of the world to shame the wise. He chooses the weak things of this world to shame the strong. He chooses the lowly things of this world and the despised things and the things that are nothing, to nullify the things that are, so that no one may boast before Him. Let him who boasts, boast in the LORD. It was not the mighty hand of Moses, but the mighty hand of God, that would free Israel from Egypt. It was not the power of Moses, but the power of God, that would achieve the rescue tried. When Moses was a mighty man with all the power and wisdom of Egypt, he had failed in his attempt to rescue his people. That was good, for now the whole world would know that it was by the power of Almighty God alone that the Jews were set free. "Not by might nor by power, but by my Spirit," says the LORD Almighty (Zechariah 4:6). This task was impossible for Moses, but with God, all things were possible. God would be with Moses. God would work through Moses.

Was Moses a weak old man now? All the better, for then he would clearly show that this all-surpassing power was from God and not from him. Yes, it was an impossible mission for Moses. It was impossible for any man, but, if God is for us, who can stand against us? If God is with us, who can work against us? And God promised Moses: *"I am with you!"*

No other word was needed. That promise alone should have given Moses the courage to go forth by faith, but God graciously gave Moses a sign too. God said, "And this will be the sign to you that it is I who have sent you: When you have brought the people out of Egypt, you will worship God on this mountain." It was a strange sign. Moses had to go and do what God commanded before he saw the sign. Once again, he had to go forward by faith, trusting that he would see the sign. He had to believe God's Word, that one day all the Israelites would be there with him on that same mountain worshipping the LORD. All that Moses could see by sight was an empty wilderness before a desolate mountain, but the sign, which Moses had to see by faith, was the great multitude of Israel, hundreds of thousands of people, camped before that mountain to worship God. The only way Moses could see this sign now was with eyes of faith. "Faith is being sure of what we hope for and certain of what we do not see" (Hebrews 11:1). Moses could see nothing, but he could believe. He could believe God, who sees and knows all things. God saw and knew what would happen in the future, because God is the one who plans or causes or predestines the future. Moses need not worry about the future; he need not worry about failure because this was God's plan. What God says, He does. What God promises, He accomplishes. Moses had only to believe and obey.

Question: Who Are You? What Is Your Name?

But Moses had many concerns. He knew that God was sending him on this mission, but how would the Israelites know? Why should they believe him? Did they still believe in God? Did they even know who God was? They had been in Egypt for 400 years, surrounded by the gods of Egypt. They knew all the gods of Egypt by name. But who was the God of Israel? Who was the God of their fathers—the God of Abraham, Isaac and Jacob? Did their God have a name? What was it? Moses himself did not know the answer to that question. What was God's name?

That was an interesting question, which Moses was not the first, nor the last, to ask. The night when Jacob wrestled with God, he asked that same question. Jacob said, "Please tell me your name." Do you remember God's answer? God said simply, "Why do you ask my name?"—and He did not tell him. (See Genesis 32:29, 30.) Another man inquired of the angel of the LORD, "What is your name?" God answered again, "Why do you ask my name? It is beyond understanding." (See Judges 13:17, 18.) In the Bible we read of the one on whom is written this Name: *King of kings and Lord of lords.* But we also read that "He has a name written on Him that no one knows but He Himself." (See Revelation 19:11–16.) The name of God is a sacred secret, but God knows our names. He even knows our secret names, which we do not know yet. When we meet with God in heaven, He will give us a white stone with a new name written on it, a name known only to the one who receives it. (See Revelation 2:17.) God also calls us by our familiar names. When the voice spoke to Moses from the burning bush, God called him by name: "Moses! Moses!" But what was God's name?

Moses did not ask this question directly. He said to God, "Suppose I go to the Israelites and say to them, 'The God of your fathers has sent me to you,' and they ask me, 'What is His name?' Then what shall I tell them?"

Answer: I Am Who I Am.

God answered Moses, "I AM WHO I AM." Imagine if you went up to a new child in the church and said, "Hi! Who are you? What's your name?" and he answered, "I AM WHO I AM." What would you think about that person? Would that person have answered your question? Would you know something about that person? Would you know his name? That was the answer God gave to Moses: "I AM WHO I AM," and because it was God who was speaking, it was a very gracious answer, for God was revealing himself to Moses; He was revealing His character to Moses. "I AM WHO I AM." God exists. He is, and His existence depends upon no man. God is WHO He is. From everlasting to everlasting He is God. The false gods of the nations are made by men and named by men and known by men, but the true God, the one and only God, even His name, the glory of His holy name, is hidden from them, unless God graciously reveals Himself to them. So God answered Moses, "I AM WHO I AM. That is what you are to say to the Israelites: 'I AM! has sent me to you.'" It was a new name for himself that God was revealing to the Israelites: I AM! God also said to Moses, "Say to the Israelites,

'The LORD, the God of your fathers—the God of Abraham, the God of Isaac and the God of Jacob—has sent me to you.' This is My name forever, the name by which I am to be remembered from generation to generation." The LORD, (which in Hebrew is Jahweh or Jehovah,) was the newly-revealed name of God. "LORD" in Hebrew sounds like "I am." Later God said to Moses, "I AM the LORD (Jahweh/Jehovah). I appeared to Abraham, to Isaac and to Jacob as God Almighty (El Shaddai), but by My name, the LORD (Jahweh/Jehovah) I did not make Myself known to them" (Exodus 6:2, 3). So, God did answer Moses' question. God did tell him His Name: I AM, the LORD, Jahweh/Jehovah.

When the Son of God came to earth and spoke to men, He also took that name for himself. Jesus said to the Jews, "I tell you the truth, before Abraham was born, I AM!" The Jews knew that He was thus claiming to be the eternal God, for He had taken God's name for himself, the name God had given to Moses from the burning bush, so they picked up stones to kill him for blasphemy. But Jesus spoke the truth. He was God! He was God the Son, who had appeared to Moses as the Angel of the LORD, in flames of fire in the burning bush.

That name, the LORD, was to be God's Name forever, the name by which He was to be remembered from generation to generation. Thousands of years have passed. We are a new generation. What do we call God? How do we worship Him? We say, "Praise the LORD!" We pray to Him as LORD and we sing for Him as LORD and we read of Him as LORD.

> I will give thanks to the LORD because of His Righteousness and will sing praise to the Name of the LORD Most High. (Psalm 7:17)

> O LORD, our Lord, how majestic is Your Name in all the earth! (Psalm 8:1)

> I will praise you, O LORD, with all my heart . . . I will be glad and rejoice in you; I will sing praise to your name, O Most High . . . Those who know your name will trust in you, for you, LORD, have never forsaken those who seek you. (Psalm 9:1, 2,10)

> We wait in hope for the LORD; He is our help and our shield. In Him our hearts rejoice, for we trust in His holy name. May your unfailing LOVE rest upon us, O LORD, even as we put our hope in you. (Psalm 33:20–22)

Glorify the LORD with me. Let us exalt His name together."(Psalm 34:3)

I will praise Your name, O LORD, for it is good. (Psalm 54:6)

Shout with joy to God, all the earth! Sing the glory of His name. Make His praise glorious. (Psalm 66:1, 2)

Sing to God; sing praise to His name. Extol Him who rides on the clouds—His name is the LORD—and rejoice before Him . . . Sing praise to the LORD. (Psalm 68:4, 32)

In God we make our boast all day long, and we will praise your name forever. (Psalm 44:8)

I trust in God's unfailing LOVE forever and ever. I will praise you forever for what you have done. In your name I will hope, for your name is good. (Psalm 52:8, 9)

Save me, O God, by your name . . . Surely God is my help; the LORD is the One who sustains me . . . I will praise your name, O LORD, for it is good. (Psalm 54:1, 4,6)

O God, you are my God . . . Because your LOVE is better than life, my lips will glorify you. I will praise you as long as I live, and in your name I will lift up my hands. (Psalm 63:1, 3,4)

I will praise God's name in song. (Psalm 69:30)

Praise be to the LORD God, the God of Israel . . . Praise be to His glorious name forever. (Psalm 72:18, 19)

Praise the LORD, O my soul; all my inmost being, praise His holy name. (Psalm 103:1)

Give thanks to the LORD. Call on His name . . . Sing to Him; sing praise to Him . . . Glory in His holy name. Let the hearts of those who seek the LORD rejoice. (Psalm 105:1–3)

Praise the LORD. Praise, O servants of the LORD. Praise the Name of the LORD. Let the name of the LORD be praised, both now and forevermore. From the rising of the sun to the place where it sets, the name of the LORD is to be praised. (Psalm 113:1–3)

Praise the LORD. Praise the name of the LORD. Praise Him you servants of the LORD . . . Praise the LORD for He is good. Sing praise to His name for that is pleasant . . . Your name, O LORD, endures forever . . . Praise the LORD . . . Praise the LORD . . . *Praise the LORD.* (Psalm 135:1, 3,13, 19–21)

I will praise you, O LORD, with all my heart . . . I will praise your name for your LOVE and faithfulness, for you have exalted above all things your name and your word. (Psalm 138:1, 2)

I will exalt you, my God and King; I will praise your name forever and ever. Every day I will praise you and extol your name forever and ever . . . My mouth will speak in praise of the LORD. Let every creature praise His holy name forever and ever. (Psalm 145:1, 2,21)

Praise the LORD . . . Let them praise the name of the LORD . . . Let them praise the name of the LORD, for His name alone is exalted. (Psalm 148:1, 5,13)

The teacher's guide for this lesson starts on page 202.

PROVISIONS FOR THE JOURNEY

• **Exodus 3:1–4:17**
• **Psalm 103**

God was sending Moses to Pharaoh to bring His people, the Israelites, out of Egypt. Moses did not feel equal to the task or ready for the work, but those feelings were irrelevant. Moses must live by faith, not by feelings. God had spent eighty years preparing Moses for this impossible mission, and God was preparing him now. God was strengthening Moses' faith. God was giving Moses provisions for his journey, things that would strengthen his heart for the hardships ahead:

1) The LORD appeared to Moses in the flames of fire in the burning bush. It was a sight that Moses would never forget. Those strange flames would burn forever in the memory of his soul.

2) The LORD spoke to Moses. Moses actually heard the voice of God calling him by name. Moses would never forget the sound.

3) The words that God spoke were words of great encouragement. The LORD assured Moses of His LOVE for His people. God

said, "I am concerned about their suffering, so I have come down to rescue them . . ." They were words of hope to strengthen Moses' heart.

4) Moses had God's clear command to go. This was not the bright thought or wild scheme or doomed plan of men. Moses was not stepping out on a whim of his own. It was God's plan. The LORD Himself was sending Moses. God said, "Go. I am sending you."

5) The LORD answered Moses' self doubts with this great promise: "I am with you." Moses had that precious promise, the promise of God's presence, to strengthen him for this most difficult task and dangerous trip.

6) God gave Moses a sign, that it really was the LORD who had sent him. God said, "When you have brought the people out of Egypt, you will worship God on this mountain." Although it was a sign that required faith in the Word of God, there was also something that Moses could see with his eyes. It was an enormous sign, one that towered above Moses. It was an entire mountain! Sometimes men would erect a pile of stones as a sign to remind them of something, but God gave Moses an entire mountain of stone, the Mountain of God, as a sign to remind him of God's Promises: "I will be with you and . . . you will worship God on this mountain." As Moses set out on his journey, whenever he looked back, he could see that sign for miles and miles, and the sight of it would strengthen his faith for the task ahead him.

7) God revealed to Moses a new name: I am, Jahweh, the LORD. The name of God, that name alone, would be a source of strength for Moses as he faced adversity. "Our help is in the name of the LORD" (Psalm 124:8).

8) God gave Moses the details of His plan. He told Moses exactly what he should do and exactly what he should say. It was not left for Moses to figure out a strategy for victory. He simply had to obey orders. The Master Mind of this plan and the General of this war was God. He told Moses, step by step, what to do and say:

STEP I: "Go, *assemble the elders of Israel* and say to them, 'The LORD, the God of your fathers—the God of Abraham, Isaac and Jacob—appeared to me and said: I have watched over you and have seen what has been done to you in Egypt. And I have promised to bring you up out of your misery in Egypt into the land of the Canaanites, Hittites, Amorites, Perrizites, Hivites and Jebusites—a land flowing with milk and honey.' "

STEP II: "Then you and the elders are to *go to the king of Egypt* and say to him, 'The LORD, the God of the Hebrews, has met with us. Let us take a three-day journey into the desert to offer sacrifices to the LORD our God.'"

STEP III: The women of Israel were to speak to the women of Egypt. God said, "*Every woman is to ask her neighbour . . . for articles of silver and gold* and for clothing, which you will put on your sons and daughters."

9) God told Moses what to do and say. Then God told Moses what would happen. Moses need not be afraid of failure, because God had promised success. What encouragement.

PROMISE I: "The elders of Israel will listen to you."

PROMISE II: "The king of Egypt will not let you go unless a mighty hand compels him. So, I will stretch out my hand and strike the Egyptians with all the wonders that I will perform among them. After that, *he will let you go!*" It was not the weathered, wrinkled, weakened hand of Moses that would wrench the Israelites from Pharaoh's grip. No, it was the hand of God Almighty that would rescue them.

PROMISE III: The women of Israel were to ask for gold and silver and God promised, "I will make the Egyptians favourably disposed toward this people, so that when you leave *you will not go empty-handed.*" The Israelites were slaves. They had nothing except the rags on their backs, but God promised they would leave Egypt with great wealth, dressed in fine clothes. It was theirs for the asking. It would not be an army of strong men that plundered Egypt. No, it would be the women who carried away the wealth of that evil empire. How? God would cause it to happen. "And so you will plunder the Egyptians," promised God.

What encouragement for Moses! God had told him, promised him, — that there would be victory! Pharaoh would be conquered. Egypt would be plundered. The Israelites would be set free by the hand of God. The LORD Himself had come down to rescue them and to bring them out of that land into a good and spacious land, a land flowing with milk and honey. Moses was not being sent to attempt a rescue; he was being sent as God's agent on a sure and certain rescue, for the LORD had spoken it. Surely now Moses would say, "Amen. I am the LORD's servant. Let me do what You have said."

But instead Moses answered with more fears and doubts. Although God had just promised success, although He had just said that the elders of Israel would listen and Pharaoh would let them go, Moses said, "What if they do not believe me or listen to me and say, 'The LORD did not appear to you'?" Why should anyone, Egyptians or Israelites, believe what he said? How could he prove that truly, the LORD had appeared to him?

10) It was a reasonable (but not a faithful) concern. So God gave Moses' three signs, three miracles, to perform before all the people. These three miracles would be like three witnesses, testifying to Moses' claim, that the LORD had appeared to him:

MIRACLE I: The LORD said to Moses, "What is that in your hand?" Moses answered, "A staff." Moses was a shepherd and an old man, who carried a staff to help him walk and work. Now this same staff would help him in his walk and work for God. "Throw it on the ground," said the LORD. Moses threw it on the ground, and it became a snake. A dead piece of wood became a living, hissing, slithering snake, a snake with fangs that could wound or kill a man. This snake was a frightening sight, and Moses ran from it. But the LORD said to him, "Reach out your hand and take it by the tail." (If you grab a snake by the tail, it will swing around and bite you. A snake must be pinned and held right behind its head, so that its fangs can't reach you. However, God told Moses to take this snake by the tail. Would Moses obey? Would Moses be bitten?) Moses reached out and took hold of the snake, and it turned back into a staff in his hand, just an ordinary, old, shepherd's crook again. "This," said the LORD, "is so that they may believe that the LORD, the God of their fathers—the God of Abraham, the God of Isaac and the God of Jacob—has appeared to you." What did this sign mean? What did it show? Perhaps it simply meant that the power of evil would not prevail. That ancient serpent, the devil, and his evil empire, Egypt, were completely controlled by the command of God. By God's Word they were created and by God's Word they would be destroyed. That snake called Satan, and all his human snakes in Egypt, could do nothing against the LORD. The poison of their fangs could not touch the hand of God's servant, Moses.

MIRACLE II: Next the LORD said, "Put your hand inside your cloak." So Moses put his hand into his cloak, and when he took it out it was white, like snow, like the hand of a leper. Moses' hand was covered with a deadly disease, the most dreaded disease of all—leprosy! This sign was more terrifying than the first, since it changed Moses' own hand into something horrible. "Now, put it back into your cloak," instructed the LORD. Moses did so, and when he took it out his hand was restored; his leprous-looking hand was healed. The God who could harm or heal a hand, the God who could destroy or restore a hand, could also harm one nation and heal another; He could destroy Egypt and restore Israel. Surely this miracle would cause His people to trust in the Almighty Power of the LORD their God. Surely they would believe Him and the one whom He had sent, the man Moses.

MIRACLE III: However, they might not. So the LORD said to Moses, "If they do not believe you or pay attention to the first miraculous sign, they may believe the second. But if they do not believe these two signs or listen to you, take some water from the Nile River and pour it on the dry ground. The water you take from the river will become blood on the ground." The Nile River was the life of Egypt, but it had been death to Israel. The Nile River was the strength of Egypt, but it was there that Israel had lost her strength, when a generation of baby boys had been drowned to death in its waters. Moses himself had been cast upon those waters, but God drew him out. By the hand of Pharaoh's daughter, God drew Moses out of that river of death, and now God, by the hand of Moses, would rescue His people. Their blood was crying out to him from the waters of the Nile River. When Moses poured the water from the river upon the ground and when it turned to blood, it would be a sign. To the Israelites it would be a sign that God was going to avenge their blood, the blood of their sons that had been spilled into the Nile River. To the Egyptians it would be the same sign: God was going to avenge the blood of His people. Their crimes had not gone unnoticed. The waters of the river had not washed that blood away. Look! There it was upon the ground for all to see. The guilt of innocent blood was upon their land.

These were all terrifying signs that God gave to Moses. These signs were not beautiful rainbows in the clouds. These were signs of death and destruction. These were terrifying signs from a terrifying God. Let all the world take warning: *Let Israel know that the LORD is God!* Let all Israel fear the LORD, for the fear of the LORD is the beginning of wisdom. Let them believe the servant of the LORD sent to them; let them believe the Word of the LORD given to them that they might live. *Let Egypt know that the LORD is God!* These were horrible signs warning them of the horrible plagues about to destroy them. Let them repent and escape. Let them turn from the false gods of Egypt to the true God of Israel before it was too late. They had been warned of the power of God by these signs, and so they were without excuse.

Moses too had seen the power of God—and felt it—as those first two miraculous signs were performed for him and through him. Surely now he was ready to go and do the LORD's will. Surely now he knew that the LORD could work with him and through him. But Moses still felt he was unfit for the task. He said, "O LORD, I have never been eloquent, neither in the past, nor since you have spoken to your servant. I am slow of speech and tongue." Even now, as he was speaking to God, he was having difficulty. Moses had some sort of speech impediment, and it continued, even now, in the presence of the LORD, as he spoke to the voice in the burning bush. How could he possibly do what God demanded?

The LORD answered Moses, "Who gave man his mouth? Who makes him deaf or mute? Who gives him sight or makes him blind? Is it not I, the LORD?" God was the One who had made Moses. God had made Moses exactly the way He wanted him to be. It is the LORD who gives us all our abilities and all our inabilities too. Both are given to us for the glory of God! When the LORD chose Moses for this task, He knew he could not speak well because God Himself had made Moses that way. It was no excuse. Moses could not claim exemption from God's service because of a speech impediment. (One way or another, draft dodgers from God's army were always recruited in the end, such as the prophet Jonah or the apostle Paul). "Now, go!" said the LORD. "I will help you speak and will teach you what to say."

11) Thus God gave Moses another word of encouragement to help him on his way. Moses' inabilities were only a problem in his own estimation; in the eyes of God there was no problem at all. Moses had to trust this promise from God: "I will help you . . . and I will teach you." What a word of blessing from a loving God.

But Moses said, "Please send someone else to do it." After all God's assurances and all God's deliverances, that was what Moses said: "Please send someone else to do it." Then the LORD's anger burned against Moses. But "the LORD is compassionate and gracious, slow to anger, abounding in LOVE . . . He does not treat us as our sins deserve . . . the LORD has compassion . . . He remembers that we are but dust" (Psalm 103). Once again the LORD gave Moses something, this time someone, to help him on his way:

12) God gave Moses a partner for this mission, a person to speak for him, his own brother. The LORD said, "What about your brother Aaron, the

Levite? I know he can speak well. He is already on his way to meet you, and his heart will be glad when he sees you. You shall speak to him and put words in his mouth. I will help both of you speak and will teach you what to do. He will speak to the people for you; it will be as if he were your mouth. And you will be as God to him." Just as God used the mouths of his prophets to speak for Him, so Moses would use the mouth of his brother to speak for him.

13) God gave Moses one more thing for his journey. Moses would have taken it anyway, but now God commanded him to take it. "Take this staff in your hand so you can perform miraculous signs with it." His old staff would have new work. Moses must stand before the king, who held a golden sceptre, the symbol of all the power of Egypt; Moses must stand before sorcerers and magicians, who waved their magic wands, symbols of all the wisdom of Egypt, and, by God's Grace, Moses must stand against them. Moses must stand against all the power and wisdom of Egypt, carrying an old wooden shepherd's crook, a sign of the power and wisdom of God. The LORD is our Shepherd. In His rod and staff we find comfort. Moses must still have a shepherd's crook, for now he was God's servant and God's shepherd, sent to lead God's people into the green pastures of the Promised Land.

The teacher's guide for this lesson starts on page 204.

THE WAY MADE SMOOTH FOR MOSES

• **Exodus 4:18–31**
• **Psalm 103**

The LORD had spoken. He would say no more at this time. He would not speak again from the burning bush. Moses must go. So, he left the mountain of God, but he did not set out for Egypt immediately. In fact, he went in the opposite direction. First he must lead the flock of sheep back to their owner, to Jethro, his father-in-law, who lived in the land of Midian. Moses had tended this man's sheep for forty years, and now he was quitting. What would Jethro say? Do you remember how much difficulty Jacob had when he left Laban? This was a similar situation. Moses' wife was Jethro's daughter; Moses' sons were Jethro's grandsons. Surely Jethro would try to dissuade Moses from going to Egypt. Should Moses tell Jethro that God had spoken to him from a burning bush? Should he say that it was the LORD who was sending him to Egypt? Surely Jethro would not believe him. So Moses said to his father-in-law, "Let me go back to my own people in Egypt to see if any of them are still alive." It was a reasonable request. Moses had not seen any of his family for forty years. Jethro answered, "Go, and I wish you well." That was easy. Moses had faced no problems there at all.

Moses was concerned that his life was still in danger; that the Egyptians were still watching and waiting to kill him. If he took his wife and two small sons, he would be risking their lives too. The LORD dealt with that concern. God spoke to Moses again, this time in the land of Midian, and said, "Go back to Egypt, for all the men who wanted to kill you are dead." That was a relief! So Moses took his wife and sons, put them on a donkey and started back to Egypt. Moses took the staff of God in his hand, remembering the LORD's final command to him on Mount Horeb: "Take this staff in your hand, so you can perform miraculous signs with it." The staff also made a good walking stick for an old man on long journey.

The little family of Moses travelled through the wilderness. They were leaving their homeland and heading for another country. Why were they going to an alien land? Because the God of their father had commanded him to go there. By faith, they were simply following their father. But there was something very wrong with Moses' family. One of his sons had not been circumcised. Had not God commanded Abraham about this long ago? God said, "You must keep my covenant, you and your descendants after you for the generations to come. This is My covenant with you and your descendants after you, the covenant you are to keep: Every male among you shall be circumcised. You are to undergo circumcision, and it will be the sign of the covenant between Me and you . . . My covenant in your flesh is to be an everlasting covenant. Any uncircumcised male, who has not been circumcised in the flesh, will be cut off from his people; he has broken my covenant" (Genesis 17:9–14). Moses had not circumcised his son. How could Moses have neglected to do what God had so clearly commanded? Perhaps his Midianite wife, Zipporah, had objected. Perhaps Zipporah had thought it was an unnecessary sign of unnecessary pain for her poor little boy, but she was wrong, and Moses was without excuse. Should Moses have listened to the words of his wife, rather than the Word of God? No, Moses ought to have done what was right, in spite of his wife's opposition. Not to circumcise his son was a very grievous sin in the sight of God. So, at a lodging place on the way, where Moses and his family stopped for the night, the LORD met Moses again, but this time, it was to kill him! What God commanded must be obeyed by everyone. Moses was no exception. He too was under the Law of God, although he was God's friend. He too must be careful, for our God is a consuming fire. God was about to destroy Moses, but Zipporah took a knife; she cut off her son's foreskin right then, right there, and she threw it at Moses' feet, saying, "Surely you are a bloody husband to me." (She called him bloody, because of the circumcision.) Zipporah was angry, but better to have his wife angry with him, than to have his God angry with him. Moses repented of his sin, and the LORD allowed Moses to live and to serve again. That was God's mercy to Moses. God forgave his sin and spared his life. Consider the LOVE of the LORD for those who trust Him and fear Him: As far as the east is distant from the west, that is how far God removes our sins from us. As high as the heavens are above the earth, that is how great God's LOVE is for us. "His anger lasts only a moment, but His grace lasts a whole lifetime. Weeping may remain for a night, but rejoicing comes in the morning" (Psalm 30:5). So Moses continued on his way. God was with him, because "the LORD's LOVE is with those who fear Him—with those who keep His covenant and remember to obey His precepts" (Psalm 103:17, 18). God was graciously removing every obstacle that stood blocking the path of Moses, and sin was the greatest obstacle of all. God commands us to "throw off everything that hinders, especially the sin that so easily entangles" and to "run with endurance the race marked out for us" (Hebrews 12:1). Moses had a great race in front of him, and God was making the way smooth for him. That dreadful confrontation, when God came to him in the night to kill him, was absolutely necessary for Moses' life and God's work, for he could not continue thus in his sin.

It may be that Zipporah left Moses at this point in the journey. It may be that Moses had to travel now on his own. Where was his partner in this venture? Where was his brother? God had said that Aaron was already on his way to meet him, but would he be able to find him? It was a vast wilderness. And after all those years, would his brother recognize him? And, the most important question of all, would Aaron be willing to join Moses on this mission? Would he believe in the ancient promise of God to their forefathers or would he only see how impossible it was? Would he say, "Yes, I'll go with you!" or would he say, "No, there are hundreds of thousands of Israelites. How can we, two old men, free all these slaves in Egypt?" Moses did not want to go to Egypt at all, and he certainly did not want to go alone. Where was Aaron? As Moses wandered through the wilderness, he must have wondered about these things. Perhaps he even worried about them, but God was taking care of all his concerns. The LORD spoke to Aaron, "Go into the desert to meet Moses." Aaron obeyed, and the LORD directed him. God had the two brothers meet each other at the perfect place. They met at the mountain of God, the mountain that was the sign of their success, the mountain where the LORD had appeared to Moses in the burning bush. Moses could even show him the place, where the ground was holy. Moses could stretch out his hands and show Aaron where the people of Israel would worship God. Yes, it was the perfect place to meet. When Aaron saw Moses, he knew who it was, and his heart was glad. He rushed up to his brother and hugged him and kissed him. Then Moses told Aaron everything the LORD had sent him to say and to do. He showed Aaron his staff and told him about the miraculous signs that God had commanded him to perform. Would Aaron believe him? Would Aaron go with him? Yes! Aaron said, "Yes!" He was willing to be the mouth for Moses. He was willing to join him on this dangerous mission. So, by faith, two old men named Aaron and Moses set off together for the land of Egypt on one of the greatest adventures in the history of this world. These two brothers set off to free their people from the power of a mighty nation. They did this by faith, trusting in the power of Almighty God to achieve the rescue tried. These two old men, walking in the wilderness, would change the world!

When Moses and Aaron arrived in Egypt, they did what God commanded them. First, they assembled the elders of Israel. Aaron spoke, since he was Moses' mouth. Aaron told the elders everything that the LORD had told Moses. He also performed the three miraculous signs before the people, and they believed. It should have been no surprise; God promised that they would. God said, "The elders of Israel will listen to you." When the elders heard that the LORD was concerned about them, when they heard that God had seen their misery, they bowed down and worshipped. They had been touched by the LOVE of God for them. Not only did they listen; not only did they believe; they bowed and worshipped. Moses must have been amazed. He was seeing the beginning of what God had promised: all Israel worshipping God!

Thus God had made the way smooth for Moses. Every concern, every problem, had been removed. Everything had gone exactly according to plan, exactly according to promise because God's plans and God's promises never fail.

The teacher's guide for this lesson starts on page 206.

THE WAY MADE ROUGH FOR MOSES

• Exodus 5:1–7:7

As God had instructed, Moses and Aaron first spoke to their own people, the Israelites. The elders of Israel listened to them and believed them. They also bowed down before the LORD and worshipped Him. But now Moses and Aaron must speak to their enemies, the Egyptians. As God had instructed, they must now go to the king of Egypt and speak to him. So Moses and Aaron went to Pharaoh and said, "This is what the LORD, the God of Israel, says: "Let My people go!" Contrary to what Pharaoh thought, he did not own the Israelites. These slaves were not his property; these people did not belong to him. They belonged to God. The Israelites were God's own possession. Now the God of Israel was commanding Pharaoh, "Let My people go, so that they may celebrate a feast to Me in the wilderness." Pharaoh did not want the Israelites celebrating and worshipping God; he wanted them labouring and working for him. Pharaoh was the lord and god of Egypt. Why should he listen to the LORD, the God of Israel, the God of his slaves? Pharaoh did not believe in Israel's God. So Pharaoh, in his pride and sin, answered, "Who is the LORD, that I should obey him and let Israel go? I do not know the LORD — and I will not let Israel go."

Pharaoh's answer should not have surprised Moses. At the mountain in the desert the LORD had warned him that "the king of Egypt will not let you go unless a mighty hand compels him" (Exodus 3:19). In the land of Midian the LORD had also warned, "I will harden his heart so that he will not let the people go" (Exodus 4:21). It should have been no surprise then that Pharaoh answered, "I will not let the people go." Moses and Aaron had to do and say what God had commanded them, whether Pharaoh listened or not. They had to proclaim God's Word, whatever Pharaoh's response might be. They had to speak the truth, whether Pharaoh believed it or not, whether he obeyed it or not. So again they appealed to the king of Egypt saying, "The God of the Hebrews has met with us. Now let us take a three-day journey into the desert to offer sacrifices to the LORD our God." That was exactly what God had commanded them to say to Pharaoh. (See Exodus 3:18.) They also added that they were afraid of what the LORD their God might do to them if they did not serve Him as He had commanded them. "He might strike us with plagues or with the sword," they said. This must have enraged Pharaoh. The Israelites should be afraid of him, the lord and god of Egypt; they should be afraid of what the king of Egypt would do to them if they did not serve him. Pharaoh answered, "Moses and Aaron, why are you taking the people away from their labour? Get back to your work!" Pharaoh was building his kingdom with the slave labour of hundreds of thousands of Israelites. He was not about to let that work grind to a halt for three whole days (or perhaps a whole week) while they served another Master. "Look," said Pharaoh, "the people of the land are now numerous, and you are stopping them from working." With that, Pharaoh dismissed God's messengers and God's message to him. The only kingdom that mattered to Pharaoh was his own earthly kingdom. The people must work to build that kingdom and no other. Pharaoh had no interest in the kingdom of God, because he had no interest in the one true God. As Pharaoh himself said, "I do not know the LORD. I will not let Israel go. Who is the LORD that I should obey Him?" However, the days were coming soon when Pharaoh would find out who the LORD was, that He should be obeyed.

Pharaoh was not concerned about the things of God, but he was concerned about the things of this world, and now Pharaoh was concerned that there might be an uprising among his slaves. The Israelites might listen to

Moses and Aaron. Pharaoh might have a full-scale rebellion on his hands. The king of Egypt must not allow that to happen. So Pharaoh devised a plan that would turn the Israelites against Moses and Aaron. That very same day Pharaoh gave this order to the Egyptian slave-drivers and task-masters: "You are no longer to supply the people with straw for making bricks; let them go and gather their own straw, but require them to make the same number of bricks as before. Don't reduce the quota. They are lazy; that is why they are crying out, 'Let us go and sacrifice to our God.' Make the work harder for the men, so that they keep working and pay no attention to lies." That was Pharaoh's assessment of the words of Moses and Aaron; that was Pharaoh's judgement of the Word of God — lies, all lies.

The servants of God had come to the Egyptians with: "This is what the LORD says." Now the servants of Pharaoh went to the Israelites with: "This is what Pharaoh says: 'I will not give you any more straw. Go and get your own straw wherever you can find it, but your work will not be reduced at all.' " The poor people must have trembled with fear when they heard this order. How could they possibly do it? Oh wretched slaves! How could they possibly obey this command from their master? They had no straw. They had no time. They worked from dawn till dusk just making the bricks. Now Pharaoh ordered them to gather straw from somewhere, yet still produce the same number of bricks each day. What could they to do? Where could they go? The people scattered all over Egypt looking for straw, but all they could find was stubble in the fields. This they gathered to use for straw, but it was so little and it took so long to get it. As the minutes ticked by, the Egyptian whips cracked and the slave drivers shouted, "Make the quota! Complete the work! Complete the work required of you for each day, just as when you had the straw. Make the quota!" But the Israelites couldn't do it. They couldn't possibly gather the straw and produce the same number of bricks. They worked from dawn to dusk, but at the end of the day, they had not made enough bricks. The Israelite foremen were asked, "Why didn't you meet your quota of bricks yesterday or today, as before?" And then they were beaten.

The Israelite foremen thought there must be some mistake. It didn't make sense. The Egyptians were supposed to supply the straw for the bricks; that was the way it had always been. Why would Pharaoh command them to do what could not be done? Why would he want to beat and kill his slaves, the ones who were building his nation? So the Israelite foremen appealed to Pharaoh. They asked, "Why have you treated your servants this way? Your servants are given no straw, yet we are told, 'Make bricks!' Your servants are being beaten, but the fault is with your own people." Surely Pharaoh would realize the injustice of their situation and correct it! But Pharaoh answered, "Lazy, that's what you are—lazy! That is why you keep saying, 'Let us go and sacrifice to the LORD.' Now get to work. You will not be given any straw, yet you must produce your full quota of bricks."

The Israelite foremen realized they were in terrible trouble. It was not a mistake. They had heard the unreasonable command from Pharaoh's own lips. He would not intervene on their behalf. Pharaoh himself had issued that dreadful decree. There was no hope now. They knew the beatings would continue. They would be beaten day after day, until they were beaten to death, because it was impossible to produce the full quota of bricks when they had no straw. Yes, the Israelite foremen knew that they were in terrible trouble, knew that they would be beaten and tortured and slaughtered, and now they knew why. It was because Moses and Aaron had spoken to Pharaoh about letting the people go to worship the LORD. That was why this terrible trouble had come upon them. As they left Pharaoh's palace, they found Moses and Aaron waiting to meet them, but now they were angry at Moses and Aaron. "This was all their fault," they thought. "May the LORD look upon you and judge you!" they said. "You have made us a stench to Pharaoh and his officials. You have put a sword in their hand to kill us."

And so the Israelites turned against Moses and Aaron, which was exactly what Pharaoh had intended. He did not want the Israelites listening to Moses and Aaron. He did not want the Israelites thinking about their God. He most certainly did not want them thinking about God's promise of deliverance. They must pay no attention to these "lies." They must concentrate on their work. Pharaoh did not want his slaves thinking about freedom. He wanted them working for him, with all their heart, soul, strength and might. Now Pharaoh had made their work so hard and their lives so cruel, that all they could think about was somehow surviving another day. That was Pharaoh's plan, and it was working.

Moses was perplexed and distressed. What was happening? What about God's plan? God's plan seemed to be failing. In his despair Moses sought the LORD. Moses turned to God in prayer and said, "O LORD, why have you brought trouble upon this people? Is this why you sent me? Ever since I went to Pharaoh to speak in your name, he has brought trouble upon this people, and you have not rescued Your people at all."

Then the LORD spoke to Moses. God said, "Now you will see what I will do to Pharaoh." Now that it had all come to a crisis, now that Pharaoh was at the height of his pride and contempt, now that His people were at the depths of their fear and despair, now God would act. Man's extremity is God's opportunity for helping and saving. The LORD said, "Now you will see what I will do to Pharaoh. Because of My mighty hand, he will let them go; because of My mighty hand he will drive them out of his country." Pharaoh said, "I will *not* let Israel go!" The LORD said, "He *will* let them go." Whose word would prove true? Two kings had spoken! Whose word would prevail?

God said to Moses, "I am the LORD!" Three times God repeated, "I am the LORD!" Did Moses forget that God was God? Did he forget who was the King of kings and Lord of lords? Who was the ruler over all nations? Was it not God? Who was in control of all things? Was it not God? Was Pharaoh all-powerful? No! "I am the LORD," said God. "I appeared to Abraham, to Isaac and to Jacob as El-Shaddai/God Almighty, but by my name, Jahweh/LORD, I did not make Myself known to them." Had Moses forgotten God's name? The LORD continued, "I also established My covenant with them to give them the land of Canaan, where they lived as aliens." Had Moses forgotten God's covenant? The LORD continued, "Moreover, I have heard the groaning of the Israelites, whom the Egyptians are enslaving, and I have remembered My covenant." Had Moses forgotten God's compassion? The LORD reminded Moses of three great things to strengthen his faith: God's Name, God's covenant and God's LOVE. Moses must not be afraid; he must only believe.

The Israelites heard Pharaoh's word, Pharaoh's wicked word; now they must hear God's Word, God's holy Word. God said to Moses:

Therefore, say to the Israelites: "*I am the* LORD . . .

1. I will bring you out from under the yoke of the Egyptians.
2. I will free you from being slaves to them . . .
3. I will redeem you with an outstretched arm and with mighty acts of judgement.
4. I will take you as my own people . . .
5. I will be your God. Then you will know that I am the LORD your God, who brought you out from under the yoke of the Egyptians.

6. I will bring you to the land I swore with uplifted hand to give
to Abraham, Isaac and Jacob.
7. I will give it to you as a possession.

I am the LORD."

The Israelites did not have to rely upon past promises given to their fore-fathers hundreds of years ago. God gave the people His great and gracious promises. God gave to them a seven-fold promise of what He would do. They must trust that promise. They too must believe.

But when Moses reported these gracious assurances and promises of God to the Israelites, they did not listen to him. They did not hear the Word of God. All they heard was the cracking of Egyptian whips and the scream-ing of Israelite slaves. By faith they did not see God or their deliverance or the land flowing with milk and honey; their eyes were closed to everything but their suffering. All they saw was Pharaoh, his soldiers, and his slave-drivers; all they saw was their cruel bondage in the land of their slavery. They felt no hope in the promises of God; no, their hearts were filled with ter-ror and despair. The Israelites did not listen to God's Word because they were so discouraged and exhausted. They felt utterly defeated. They did not say, "With God we will gain the victory, He will trample down our en-emies." (Psalm 108:13) No, their hope was gone, and they did not listen to God's Word for them, which would have filled them with an enduring hope. The Israelites were living by fear, rather than by faith. They were liv-ing by sight, by what appeared to be, rather than by faith, by what God as-sured would be. However, the LORD was going to rescue them. That was God's covenant promise!

Now Moses was disheartened too, for the Israelites were no longer lis-tening to him. God's plan seemed to be failing. When God told Moses the next step, he didn't want to take it. The LORD said to Moses, "Go tell Pharaoh king of Egypt to let the Israelites go out of his country." Again? Didn't God see that this was not working? Didn't God see that even the Israelites were not listening to him? Moses said to the LORD, "If the Israelites will not lis-ten to me, why would Pharaoh listen to me, since I speak with faltering lips." Moses thought that God's plan was failing because of him, because of his inability to speak well. The Israelites had blamed him for all the trouble, and now Moses was blaming himself. Moses thought no one was listening because of the way he was speaking.

But God's plan was working. Moses had only to do what God told him to do. The LORD said to Moses, "See, I have made you like God to Pharaoh, and your brother Aaron will be your prophet. You are to say everything I command you, and your brother Aaron is to tell Pharaoh to let the Israelites go out of his country." Would Pharaoh listen this time? No! That was part of God's plan. The LORD said, "But I will harden Pharaoh's heart." God would harden Pharaoh's heart so that he would not listen, so that he would not be saved. It was God's judgement upon that wicked man. Four hundred years ago God had promised Abraham, "Whoever curses you, I will curse" (Genesis 12:3). Pharaoh had cursed God's people; now God would curse Pharaoh. The worst of that curse was that God would harden Pharaoh's heart to both the words and the works of God. The LORD said, "Though I multiply my miraculous signs and wonders in Egypt, he will not listen to you. Then I will lay my hand on Egypt and with mighty acts of judgment I will bring out my divisions, my people, the Israelites. And the Egyptians will know that I am the LORD when I stretch out my hand against Egypt and bring the Israelites out of it."

Then Moses and Aaron obeyed the LORD and did just as the LORD commanded them. Again they went and spoke to Pharaoh. Although they were such old men, they pressed forward in the battle by faith. Their fight was not merely against flesh and blood, against the king of Egypt who was only a man; their fight was also against the spiritual forces of evil in the heavenly realms. Their fight was against Satan himself, who wanted to destroy the people and the praises of God. All hell would be fighting against Moses and Aaron, but they went forward by faith, proclaiming God's Word and doing just as the LORD commanded them.

To summarize, the way was made rough for Moses by the many beings (both human and demon) blocking his path:

1. The devil and the hordes of hell were the demonic powers fighting against Moses in the invisible realms. Moses' struggle was not merely against human adversaries, but "against the powers of this dark world and against the spiritual forces of evil in the heavenly realms" (Ephesians 6:12).

2. Pharaoh was a human "prince of darkness," a liar and a murderer like his father the devil. Pharaoh was the evil king who hardened his heart against Moses and against the LORD.

3. The Egyptians were a whole nation of people in opposition to Moses and in rebellion against God.

4. Even the Israelites turned against Moses.

5. Sometimes Moses himself got in the way. His weaknesses hindered his progress and he blocked his own path by his lack of faith. God urges all of us to "throw off anything that hinders and the sin that so easily entangles." God urges us to "run with endurance the race marked out for us" (Hebrews 12:1).

The teacher's guide for this lesson starts on page 208.

TWO KINGDOMS IN COLLISION

- **Exodus 7:1–13**
- **Matthew 24:24**
- **Romans 1:18–32**
- **Ephesians 6:10–13**
- **II Thessalonians 2:9–12**
- **Revelation 16:13, 14**

In those days the world was filled with people, creatures made in the image of God, but there were very few who glorified God, very few who bowed down in worship before the LORD their maker. The whole world was divided into nations, but not one of all these nations acknowledged the LORD. In which land could one hear the praises of God being sung from the lips of its people? There was no such land. The faithful were few upon the earth and the praises of God were seldom heard. This was Satan's plan from the beginning—to silence the praises of God. Yes, Satan wanted to erase the worship of the one and only God from the face of the entire earth. Satan appeared to have succeeded in his plan, for he had deceived every nation, tribe, people and language. Every nation had its false gods and worthless idols. Some of these nations worshipped the sun, the moon and the stars. Other nations worshipped the earth. They worshipped the rivers and the mountains, the plants and the trees. They worshipped all sorts of animals too and made idols in the forms of these animals. They bowed down before images of frogs and snakes, bulls and goats, cats and dogs, bears and wolves. They called upon the names of dragons and demons. They put their trust and their hope in the dead. They followed after mere men, who claimed to be gods. They bowed before statues of men and women, declaring them to be gods and goddesses. Because they exchanged the truth of God for a lie, and worshipped and served created things rather than the Creator—who is forever praised—God gave them over to their foolishness and godlessness and wickedness. God gave them over to the domain of darkness, which they loved, and the Prince of Demons, whom they served. Their lands were filled with all the depravity and perversity and atrocity that people commit who have forgotten the true God. Satan seemed to winning the war on earth.

From the beginning, however, before the foundation of the world, God had a plan. God wanted a people for Himself, a people who would love Him and follow Him, a people who would serve Him and worship Him. God's plan was that the knowledge of God would cover the earth as the waters cover the sea. God's plan included a great multitude from every nation, tribe, people and language worshipping before the throne of God in heaven. God's plan was to save a people for Himself, to save them from sin and death. God's plan was to rescue them from the devil and his domain of darkness. God's plan was to deliver His people into the glorious and eternal kingdom of light, the kingdom of His Son, Jesus Christ. But God seemed to be losing the war on earth.

Now at this point in the world war between God and Satan, a great battle was brewing, and it was brewing in the land of Egypt. God declared, "I am the LORD!" It was in Egypt that God would show the whole world that this was true. "I am the LORD and there is no other!" There, in that nation, God was going to smash the power of Satan. There God was going to smash the power of man. Idols and armies would be destroyed. There in the sight of every nation God would show His mighty acts and awesome signs. There God would save His people, and all the earth would see His great salvation.

God had chosen a people to make into a great nation for Himself, a nation that would worship Him alone, the one true God. But the people whom God had chosen, the Israelites, were trapped as slaves in the land of Egypt. The God of Israel said to the king of Egypt, "Let My people go, so that they may worship Me." But Pharaoh answered, "Who is the LORD, that I should obey Him and let Israel go? I do not know the LORD and I will not let Israel go." Who is the LORD? Now God was going to show Pharaoh, and all of

Egypt, and the whole world, who He was! The LORD said to Moses, "You are to say everything I command you, and your brother Aaron is to tell Pharaoh to let the Israelites go out of his country. But I will harden Pharaoh's heart, and though I multiply my miraculous signs and wonders in Egypt, he will not listen to you. Then I will lay my hand on Egypt and with mighty acts of judgement I will bring out my divisions, my people, the Israelites. *and the Egyptians will know that I am the Lord . . ."*

So Moses and Aaron did just as the LORD commanded them. They went back to Pharaoh with the same message. "Thus says the LORD, the God of Israel, *'Let my people go!'* " This time Pharaoh asked for proof. They claimed to have been sent from God. "Prove it," said Pharaoh. "Perform a miracle." God had told Moses and Aaron what to do. Aaron threw his staff down in front of Pharaoh and his officials, and the staff became a snake! But Pharaoh was not frightened. The sight which had caused Moses to run in fear, did not move Pharaoh in the least. His heart was hard. There was no fear of the LORD. Pharaoh's heart was as hard as stone, yielding not, trembling not, before the LORD. This slithering serpent was a frightening sign from Almighty God, but Pharaoh believed it not. He hardened his heart. Pharaoh hardened his heart against God, against God's sign and against God's Word.

God had warned Moses and Aaron that this would happen. God had told them beforehand, "I will harden Pharaoh's heart, and though I multiply my miraculous signs and wonders in Egypt, he will not listen to you." However, God had not warned them about what Pharaoh would do next: Pharaoh summoned his sorcerers and magicians and they were able to do the same things and show the same signs by their secret arts. One by one they threw down their staffs, and they also became snakes! How was this possible? Moses and Aaron must have been shocked. How could these wicked men have performed these awesome signs? These men were not servants of the Most High God, yet every one of them had produced the same miracle. How was this possible? The Bible speaks of "evil spirits" and the "spirits of demons performing miraculous signs" (Revelation 16:13, 14). Egypt's sorcerers and magicians did what they did by the power of Satan. They didn't just dabble in the demonic; they had fathomed the darkest depths of the occult regions. They were the masters of "Satan's deep secrets" (Revelation 2:24). What they did was "in accordance with the work of Satan displayed in all kinds of counterfeit miracles, signs and wonders and in every sort of evil that deceives those who are perishing. They perish because they refused to love the truth and so be saved. For this reason God sends them a power-ful delusion, so that they will believe the lie and so that all will be con-demned who have not believed the truth but have delighted in wickedness" (II Thessalonians 2:9–12). God's signs are given to bear witness to the truth, but Satan's signs are given to deceive. These sorcerers were Pharaoh's "false prophets" who had appeared and performed "great signs and miracles to de-ceive even the elect—if that were possible" (Matthew 24:24). As snake af-ter snake after snake appeared when each magician threw down his staff, Moses and Aaron had to stand firm in their faith, believing in the power of Almighty God to prevail, believing that this too was part of God's plan.

Moses and Aaron were in a terrible battle that day. They were not strug-gling against mere men, creatures of flesh and blood like themselves. No, their struggle was against unseen forces of darkness and invisible powers of wickedness in the heavenly realms. This was not just a battle between two men, Pharaoh and Moses, or between two nations, Egypt and Israel. This was part of the great war in heaven between Lucifer and our LORD. What God's servants were witnessing that day was the collision of two kingdoms. It was part of the colossal contest between the Kingdom of Darkness and the Kingdom of Light. Who would win? On that day, which kingdom would conquer? At first it seemed that Satan would prevail, as snake after snake af-ter snake appeared from the pits of hell. There was only one serpent repre-senting the power of God, but there were dozens of snakes, a whole brood of vipers, representing the power of Satan. But God's serpent swallowed up all the others. Aaron's staff devoured all the other staffs. The message was clear: Satan is powerful, but God is *all powerful*. He alone is the Almighty. The message was clear, but Pharaoh hardened his heart against it. He re-fused to believe what he saw with his own eyes:

God could destroy the power of Egypt. Pharaoh refused to listen to this early warning. His heart became hard and he would not listen to Moses and Aaron, just as the LORD had said. Pharaoh would not let the Israelites go. Moses and Aaron were sent away, but it was Egypt's sorcerers and magicians who left empty-handed. Aaron carried his staff in his hand, but their staffs were gone. It was a picture of what was to come. Soon the power of God's enemies would be swallowed up. Soon Pharaoh would be robbed of every-thing and Egypt would be left with nothing.

The teacher's guide for this lesson starts on page 210.

THE JUST JUDGEMENTS OF GOD: THE TEN PLAGUES

• Exodus 7:14–24
• Revelation 16:1, 3–7

PLAGUE 1: A River of Blood (Exodus 7:14–24; Revelation 16:1, 3–7)

B y the sign of the snake it was demonstrated to Pharaoh that Moses and Aaron were messengers sent to him from God Almighty, but Pharaoh's heart was unyielding, and he refused to let the Israelites go. So the LORD sent his two servants to the bank of the Nile River to wait for Pharaoh. Every morning Pharaoh came down to the water of the Nile River, which was the life-flow of Egypt. Perhaps the reason why Pharaoh came down to the water early each day was to pray to his god, the great god of Egypt, the Nile River. All the streams and canals and ponds and reservoirs of that country were connected to the Nile River. Every living thing in Egypt depended upon it. The crops were irrigated by it and the livestock was watered at it; the people boated on it, fished from it, bathed in it and drank from it. Even the King of Egypt went down to the Nile River every day. It was the "river of life" for Egypt, and the people bowed down before that river in worship. But the LORD, who is *life* and from whom flows living water, the only true God, He would destroy their false god. The God of Israel, the God of all the earth, who created and controlled this river-god of Egypt, He only had to touch its water and it would become a curse to them. By the Word of the LORD the Nile River would become the curse, rather than the life, of Egypt. God would show Pharaoh and all the Egyptians that He was the LORD, that He alone was the One before whom every nation and every knee should bow.

So, when Pharaoh and his officials arrived at the riverside the next morning, Moses and Aaron were waiting for them. Then they did just as the LORD commanded them. First Moses spoke to Pharaoh saying, "The LORD, the God of the Hebrews, has sent me to you: *Let my people go, so that they may worship me* in the desert. But until now you have not listened. So, this is what the LORD says: By this you will know that I am the LORD: With the staff that is in my hand I will strike the water of the Nile, and it will be changed into blood. The fish in the Nile will die and the river will stink. The Egyptians will not be able to drink its water." Then Aaron took his staff, the one that had become a snake, and he raised it up before Pharaoh and his officials. Aaron stretched it out over all the waters of Egypt and then he struck the water of the Nile River with it, and instantly it turned into blood. Now Pharaoh saw blood splashing at his feet and he saw blood as he gazed along the length of the river. In front of his very eyes Pharaoh had seen the river he loved changed from clear blue water to thick red blood. Before his very eyes Pharaoh had seen the water he worshipped changed from a beautiful, shimmering source of life to a horrible, frightening sign of death.

Drops of blood dripped from Aaron's staff and blood was splattered on his robe. Who was this old man, who dared to strike the god of Egypt? Moses, whose trembling voice and faltering lips had told of this plague, stood near him. Who was this old man who dared to warn the king of Egypt? Pharaoh could have answered truly, "They are servants of the Most High God." But Pharaoh thought, "They are just magicians. They are no different than my own sorcerers." If that were so, then Pharaoh should command his wise men to change the river back to water. He should command them to bring the Nile back to life. But all his magicians could do was to mimic the miracle of Moses. Pharaoh's sorcerers did the same thing by their secret arts and occult tricks: They too changed water into blood. And Pharaoh was absurdly pleased that his own servants had polluted the last little bit of drinking water left in Egypt. He was pleased because now he did not have to listen to

Moses and Aaron; he could ignore them. Now he could discount the miracle he had witnessed. Now he could deny that these two old men were sent from God. Pharaoh's heart became hard, just as the LORD had said, and he did not believe the truth of God. Pharaoh refused to love the truth and so be saved. Because Pharaoh delighted in wickedness, he allowed himself to be deceived by Satan's counterfeit sign. Pharaoh would not listen to Moses and Aaron. He would not let the Israelites go, although the Nile River, the very life of his nation, had been turned into blood. Pharaoh simply turned away from God's messengers; he turned his back on God's Word, and proudly strode into his palace, assuring himself that he had nothing to fear.

While Pharaoh sat undisturbed in his fine palace sipping choice wines, his country was in chaos. His own people had no water to drink. Every stream and every canal, all the ponds and all the reservoirs, even the water in the wooden buckets and stone jars, had been turned to blood. The people had to find water to drink or they would die. Already the land reeked of death. All the fish had died and the stench of their decaying flesh mixed with the putrid smell of old blood was nauseating. Now when the Egyptians came near the Nile River, they bowed forward not to worship, but to vomit. The smell was sickening. That was what the LORD did to their god: He made it a stench to their nostrils, an offense to their eyes, a revulsion to their stomachs. That was what the LORD did to the Egyptians: He gave this blood-thirsty people blood to drink. Was it not a just punishment? The river, which once drank the blood of the Israelite babies, now became blood for the Egyptians to drink. If the Egyptians did not find water soon, they too would die. They began frantically digging holes along the Nile in their search for water. God, in His Mercy, allowed them to find water to drink in these many little wells.

That day, as Moses stood on the bank of the Nile River, he must have been deeply moved as he witnessed the LORD turn its water into blood. Long, long ago, as a baby, Moses had been condemned to die in the waters of that river, by the command of Pharaoh, but God had graciously spared his life. Now Moses was the one who condemned that river to die, by the command of the LORD. Moses' life, even his name, was intimately connected with that river. That day Moses watched as the LORD put a plague upon the great Nile River. The staff of Aaron was like the finger of God, touching it, cursing it, killing it. How awesome are the works of God, how terrible are His judgements. Moses must have left the river of blood that day with the words of the angel and the response of the altar in his heart:

You are just in these judgements . . . Holy One . . .
for they have shed the blood of your saints and prophets,
and You have given them blood to drink, as they deserve.
Yes, Lord God Almighty, true and just are Your judgements.

Revelation 16:5–7

PLAGUE 2: An Army of Frogs (Exodus 8:1–15)

Seven days passed after the LORD struck the Nile River, but even a river of blood flowing through his country did not bring Pharaoh to his knees before the LORD. No, the king of Egypt refused to repent. He refused to let the Israelites go to worship their God. Then the LORD said to Moses, "Go to Pharaoh and say to him, 'Thus says the LORD: *Let my people go, so that they may worship me.* If you refuse to let them go, I will plague your whole country with frogs. The Nile will teem with frogs . . .' " Now God would cause this river, which had been dead for seven days, to miraculously come back to life. This river of blood, in which all the fish had died, would suddenly teem with life again in the form of millions upon millions of frogs. These frogs would not stay in the Nile River or along its banks; no, they would cover the whole land of Egypt! The land would be filled with frogs and the houses would be filled with them too. God said, "They will come up into your houses and onto your people." Not only the land would be covered with frogs; the people would be covered with them too, and this time Pharaoh would not escape the plague that faced his people. The king himself would be touched by it. God told Moses to warn Pharaoh about these frogs: "They will come up into your palace and into your bedroom and onto your bed . . . The frogs will go up on *you!*"

So Moses and Aaron went to Pharaoh again with God's Word. And Aaron did as the LORD commanded. He stretched out his hand with his staff over the waters of Egypt and frogs came up from the Nile River and from all Egypt's streams and canals and ponds. Frogs covered the land.

Perhaps you think that frogs are cute little creatures. They are. They are so pretty with their big black eyes and bright green skin, flecked and striped with gold. Have you ever watched a frog swim or jump? They are amazing athletes. Have you ever listened to a chorus of frogs peeping from the swamps on a warm spring night? They are beautiful singers. Even a big, fat, bullfrog croaking on a lilypad glorifies the LORD. God made these creatures, and they hop and sing and swim to the glory of God. "Let everything that has breath praise the LORD. Praise the LORD" (Psalm 150:6). However, on that day in Egypt, God would use frogs to praise His Name in another way. On that day, what the people of Egypt saw was not natural or beautiful. What they witnessed was uncanny, a miracle both awful and dreadful, a plague sent from Almighty God, "frogs that devastated them" (Psalm 78:45). How could this be? Frogs are harmless little creatures. Even small children like to catch them and hold them in their hands. Yet these frogs would conquer a king and a nation. "God chose the foolish things of the world to shame the wise; God chose the weak things of the world to shame the strong. He chose the lowly things of this world and the despised things and the things that are not, to nullify the things that are, so that no one may boast before Him" (I Corinthians 1:27–29). Pharaoh's boast before the LORD would come to nothing. All the wisdom and power of Egypt would not be able to stop these frogs. God would use a humble little creature of the earth to humble Pharaoh.

On that day in Egypt an unseen general gave the command for His troops to march. By God's Word an army of frogs advanced into enemy territory. These small green soldiers, without weapons and without armour, invaded the entire land of Egypt, and nothing could stop them. Pharaoh's soldiers and chariots were useless; their swords and their shields could do nothing. Millions of frogs just kept coming up out of the water and onto the land of Egypt. God's army of frogs marched forward. They hopped right into the houses. They leapt right past Pharaoh's guards and into his palace. They could not be kept out. There were too many of them. The frogs outnumbered Pharaoh's people; they over-powered his soldiers. There were frogs everywhere . . . *everywhere!* They were squashed on the floors of the palace like a slimy carpet. They squatted on the king's table and perched on his plates. They sat in his food and swam in his wine. They fell into the bread dough and were baked in the ovens. Pharaoh was disgusted. He could not eat. He left that miserable meal and went into his bedroom, but even there the king of Egypt could not escape from the plague. Frogs were climbing up his curtains and crawling across his covers. God's little green soldiers were hopping on his pillows and bouncing on his bed. Pharaoh shrieked at his servants to shake out the sheets. They obeyed, but that night Pharaoh would not be sleeping. He had barely stretched out his legs and closed his eyes, when he felt those creepy creatures on him. How dare they do such a thing? How dare they flop themselves on Pharaoh's face? How dare they hop on the king's head? How dare they rest on the royal rump? Pharaoh was in a rage. He was hopping mad, frog-hopping mad! He leapt out of bed and raced to his courtroom. Frogs were sitting on his throne. After they were brushed off, Pharaoh sat down and summoned his sorcerers. The magicians imitated the miracle of Moses. They very cleverly conjured up more frogs. Great! Just what Pharaoh wanted. Just what Egypt needed. More frogs! This time the king was not amused or impressed by the powers of his sorcerers and magicians. Why didn't they order the frogs to leave? Why didn't they command the frogs to vanish? They didn't, because they couldn't. Their power was limited. Satan and his servants could accomplish only what God permitted. The LORD had not ordered his army of frogs to retreat. They would remain in Egypt until God removed them.

Pharaoh began to understand this. He understood that the power and wisdom of Egypt had failed, failed in the face of these small frogs with their wide grins, who were driving him crazy. There was only one thing to do, one way to be rid of them. Pharaoh summoned Moses and Aaron. He wanted relief. Pharaoh, mighty Pharaoh, begged for God's mercy and Moses' prayers. "Pray to the LORD to take the frogs away from me and my people, and I will let your people go to offer sacrifices to the LORD."

Moses must have been very excited. At last the exodus would begin. At last the Israelites would be free! "When should I pray?" asked Moses. "I leave to you the honour of setting the time for me to pray for you . . ." "To-morrow," answered Pharaoh. Moses replied, "It will be as you say, so that you may know that there is no one like the LORD our God. The frogs will leave you and your houses, your officials and your people. They will remain only in the Nile River." Pharaoh must see that neither the frogs coming or leaving was an accident, a mere occurrence of nature. He must see that this army's advance and retreat was a direct act of God commanded by the LORD of hosts. God speaks, and even the frogs obey Him.

Moses did pray for Egypt's relief. After he left Pharaoh's palace, Moses cried out to the LORD about the frogs he had brought on Pharaoh. And the LORD did what Moses asked. The frogs died. They died in the homes, in the yards, in the fields. They died all over the land of Egypt. Their bodies were piled into heaps of rotting, stinking flesh. But they were gone. The ugly piles and awful smells would remind the Egyptians of God's plague lest they forget what God could do.

But Pharaoh had already forgotten. When he saw that there was relief, when he realized that the army of frogs was dead, he hardened his heart one more time. He refused to listen to Moses and Aaron. He refused to listen to God. He broke his promise, and he would not let the Israelites go.

Moses must have been upset, but God had warned him that this would happen. God told him at the beginning: "I will harden Pharaoh's heart, and though I multiply my miracles, signs and wonders in Egypt, he will not listen to you . . . but I will bring out My people, the Israelites . . . And the Egyptians will know that I am the LORD" (Exodus 7:3–5). It was all part of God's plan. The LORD had many more miracles to perform before the exodus would take place.

PLAGUE 3: Legions of Lice (Exodus 8:16–19; Psalm 2)

God granted Pharaoh's request. Pharaoh said, "Pray to the LORD to take the frogs away, and I will let your people go . . ." So Moses cried out to the LORD and the LORD in His mercy removed the frogs. But God's mercy did not soften Pharaoh's heart. No, the king of Egypt's response to the relief was to harden his heart again. Unless God created in Pharaoh a new heart, neither the judgements of God nor the mercies of God, would bring Pharaoh to a true repentance. His heart would grow harder and harder and harder. Pharaoh promised to let God's people go, but he broke that promise. Did Pharaoh really think that he could cheat God? The LORD must have laughed in heaven at this foolish little king of the earth. Was he not afraid of what the LORD would do next? No, Pharaoh was not a wise man; he did not even have the beginning of wisdom, for Pharaoh did not fear the LORD.

> Be wise, you kings. Be warned, you rulers of the earth. Serve the
> LORD with fear and rejoice with trembling. Kiss the Son, lest He
> be angry and you be destroyed in your way, for His wrath can flare
> up in a moment . . . (Psalm 2:10–12)

God's wrath did flare up, and this time without a warning. God spoke to Moses and told him what Aaron must do. Aaron must stretch out his hand with his staff one last time. This time he must strike the earth, not the water, of Egypt. The LORD said, "Strike the dust of the ground and throughout the land of Egypt the dust will become lice." Moses and Aaron did as the LORD commanded. Aaron stretched out his hand with the staff and struck the dust of the ground. Immediately all the dust throughout the land of Egypt became lice. Immediately lice came upon both animals and people. Lice came upon the king himself.

What are lice? They are tiny insects that live and feed on the bodies of people and animals. They bite; they hurt; they itch. They burrow into the flesh and lay eggs in the hair of their hosts. They cause weakness and sickness and madness. They drive people crazy with itching and scratching. Once a place is infested with lice, it is almost impossible to get rid of them!

Now the whole land of Egypt was infested with this pest, this plague. Like the dust on the ground were the lice on the people. Once before God had brought forth living creatures from the dust of the earth. In the beginning God said, "Let the land produce living creatures . . ." and it was so. When God speaks, even the dust on the ground obeys Him. This time, God brought forth legions of lice to glorify Himself. The God of armies can conscript angels or insects into His service. The LORD of hosts can call even the tiniest of creatures into action. With every bite these tiny torturers had a message: "Let my people go."

Not yet would Pharaoh let God's people go. First, he must see if his own sorcerers and magicians could remedy the situation. Surely the power and wisdom of Egypt was greater than that of these miserable lice brought by these miserable slaves. Pharaoh called for his wisemen, but they could neither produce, nor remove, the lice. They could neither create them, nor destroy them. They struck the ground, but nothing happened. The dust remained dust, and the lice remained on both man and beast. Their secret arts and occult tricks had failed them. Their source of power had failed them. Satan could go only as far as God permitted him to go. He was a roaring lion—on a leash. These wisemen, wicked though they were, understood something very important that day. They explained to Pharaoh about the plague: "This is the finger of God." Even these servants of Satan understood that God rules, that His power is supreme, that He is Almighty. "This is the finger of God," they said, for the first time admitting defeat, for the first time speaking the truth to their king. "This is the finger of God," they said, which was also a warning. This was only the finger of God, a mere touch of His punishment. Beware, Pharaoh! If this is the finger of God, beware of an angry blow by God's mighty hand and outstretched arm. Beware!

Pharaoh's wisemen were finally becoming wise, (as they began to know and fear the LORD,) but Pharaoh would not listen to them. His own sorcerers and magicians, who had before deceived him, now said enough to undeceive him: "This is the finger of God." They spoke the truth, but Pharaoh's heart was hard and he would not listen, just as the LORD had said.

PLAGUE 4: Swarms of Flies (Exodus 8:20–32)

God had struck the land of Egypt with three plagues, but Pharaoh had not listened or yielded to the Word of the LORD. Then the LORD told Moses to get up early in the morning and confront Pharaoh again as he went down to the water. God's message had not changed. Pharaoh's heart was hard, but God's Word was firm. "Thus says the LORD: '*Let my people go that they may worship me.*'" It was the same command. Perhaps Pharaoh thought he was winning this war, because he had withstood three plagues. He had not surrendered to God's command; he had not surrendered so much as a single slave. But Pharaoh was deceived; he was losing battle after battle after battle. No one can fight against God and win. God was being glorified through Pharaoh's hardness of heart. Even the wrath of man praises God!

Pharaoh was being given another chance. He had an opportunity to say "yes" to God, before Egypt was struck with another plague. Moses warned, "Thus says the LORD: 'Let My people go, so that they may worship Me. If you do not let My people go, I will send swarms of flies . . .'" Moses warned Pharaoh that these flies would be a plague upon Egypt. They would crawl all over his people—without exception. The king of Egypt would not be spared. God said, "I will send swarms of flies on *you*." Moses warned that the homes of the Egyptians would be full of flies. The peasants' huts, the nobles' houses, the king's palace—none of them would escape the plague of flies. Even the ground would be covered with masses of crawling buzzing flies.

This plague would be different than the preceding ones. This time, God would spare His people. There would be no flies in the Goshen Ghetto. The Israelites had suffered the lice epidemic, the water crisis and the frog problem along with their enemies, but now God said, "On that day I will deal differently with the land of Goshen, where My people live. No swarms of flies will be there, so that you will know that I, the LORD, am in this land. I will make a distinction between My people and your people. This miraculous sign will occur tomorrow."

Pharaoh had been warned. He had been given by God another day of grace, one more full day (plague-free) in which to consider the Word of God and repent of his sin. He had been given time to let God's people go, but Pharaoh did not obey the command of the LORD. So, the LORD sent swarms of flies into Egypt. "He spoke, and there came swarms of flies . . . throughout their country" (Psalm 105:31). "The LORD will whistle for flies . . . and for bees . . . and they will all come" to accomplish His purposes (Isaiah 7:18, 19). Yes, even the flies obey Him.

What greeted Pharaoh the following day was a horrible sight and sound. Dense swarms of flies poured into Pharaoh's palace and into the houses of all his people. The walls and the floors were black with the moving creatures. The air was thick with the humming insects. Flies buzzed in their ears, stuck in their eyes, flew into their mouths. The Bible says that "the land was *ruined* by flies." The Bible says that God sent "swarms of flies that *devoured* them" (Psalm 78:45). Egypt was being destroyed.

Pharaoh saw what was happening to his country, so he summoned Moses and Aaron. He was not yet willing to obey God, but he was willing to bargain with Him. "Go," said Pharaoh. "Sacrifice to your God, but do it here, in the land of Egypt."Moses said that would not be right and he told him why:

1) The first reason was that there was no such thing as religious tolerance in Egypt. The way the Israelites worshipped the LORD their God would be detestable to the Egyptians and would cause riots. The Israelites slaughtered sheep and sprinkled blood. They also slaughtered bulls and goats for sacrifice, animals which the Egyptians worshipped. When the Egyptians saw the Israelites killing animals which they considered sacred, they would stone them to death.

2) A more important reason was that God had commanded the Israelites to take a three-day journey into the desert. They must obey the LORD. They must worship their God exactly as He commanded and not as the king (or anyone else) suggested. Moses was not going to compromise. He was not going to bargain with the king of Egypt. Had anyone ever dared to say "no" to Pharaoh before this day? Yet here stood this old man, Moses, saying "no" to his offer and his order: "Sacrifice to your God here." Pharaoh, of course, did not have to accept Moses' refusal, but then he would have to continue listening to these flies, which were buzzing all around him. Pharaoh could

not stand it a minute longer. He yielded. He said, "I will let you go to offer sacrifices to the LORD your God in the desert, but you must not go very far." (Pharaoh wanted to make sure that he would get all his slaves back again!) "Now pray for me," demanded Pharaoh. Moses answered, "As soon as I leave you, I will pray to the LORD, and tomorrow the flies will leave Pharaoh and his people. Only be sure that Pharaoh does not act deceitfully again by not letting the people go to offer sacrifices to the LORD."

Pharaoh had a fly-filled day to think about that warning. With the flies still plaguing him and his country, Pharaoh could think about what he was going to do. Would he really repent? Would he really let the people go this time? Would he really obey God's Word? What would happen if he didn't? Was he not afraid that the God who could whistle for flies could just as easily whistle for bees—or something worse? Could not the God of Israel send swarms of killer bees into Egypt to sting his people to death as easily as He had sent the flies? Of course God could do this. (See Isaiah 7:18.) It was the grace of God that had spared Pharaoh and his country so far. These first plagues had been annoying and distressing, even alarming and ruining, but so far no one had died. God had been merciful to Egypt. But if Pharaoh disobeyed again, what would the God of Israel do next? If the plague were removed, how would Pharaoh respond to God's mercy this time? Pharaoh had a full day to ask himself such questions, and he had a full day to come up with the right answers.

Meanwhile, Moses left Pharaoh and he prayed to the LORD to remove the plague of flies. The LORD answered Moses' prayer. The LORD did what Moses asked. He sent the flies out of Egypt. As quickly as they appeared, they vanished. Not a single fly remained. Not only was the plague gone; every single little pest was gone too. Even we have to put up with a few flies where we live, but in Egypt "not a fly remained." It was remarkable! Their removal was as amazing as their arrival. Surely now Pharaoh would see that this was the work of God. But Pharaoh hardened his heart. He would not believe; he would not obey, and he would not let God's people go.

It was strangely quiet in Egypt that day. The constant buzzing , buzzing, buzzzzzzzzzing had ceased, and the whole land felt a tremendous relief, but in spite of the stillness, something hung heavily and invisibly over the land. What was it? There was peace in Egypt from the flies, but there was no peace with God. His wrath remained upon them.

PLAGUE 5: A Deadly Disease (Exodus 9:1–7)

Was Pharaoh not yet afraid of what the LORD would do to him and his people? Again he deceived Moses. Again he disobeyed God. What would happen now? The LORD sent Moses to Pharaoh with the same message. "This is what the LORD, the God of the Hebrews, says: *'Let my people go, so that they may worship me.'* If you refuse to let them go and continue to hold them back, the hand of the LORD will bring a terrible plague on your livestock in the field, on your horses and donkeys and camels, on your cows and sheep and goats. But the LORD will make a distinction between the livestock of Israel and that of Egypt, so that no animal belonging to the Israelites will die." This time it was not the "finger of God," but the "hand of the LORD," that would strike Egypt . . . and the fierce hand that struck Egypt with this deadly disease was the same kind hand that would shield Israel from it. Not only would God preserve His people; He would protect their animals too.

The LORD set a time and said, "Tomorrow the LORD will do this in the land." And the next day the LORD did it. What God says, He does. God's Word does not fail. The Israelites could count on the Promises of God, and so could the Egyptians. God's Word is true, both in blessing and in cursing, in salvation and in destruction. The LORD did what He said: All the livestock of the Egyptians died.

The loss of the livestock was a national disaster in Egypt. All the beasts that made her rich and strong were wiped out in one day. The horses for Egypt's army, the camels for her trade, the donkeys for her labour, they all lay lifeless in the fields and along the roads. The cows and sheep and goats — all the animals that supplied Egypt with food and clothing — these died by the thousands, by tens of thousands, by hundreds of thousands. Pharaoh must have sat in stunned silence as the reports came to him from all over the country. From the majestic stallion of Pharaoh himself to the scrawniest goat of the poorest peasant, all the animals were struck by the deadly disease.

Was there not one animal of all the livestock left standing in the entire land? Yes, there were many of these animals left. In the Goshen ghetto, in the area where the Israelites lived, you could still hear the baaing of sheep and the bleating of goats. Pharaoh suddenly remembered the words of Moses and the Word of God: "No animal belonging to the Israelites will die." Pharaoh sent men to investigate. Was it true? Yes, their livestock was still alive —all of it. The plague had not sickened or weakened even one animal belonging to the Israelites. They were all well and strong.

How could this be? The livestock of the Israelites breathed the same air, drank the same water, ate the same grass, yet this deadly disease had not touched them. How could this be? Pharaoh knew the answer, but he suppressed the truth in unrighteousness. Pharaoh refused to acknowledge God. He refused to submit to the Lord. His heart was unyielding even now. Pharaoh would not let God's people go.

It is hard to comprehend the wickedness and foolishness of Pharaoh. Did he not realize that the one who could destroy the animals of Egypt, could also destroy the people? Had he not been shown that when the God of Israel spoke, even a deadly disease obeyed Him? Did Pharaoh not realize that even his own life was in the hands of this God? Did he not think that the hand of the LORD could strike him too, that he could be struck down dead, as easily as his horse? Did all Egypt's dead animals (or all Israel's live ones) not make him see that this God controlled life and death itself?

What about the rest of the Egyptians? Did they not see the vanity of their own gods? The animals that the LORD struck down were the creatures that they loved and the idols that they worshipped. They bowed before golden calves and silver goats, but now these gods of Egypt lay dead. Their rotting corpses polluted the land, as surely as their shining images defiled it. However, while the gods of Egypt were being smashed, perhaps unbelief was crumbling in people's hearts too. Perhaps some of the people in Egypt were turning to the God of Israel in fear and faith. Perhaps some hearts in Egypt were being softened, even while their king continued to harden his heart.

Once again God had shown mercy to Egypt. He had struck their animals; He had struck their gods, but He had not yet struck them. They were still alive. They had seen the hand of God at work in their land, like no other people on the face of the earth. They had been given another opportunity to repent, another opportunity to turn from their sins and their gods, another opportunity to believe in the LORD—and live. But would they choose life?

What about the Israelites? Did they trust now in their God? Did they know for certain that God could and would rescue them? As the Israelites looked upon the thousands and thousands of dead animals belonging to their enemies, did they say in their hearts about the LORD, "He is my refuge and my fortress, my God, in whom I trust. Surely He will save you . . . from the deadly pestilence. He will cover you with His feathers and under His wings you will find refuge. His faithfulness will be your shield . . . You will not fear the terror of night . . . nor the pestilence that stalks in the darkness, nor the plague that destroys at midday. A thousand may fall at your side, ten thousand at your right hand, but it will not come near you. You will only observe it with your eyes and see the punishment of the wicked" (Psalm 91:1–8). Hallelujah! Did the Israelites offer thanks and shouts of praise to their God?

PLAGUE 6: An Outbreak of Boils (Exodus 9:8–12; Revelation 16:2, 11)

The livestock of Egypt had become deadstock. This time Pharaoh did not summon God's servants, for he thought that the prayers of Moses could not reverse this plague, nor could the rod of Aaron raise the dead. There was no way to recover the loss of Egypt's animals. They were all dead. The plague was done, so Pharaoh made no promises. In fact, since Egypt's beasts of burden were gone, he was more determined than ever to keep his slaves. Let the Israelites do the work of the horses. Let them bear the loads of the donkeys. Pharaoh would not let God's people go!

Did Pharaoh think that the servants of God were like his own sorcerers and magicians; that their power too must come to an end? Did Pharaoh think that Israel's God was growing tired and would soon give up the fight? Did Pharaoh think he was winning because he was still standing? How could Pharaoh not yet fear the LORD? Did he really think that there was nothing else or nothing worse that God could do? Oh foolish Pharaoh.

Out of the furnace of His people's affliction, God would afflict His enemies. The LORD said to Moses and Aaron, "Take handfuls of soot from a furnace." (Perhaps it was from one of the furnaces were the Israelite slaves baked bricks from morning till night to feed Pharaoh's fancies). "Take handfuls of soot from a furnace," said the LORD, "and have Moses toss it into the air in the presence of Pharaoh. It will become fine dust over the whole land of Egypt, and festering boils will break out on men and animals throughout the land."

Moses and Aaron obeyed the LORD. Again they went to Pharaoh, this time carrying something very strange in their hands—ashes. Moses stood before the king and tossed the ashes into the air. Instantly, festering boils broke out on all the powerful men and beautiful women of Pharaoh's court. Large, red, ugly, painful sores covered their bodies and faces. The king screamed for his wisemen to do something, but the king's magicians and sorcerers had been struck so forcefully by the angry hand of God, that they could not face Moses; they could not even stand. Satan's servants had a small taste of hell. They were in such torment because of the boils, that they could not get up from the floor where they writhed in agony.

While this was happening in Pharaoh's palace, a fine grey dust was spreading mysteriously over the whole land of Egypt. Dust to dust. Ashes to ashes. The people must have wondered what it was, but soon their confused looks turned to alarmed shouts. Oozing, itching, bleeding sores broke out on all the people. This time the LORD struck the Egyptians themselves, attacking their health and their strength and afflicting them with terrible pain. The LORD also attacked their pride, turning their beautiful, powerful bodies into useless heaps of flesh — heaps of stinking, disgusting, nauseating, excruciating flesh. The Egyptians cried and screamed because of the pain of that plague, but even the weeping and moaning of his own people did not soften Pharaoh's heart. His heart was as hard as stone, encrusted with the cement of sin. Not even the sighs and tears of his own children penetrated Pharaoh's heart. He was unyielding. He would not let God's people go.

Pharaoh refused to believe and obey the Word of the LORD. He must have cursed the God of Israel because of his pains and his sores. He must have cursed the name of God, who had control over these plagues, but he refused to repent. He refused to glorify God, though he himself was in agony.

Then we read of a judgement upon Pharaoh far worse than any plague. The Bible says: "The LORD hardened Pharaoh's heart." For many years Pharaoh's heart was hard, and that was bad enough. During these plagues Pharaoh had actively and consciously hardened his own heart, and that was even worse. But now we read that God hardened Pharaoh's heart. That condition was the worst. What God hardens, who can soften? There was no longer hope for Pharaoh, for the LORD God Himself hardened Pharaoh's heart. God had given Pharaoh over to the hardness for which there was no forgiveness. The sentence of death had been pronounced by God upon Pharaoh's heart. Dust to dust. Ashes to ashes. There would be no mercy. The LORD hardened Pharaoh's heart.

PLAGUE 7: A Hammering of Hail (Exodus 9:13–35; Psalm 78:47–50; 105:32, 33; Revelation 16:21)

The LORD sent Moses to Pharaoh again. As God commanded him, Moses appeared before the king of Egypt early in the morning and confronted him with the Word of God. This was the message that Moses proclaimed: "Thus says the LORD, the God of the Hebrews: *Let my people go, so that they may worship me . . .*" Pharaoh had heard that same message many times and had not obeyed it. Why should he listen this time? God told him why. God said, "This time I will send *the full force of my plagues* against you and against your officials and against your people, so that you may know that there is no one like Me in all the earth. For by now I could have stretched out my hand and struck you and your people with a plague that would have wiped you off the face of the earth. But I have raised you up for this very purpose, that I might show you My power and that My name might be proclaimed in all the earth . . ."

This time God warned Pharaoh that, if the Israelites were not set free, the Egyptians and their king would have to face the full force of God's plagues against them. If Pharaoh thought the plagues were subsiding, if he thought they would soon be ending, if he thought he could succeed in resisting, if he thought he was possibly winning, God was telling him that he was wrong. More plagues and worse plagues were yet to come. It was true that Pharaoh had not yielded, that he had not surrendered even one of his slaves; it was true that he had resisted the commands of God Almighty and that he had not weakened under the assaults or crumbled under the attacks against him, but that was not because of Pharaoh's strength. That was because of God's mercy. Pharaoh had not faced the full force of God's fury. God had restrained Himself. Had God not done so, Pharaoh and his people would have been wiped off the face of the earth by now.

Pharaoh was a fool. He neither feared the fury of God nor fled to the mercy of God. His heart was hard. His mind was dark. He took his stand against God and was proud that he was still standing. Six plagues had not moved him. Pharaoh laughed. He was a mighty king, who sat on Egypt's throne; no one, not even God, would tell him what to do. "But the one enthroned in heaven laughs; the LORD scoffs" at the kings of the earth. "Then He rebukes them in his anger and terrifies them in His wrath . . ." (Psalm 2:4, 5).

God told Pharaoh that day why he was the king of Egypt and why he was still allowed to sit alive upon his throne. God was the one who had placed him there and God was the one who allowed him to remain there, (for just a little while longer). God had raised Pharaoh to this high position, as the greatest king in the world, for one purpose, for these plagues that were now happening: "that I might show you My power and that *my* name might be proclaimed in all the earth!" All this was for God's own glory! God was using Pharaoh (and Pharaoh's hard-heartedness and Pharaoh's vile wickedness) to glorify Himself. God was using Pharaoh for His own purposes. Even Pharaoh's stubborn rebellion against God was part of God's plan. It would all be used to praise and worship and glorify the LORD! No person, not even the greatest king in the world or the mightiest angel in the universe, can thwart the purposes and promises of God.

What God said that day to Pharaoh surely came to pass. Even now, thousands of years later . . . even here, thousands of miles away . . . we know of the power of God because of what He did to this Pharaoh in the land of Egypt. At that time the news of what God did travelled throughout the nations, and that news is still travelling, to this very day. We read about these plagues; we even sing about them; and we glorify God because of them. That was why God rescued His people in this way. God wanted people in every land, in every age, to know of His power through the signs, wonders and miracles that He performed in Egypt. God wanted people to know Him and fear Him; He wanted people to trust Him and love Him; God wanted people to believe Him and obey Him and worship Him, that they might be saved. God our Saviour, "wants all men to be saved and to come to a knowledge of the truth" (II Timothy 2:4). That was why God created human beings, to enjoy Him and worship Him forever. These plagues were all part of God's great plan of salvation. "Therefore, be wise, you kings! Be warned, you rulers [and peoples] of the earth! Serve the LORD with fear . . . Kiss the Son, lest He be angry and you be destroyed . . . for His wrath can flare up in a moment. Blessed are all who take refuge in Him" (Psalm 2:10–12). It was a message for the whole world!

That was the long-range forecast, but God had something to say to Pharaoh for the very next day: "You still set yourself against My people and will not let them go. Therefore, at this time tomorrow I will send the worst hailstorm that has ever fallen on Egypt, from the day it was founded until now. Give an order to bring your livestock and everything you have in the field to a place of shelter, because the hail will fall on every man and animal that has not been brought in and is still out in the field, and they will die."

Not one more animal needed to die. Not one human life needed to be lost. God had given Egypt an escape from the disaster that was about to strike. They had twenty-four hours of warning before the fatal hail began to fall. Only one thing was required—faith! They had to have faith that Moses was indeed a prophet sent from God. They had to have faith that this message was in truth the Word of God. They had to have faith in the God of Israel, that He was God Almighty, whom even the storm clouds and hail stones obeyed. In this plague God was making a distinction not just between Israelite and Egyptian; this time God was making a distinction between Egyptian and Egyptian, between those who believed God's Word and those who did not believe God's Word. This time the dividing line was faith. We read in the Bible that the officials of Pharaoh, who feared the Word of the LORD, hurried to bring their servants and their animals inside. But those who ignored the Word of the LORD left their servants and animals outside.

The next day the LORD said to Moses, "Stretch out your hand toward the sky so that hail will fall all over Egypt—on men and animals and on everything growing in the fields of Egypt." When Moses stretched out his staff towards the sky, the LORD sent the worst storm that had ever raged in the land of Egypt. The sky grew black. Thunder crashed in the clouds and lightening flashed to the ground. Trees were shattered. Bolts of lightening struck both man and beast. Rain poured down heavily on the land. Then the rain turned to sleet and the sleet turned to hail. Huge hailstones beat furiously upon every living thing. The hailstones were ice bullets, shredding the crops and stripping the trees. The hailstones were canon balls, slaughtering men and beasts and damaging homes and barns. Egypt had fought in many wars, but never had such deadly and destructive ammunition been used against the land. The barrage went on and on and on. Would anything be left standing? Even Pharaoh began to wonder. As hour after dark hour passed, the storm continued. Huge hailstones smashed against the palace walls. Even Pharaoh feared for his life.

Meanwhile, in the Goshen ghetto, the Israelites stood in the sunshine of God's LOVE, "for God, the LORD, is shield and sun" (Psalm 84:11). The Israelites found shelter in the Most High God. They hid in the shadow of the Almighty, while the storm of God's wrath rained down upon their enemies. For hundreds of years the Israelites had heard the crack of Egyptian whips. Now they heard a pleasant sound; they heard the *crack* of thunder in the distance as God lashed their Egyptian tormentors with lightening. The Israelites could see the whips of fire striking their enemies again and again. It was a pleasant sight. For hundreds of years the Israelites had been beaten by the hands of the Egyptians. Now the Egyptians were being beaten by the mighty arm of their God. The God of vengeance, the LORD of justice, was punishing the wicked, and His people were right to rejoice in it. Now it was Egypt's turn to plead for mercy.

Pharaoh could stand the beating no longer. Hailstorms were usually brief, but this one was not stopping or moving. The black thunderclouds were not rolling onwards. They had been stationed above Egypt and there they would stay. They had not received a cease-fire order from God their commander. The storm would continue until Pharaoh was ready to surrender.

Pharaoh was ready. He summoned Moses and Aaron and confessed to them, "This time I have sinned. The LORD is in the right and I and my people are in the wrong. Pray to the LORD, for we have had enough thunder and hail. *I will let you go!* You don't have to stay any longer." Moses replied, "When I have gone out of the city, I will spread out my hands in prayer to the LORD. The thunder will stop and there will be no more hail, so that you may know that the earth is the LORD's! But I know that you and your officials still do not believe the LORD God."

Then Moses left Pharaoh and went out of the city. Moses was not afraid to walk out in the storm. The LORD his God would not strike his servant with a hailstone. Each one was directed by God. There would be no stray bullets. When he was outside the city, Moses spread out his hands toward the LORD. Immediately, the thunder and hail stopped and the rain no longer poured down on the land.

When Pharaoh saw that the storm had stopped, did he rejoice? Yes. Did he give thanks to God? No. When Pharaoh saw that the danger had passed, he sinned again. He and his officials hardened their hearts. Because Pharaoh's heart was hard, harder than ever, he would not let the Israelites go.

"Blessed is the man who always fears the LORD, but he who hardens his heart falls into trouble" (Proverbs 28:14). Pharaoh was in trouble, trouble that eventually would lead to his death.

PLAGUE 8: An Invasion of Insects (Exodus 10:1–20; Psalm 105:34, 35; Joel 2:1–11; Revelation 9:1–12)

Once again the LORD said to Moses, "Go to Pharaoh." Moses must have wondered: Why? Why go to Pharaoh again? What could he say, what could God do, that would make Pharaoh let the Israelites go? Egypt was already ruined. The hail storm had destroyed almost all of the crops, and still Pharaoh had refused to let God's people go. Now he had little left to lose. What was the purpose of going to Pharaoh again, especially when the LORD's next words made the task seem utterly futile. God said to Moses, "Go to Pharaoh, for I have hardened his heart." Then there was no hope. Pharaoh's hard heart would never respond to the Word of God. So why go to Pharaoh again, why preach to him again, if his heart was hard? God told Moses why. The LORD not only had good reasons; He had great and glorious reasons. God said, "I have hardened Pharaoh's heart . . ."

1. So that I may perform these miraculous signs among them

2. So that you may tell your children and grandchildren

3. So that you may know that I am the LORD.

God had hardened Pharaoh's heart so that He could multiply His signs and wonders and miracles for all the world to see and to know that He was the LORD. God had determined the perfect number of plagues to be performed. These ten plagues were inflicted, so that they might be recorded, so that there might be undeniable proof for the generations to come, that the God of Israel is the LORD of all the earth! He was the LORD over nature. The waters listened to His Voice. The winds and the clouds obeyed Him. The tiniest creatures responded to the Word of the LORD. Even the darkness and the powers of darkness were under His sovereign rule. These plagues would be a warning to unbelievers in every age to repent of their unbelief. These plagues would be a strengthening to believers in every age to persevere in their faith, because great is the LORD and "great are the works of the LORD" (Psalm 111:2).

So Moses and Aaron went to Pharaoh again, just as God had commanded them, and said, "Thus says the LORD, the God of the Hebrews, "How long will you refuse to humble yourself before Me? *Let my people go so that they may worship me.* If you refuse to let them go, I will bring locusts into your country tomorrow. They will cover the face of the ground, so that it cannot be seen. They will devour what little you have left after the hail, including every tree that is growing in your fields. They will fill your houses and the houses of all the Egyptians, something neither your fathers nor your forefathers have ever seen from the day they settled in this land until now."

When Moses said what he had been sent to say, he turned and left. He was not interested in pleading or begging, bargaining or arguing with Pharaoh. He had warned the king of Egypt what his continuing disobedience to the God of Israel would bring: An invasion of insects!

Pharaoh's officials were afraid. They now feared the Word of the LORD that came through Moses. They knew that what he fore-warned, not only happened, but was worse than what they imagined. They said to Pharaoh, "How long will this man be a snare to us? Let the people go, so that they may worship the LORD their God. Do you not yet realize that Egypt is ruined?" Pharaoh had not yet surrendered, but his country was already conquered. Even Pharaoh's advisors knew this. Famine faced Egypt. Most of their livestock had been killed by disease. The few that were left were slaughtered in the storm. Most of the crops had been ruined by the hail. The little that was left would be devoured by the locusts. Egypt was ruined. Even Pharaoh's advisors were echoing Moses' message: "*Let the people go, so that they may worship the LORD their God.*"

Pharaoh refused to listen to the Word of God spoken through Moses and Aaron, but he considered listening to his own advisors. He summoned God's servants to return to him. He said to Moses and Aaron, "Go, worship the LORD your God." Moses could hardly believe his ears. Was that long-awaited order to go really coming from the lips of Pharaoh? Yes, but that joyful command did not last long. Immediately following came a suspicious question from those same lips. "But just who will be going?" asked Pharaoh. Moses answered, "We will be going with our young and old, with our sons and daughters, with our flocks and herds, because we are to celebrate a festival to the LORD." Pharaoh was enraged. Never. Never would he allow everyone to go. Pharaoh said, "The LORD *is* with you— if I let you go with your women and children! Clearly you are bent on evil. No! Have only the men go and worship the LORD, since that is what you have been asking." Pharaoh knew that he would never see his slaves again, if they left with their families. Thus Pharaoh wanted to keep the women and children back in Egypt as hostages, to ensure that the men would return. He was willing now to let the men slaves go for three days to worship their God, but then he wanted them back again. Keeping the women and children would ensure the return of his slaves. That was all Pharaoh was willing to give, an offer which was not acceptable to God. God is not pleased if only men worship Him. God wants the praises of women and children too. Their voices, singing forth the honour and glory of His Name, are as sweet to the LORD as the lower toned sounds of the men. All God's people—young and old, men and women—must worship the LORD their God. So Moses rejected Pharaoh's offer. Then the king of Egypt had these two Israelites, who were servants of the Most High God, driven from his presence. Let them feel the sting of his whips, along with the rest of his slaves. Pharaoh would show them who was lord in Egypt.

Then the LORD said to Moses, "Stretch out your hand over Egypt so that locusts will swarm over the land and devour everything growing in the fields, everything left by the hail." So Moses stretched out his staff over Egypt, and the LORD made an east wind blow across the land all that day and all that night. By morning, the wind had brought the locusts. They invaded all Egypt. What was this invasion like? "Like dawn, spreading across the mountains, a large and mighty army comes . . . Before them the land is like the garden of Eden, behind them, a desert waste—nothing escapes them. They have the appearance of horses; they gallop along like cavalry. With a noise like that of chariots, they leap over the mountaintops, like a crackling fire consuming stubble, like a mighty army drawn up for battle. At the sight of them, nations are in anguish. Every face turns pale. They charge like warriors; they scale walls like soldiers. They all march in line, not swerving from their course. They do not jostle each other; each marches straight ahead. They plunge through defences without breaking ranks. They rush upon the city. They run along the wall. They climb into the houses; like thieves they enter through the windows. Before them the earth shakes. The sky trembles. The sun and moon are darkened and the stars do not shine. The LORD thunders at the head of His army. His forces are beyond number and mighty are those who obey His command" (Joel 2:2–11). Yes, God commanded, and His army of locusts flew with the wind into Egypt. Nothing could stop them. They could fly over oceans and deserts and mountains. They settled down in every area of the country in great numbers. Never before had there been such a plague of locusts, nor will there ever be again. They covered all the ground until it was black. "[God] spoke, and the locusts came, grasshoppers without number; they ate up every green thing in their land . . ." (Psalm 105:34, 35). They devoured all that was left after the hail, every growing thing that was left. You could hear the horrible sound of their tiny jaws gnawing. Yes, you could hear the millions of locusts' mouths chewing and chewing, as they ate up the last of Egypt's food. "God gave their crops to the grasshopper, their produce to the locust" (Psalm 78:46). The whole land was left brown and bare. Nothing green remained anywhere in Egypt: no grass, no plants, no trees. The land was utterly ruined.

Pharaoh was stunned when he saw the devastation. The beauty and the plenty of his beloved country was gone. Egypt had become a wasteland. Quickly he summoned Moses and Aaron. He confessed, "I have sinned against the LORD your God and against you. Now forgive my sin once more and pray to the LORD your God to take this deadly plague away from me." At last Pharaoh had seen the connection between sin and death. His sin (the oppression of God's people and rebellion against God) had led to death (the destruction of Egypt.) Pharaoh begged for forgiveness and asked for the deadly plague to be removed, but was he willing to repent? It was not the plague of locusts, but the sin of hard-heartedness, that was the problem. Was Pharaoh willing to repent of that sin? This time, Pharaoh made no promises.

Nonetheless, Moses was willing to pray to the LORD and the LORD, Who is quick to forgive and swift to show mercy (although He knew what was in Pharaoh's heart), was willing to withdraw His troops. The LORD changed the wind to a very strong west wind, which caught up the locusts and carried them into the Red Sea. Take warning, Pharaoh! Take warning! By God's hand, the army of Egypt can thus be driven to destruction as easily as these legions of locusts. Take warning, Pharaoh! Take warning! If the airforce of the Almighty can be drowned in the Red Sea, so can the soldiers and chariots of Egypt's army.

God was merciful to Pharaoh one more time. He had sent this plague of locusts, but they were only locusts of the earth, not locusts out of hell. The Bible declares that a day is coming when God will send locusts out of hell's smoke to torture the wicked. These locusts will not harm the grass or plants or trees, but they will sting the wicked, like the sting of a scorpion. During those days men will long to die, because of the agony they suffer. God was merciful, in that the plague could have been worse, much worse! God was merciful in that He again showed Pharaoh and all Egypt who He was. "I am the LORD and there is no other." In this plague, Pharaoh and his people again had an opportunity to repent of their wicked unbelief. God was merciful in that He removed the plague at Pharaoh's request, so that not a single locust was left anywhere in Egypt. But the LORD hardened Pharaoh's heart, and Pharaoh would not let the Israelites go.

PLAGUE 9: A Dreadful Darkness (Exodus 10:21–29; Psalm 105:26–28; Isaiah 13:9–11; Amos 5:20 & 8:9; Zephaniah 1:14, 15; Revelation 16:10)

Egypt was completely ruined, but Pharaoh's heart remained hardened and darkened. Still he refused to acknowledge God. Still he refused to obey God's command to let God's people go. Perhaps Pharaoh felt that he had nothing left to lose, that God had nothing else to take, so why should he let his slaves go? He needed his slaves now, more than ever, to work at restoring his ruined country. But Pharaoh was wrong. Was there really nothing left for God to take?

In the beginning God said, "Let there be light," and there was light. God saw that the light was good and God separated the light from the darkness. God also said, "Let there be lights in the expanse of the sky . . . to give light on the earth." And it was so. God made the sun to blaze during the day; at night the moon shimmered on the waters and stars twinkled in the heavens. In between day and night, at dawn and at dusk, there was twilight. God also gave the earth the magnificent splendour of sunrises and sunsets, making the heavens flame with radiant reds and glorious golds for the eyes of men to behold with wonder and for the lips of men to give thanks to God, whose glory crowns the sky. God gave these good gifts to all mankind. In His mercy He caused the sun to shine on both the righteous and the wicked. By God's grace evil men could also see the light of day. But the God who said, "Let there be light" could just as easily say, "Let there be darkness"— and it would be so.

Was there really nothing else for God to take from Egypt? Yes, there was. God could take light from the land, and that is exactly what God did. The LORD said to Moses, "Stretch out your hand toward the sky so that darkness will spread over Egypt—darkness that can be felt." Moses did as God commanded. He stretched out his hand toward the sky and total darkness covered all Egypt for three days. The Egyptians could not see anyone or go anywhere. They were trapped by it, blinded by it, terrified by it. They could not see to work or even to move. "Light the lamps!" Pharaoh shouted to his servants, but still there was no light. Perhaps the darkness was so thick and so black that their feeble lights could not penetrate it. Perhaps the darkness was like a cold, wet, thick, black, fog, a darkness that could be felt, a darkness that snuffed out any flame that tried to flicker in it. "Light the lamps!"

Pharaoh screamed . . . but there was only darkness. Did the king of Egypt think he could command light when the King of kings had commanded darkness? God says, "I am the LORD and there is no other; apart from Me there is no God . . . I form the light and create darkness" (Isaiah 45:5, 7). This little god of Egypt could shriek in fear and rage, "Light the lamps," but both the light and the darkness obeyed the LORD. Total darkness covered all the land . . . and it was *terrifying*!

Most people are afraid of the dark, but few people have experienced total darkness. There is always a little light shining somewhere, even if it is just a crack of light by the door or the wink of a star in the sky. What you experience is greyness, not blackness, and as your eyes become accustomed to the dark you begin to see shadowy forms. You acquire night vision. But this did not happen to the Egyptians. No matter how long they waited or how long they stared, they still could see nothing. Their eyes could not adjust to such darkness.

Once I experienced total darkness when I was touring some caverns deep underground. The guide turned off all the lights, and we were plunged into total darkness. There was not a pinpoint of light anywhere. You could see nothing, not even your hand right in front of your face. After three minutes, the guide switched the lights on again. She did not wait longer, because very quickly people panic in total darkness. I had to pray to the LORD to keep myself from screaming during the last long minute of that underground blackness.

But back in Egypt, during the plague of darkness, God did not restore light to the Egyptians after a few terrifying minutes. No. Hour after hour passed and there was no light. Twenty-four hours passed. Surely a new day would bring new light, but the darkness remained. Hour after agonizing hour, the darkness pressed upon them. They could actually feel it, like the cold, clammy fingers of death trying to crush them or choke them. This was no ordinary darkness, like the darkness of night, which is given to us for rest and sleep. This was an eerie, evil, unnatural darkness, one in which there was no peace, one which was filled with the horror and terror of God's judgement. Perhaps it was a darkness filled with the dread of demons. Perhaps evil spirits slithered into that blackness like serpents from the pits of hell. Perhaps it was a darkness filled with the visions of their own damnable deeds, now accusing them, now condemning them, and there was nowhere to run. The Egyptians were trapped in their houses, trapped in the darkness of their own guilty consciences. There was no way to escape it. How long must they endure it?

Another "day" began; it "dawned" as black as the two preceding ones. What were the Egyptians thinking? Were their minds wandering to the God of Israel, whose mercies are new every morning, like the light of dawn, for which they had never once given Him thanks. Were they thinking of the gods of Egypt, the sun, which they worshipped? Where was their god now? In one instant, with one command, the God of Israel had blotted out the sun. Who was this God, that even the sun and the moon in the heavens obeyed Him? Who was this God, that even the little flames on earth listened to His Voice? Perhaps some of the Egyptians, even in the darkness of those dreadful "days," turned their hearts to the LORD, the God of Israel, forsaking their own gods, the false gods, of Egypt. Perhaps some of the Egyptians whispered in the dark, "LORD, the God of Israel, let the light of your countenance shine on us too, we pray." God in His mercy had given the Egyptians one more day of darkness, one more terrifying plague to bring about repentance, one more mighty miracle that they might know He alone was the LORD. God gave them one more sign, that they might turn from their wickedness and live, that they might be spared from the eternal darkness that awaited them.

What about the Israelites? Did they have any light during these three days. Yes. The Bible records that all the Israelites had light in the places where they lived. In every window of every house in the Goshen ghetto, lamplight shone in the darkness, although the Egyptians saw it not. They had not the comfort even of those poor, faint, little lights shining in the hovels of their slaves. Once again, God dealt differently with the land of Goshen, where His people lived. God had warned Pharaoh earlier, "I will make a distinction between My people and your people" (Exodus 8:22, 23). "The LORD's curse is on the house of the wicked, but He blesses the home of the righteous" (Proverbs 3:33).

In the palace of Pharaoh there was no light. Three days of darkness had passed, and Pharaoh could stand it no longer. He called for Moses. Perhaps Moses carried a lamp into the black palace, for surely God would allow his beloved servant the blessing of light. Pharaoh must have been amazed and relieved to see light again, and what he would have seen shining in the darkness was the face of Moses, illuminated by the lamp in his hand. If Pharaoh could only see that Moses carried with him a far greater light, the light of

God's Word, which is "a lamp to our feet and a light to our path" (Psalm 119:105). But Pharaoh was only concerned with ridding himself of this present physical darkness, which he could endure no longer. "Go." said Pharaoh. "Go. Worship the LORD. Even your women and children may go with you." Was this the moment? Was it the time for Israel to leave Egypt? Moses knew it was not. Pharaoh had more to say: "Go . . . Only leave your flocks and herds behind." Pharaoh knew that these flocks and herds were Israel's only wealth and their only way of life. So many hundreds of thousands of people could not survive long in the desert without their animals. Pharaoh was risking a mass escape of his slaves with this offer, but he was not risking much. His slaves would surely return if they left empty-handed, with no way to support themselves in the world. No, they would need their animals. Moses was no fool. He did not jump at Pharaoh's offer. He simply said, "You must allow us to have sacrifices and burnt offerings to the LORD our God. Our livestock too must go with us." And then Moses said a remarkable thing. He did not suggest that they should take a few sheep and goats for the ceremony. Oh no! Moses said, "Not a hoof is to be left behind." Moses wanted to take all their animals, not leaving a single one behind. Moses said, "We have to use some of them in worshipping the LORD our God, and until we get there, we will not know what we are to use to worship the LORD."

Pharaoh was outraged. How dare Moses reject his offer? How dare Moses make such demands? Did he think that Pharaoh was stupid? The Israelites would leave and never come back! Now that there was light again, Pharaoh was unwilling to let God's people go. "Get out of my sight!" screamed Pharaoh, as he looked with rage at the face shining before him. "Get out of my sight! Make sure you do not appear before me again! The day you see my face, you will die!" "Just as you say," replied Moses. "I will never appear before you again." In banishing Moses, Pharaoh was consigning himself to the spiritual darkness, which he loved, and the eternal darkness, which he deserved. God had hardened Pharaoh's heart, and there was no hope left for him.

Darkness always accompanies God's judgement. Do you know another time when darkness covered another land, not for three days, but for three hours? We read in the Gospels that when Jesus hung on the cross "darkness came over all the land" (Matthew 27:45; Mark 15:33; Luke 23:44, 45). It was the time of judgement, when God's wrath fell upon Jesus because He had taken upon Himself our sins. He cried out from the cross, "My God,

My God, Why have You forsaken me?" Why? "He was pierced for *our* transgressions; He was crushed for *our* iniquities . . . He bore the sin of many" (Isaiah 53:5, 12).

Do you know another time when the kingdoms of this world will be plunged into darkness? When God comes to judge the earth, on the great and terrible day of the LORD, darkness will be part of that judgement. Listen to the warnings of God's prophets:

"See, the Day of the LORD is coming—a cruel day with wrath and fierce anger—to make the land desolate and destroy the sinners within it. The stars of heaven and their constellations will not show their light. The rising sun will be darkened and the moon will not give its light. I will punish the world for its evil, the wicked for their sins . . ." says the LORD Almighty. (Isaiah 13:9–11)

"Will not the Day of the LORD be darkness, not light—pitch dark, without a ray of brightness?" (Amos 5:20)

"In that day," declares the Sovereign LORD, "I will make the sun go down at noon and darken the earth in broad daylight." (Amos 8:9)

"The great Day of the LORD is near—near and coming quickly. Listen! The cry of the Day of the LORD will be bitter . . . That day will be a day of wrath, a day of distress and anguish, a day of trouble and ruin, a day of darkness and gloom, a day of clouds and blackness . . ." (Zephaniah 1:14, 15)

How can we escape that dreadful day of darkness that is fast approaching? The Bible says, "Give glory to the LORD your God before He brings the darkness . . . thick darkness and deep gloom" (Jeremiah 13:16). The Bible also says, "The people walking in darkness have seen a great light; on those living in the land of the shadow of death a light has dawned . . . For to us a child is born; to us a son is given . . . and He will be called Wonderful Counselor, Mighty God, Everlasting Father, Prince of Peace" (Isaiah 9:2, 6). Who was this great light? Jesus Christ! Jesus said, "I am the light of the world. Whoever follows Me will never walk in darkness, but will have the light of life" (John 8:12). The Bible says, "Believe in the Lord Jesus Christ, and you will be saved." That dreadful day of darkness is the day when God punishes the world for its evil and the wicked for their sins. There is a way, however, that the punishment for your sins can be placed on someone else, so that you will not be swept away in God's judgement. Listen to what the Word of God declares, not to Pharaoh in Egypt long ago, but to *you*, right now:

"He was pierced for our transgressions; He was crushed for our iniquities; the punishment that brought us peace was upon Him . . . the LORD has laid on Him the iniquity of us all." (Isaiah 53:5, 6)

Do you believe this? Do you believe in the one, who died on the cross to save us from our sins and to deliver us from that day of darkness and that eternity of darkness, in which there is no light at all. Do you believe in Jesus? The Word of God says, "For God so loved the world, that He gave His one and only Son, that whoever believes in Him, shall not perish, but have eternal life. For God did not send His Son into the world to condemn the world, but to save the world through Him" (John 3:16, 17). Jesus. He is the Light of the world, and in Him there is no darkness at all.

PLAGUE 10: A Miracle at Midnight (Exodus 11, 12 & 13:19; Numbers 33:3; Hebrews 11:28)

Pharaoh still refused to let God's people go. How many more plagues could Egypt and Pharaoh endure? The LORD had told Moses, "One more. I will bring one more plague on Pharaoh and on Egypt. After that, he will let you go from here." This last plague would be the worst one of all. Moses had known about it for a long time. On his way to Egypt God had told him what would happen at the end. Yes, long before the first nine plagues, Moses had known about the tenth and most terrible plague, for God had told him on the journey what He was going to do. The LORD said, "When you return to Egypt, see to it that you perform before Pharaoh all the wonders I have given you the power to do. But I will harden his heart so that he will not let the people go. Then say to Pharaoh, 'This is what the LORD says: *Israel is my firstborn son,* and I told you: *Let my son go, so he may worship me,* but you refused to let him go; *so I will kill your firstborn son!*' " (Exodus 4:21–23).

The time had come for Moses to warn Pharaoh of this sentence of death which lay over the lives of every firstborn son in the land. Pharaoh said, "Get out of my sight," but Moses had one final message before he left. Moses said, "This is what the LORD says: 'About midnight I will go throughout Egypt. Every firstborn son in Egypt will die, from the firstborn son of Pharaoh, who sits on his throne, to the firstborn son of the slave girl, who works at her mill (and all the firstborn of the cattle as well). There will be loud wailing throughout Egypt—worse than there has ever been or ever will be again.' "

Was Pharaoh not afraid of this word from the LORD? Did he not yet fear

God? Did he not yet know, from all the other plagues, that what God says, He does? Was Pharaoh not afraid that he would lose his own beloved first-born son, the prince of Egypt and heir to the throne? No one was too mighty (not even the king himself), and no one was too lowly (not even a slave girl), to escape this plague. Every household in Egypt would be touched by death; every family in Egypt would lose a son. Would no one in all the land escape this plague? Yes, in the Goshen ghetto, the firstborn sons of Israel would be spared. God Himself would strike down the Egyptians, but, as Moses told Pharaoh, "Among the Israelites, not even a dog will bark at man or animal." Among the Egyptians God would unleash "a band of destroying angels" (Psalm 78:49) and among the Egyptians a deadly plague would stalk through the darkness, but nothing would harm or even scare the Israelites, not even a barking dog. "Then you will know that the LORD makes a distinction between Egypt and Israel," said Moses. And after that terrible plague, what would happen? The Egyptians would all beg the Israelites to leave. The king himself would drive them out of his country. Moses said to Pharaoh, "All these officials of yours will come to me, bowing down before me and saying, 'Go, you and all the people who follow you, go!' " Moses declared, "After that, *I will leave.*" Moses had warned Pharaoh what was about to happen. Then Moses, hot with anger, left Pharaoh.

Oh foolish Pharaoh. Do you not yet realize what will happen? The Israelites will leave anyway, so why not let them go now? Why not listen to the words of Moses and the Word of God? Let God's people go, before it is too late, before all the firstborn sons of Egypt die. Listen Pharaoh; you can stop this plague before it happens. You can spare the sons of Egypt from death. You can save the life of your own child. All you have to do is say one small word: "Go!" All you have to do is obey the LORD. But Pharaoh's heart was hard. Yes, the LORD hardened Pharaoh's heart, and he would not let the Israelites go out of his country. Even this final warning of this tragic killing did not change his heart. God told Moses, "Pharaoh will refuse to listen to you—so that my wonders may be multiplied in Egypt." The greatest miracle of all was about to happen that very night. The exodus was about to take place!

The LORD had given Moses instructions about this night, for the Israelites must be ready to leave the country. On their last night in Egypt, what do you think God commanded them to do? How must they prepare for their exodus from Egypt? It was a very strange thing that God commanded them. God told the Israelites to paint the doorways of their houses with blood! Every Israelite household was to select a lamb, slaughter it, collect the blood in a basin, dip a branch in the blood, and sprinkle it around the sides and tops of their doorways. After that they were to roast the meat and eat it, along with bitter herbs and unleavened bread. They were to eat this meal quickly in their blood-splattered houses and they were not to go outside at all. However, they were to be all dressed and ready for a long journey into the night. Imagine sitting down to a meal with your coats buttoned warmly and your boots buckled tightly and your knapsack strapped firmly to your back. Is that how you eat your dinner? Of course not, but God commanded the Israelites for this special meal to eat it that way—with their cloaks tucked into their belts, their sandals on their feet and their staffs in their hands. This meal was to be eaten in haste.

The lamb, whose blood was sprinkled and whose body was eaten, was to be called the Passover lamb. The meal would be called "The LORD's Passover." Why? God explained: "On that same night I will pass through Egypt and strike down every firstborn (both men and animals) and I will bring judgement on all the gods of Egypt. I am the LORD. The blood will be a sign for you on the houses were you are; and when I see the blood, I will *pass over* you. No destructive plague will touch you when I strike Egypt."

This was the first time God commanded His people to do something to be spared from a plague. They must do it by faith. They too must obey the Word of the LORD. They too must fear God. Moses summoned all the elders of Israel and said to them, "Go at once and select the animals for your families and slaughter the Passover lamb. Take a bunch of hyssop, dip it into the blood in the basin and put some of the blood on the top and on both sides of the doorframe. Not one of you shall go out the door of his house until morning. When the LORD goes through the land to strike down the Egyptians, He will see the blood on the top and sides of the doorframe and will *pass over* that doorway, and He will not permit the destroyer to enter your houses and strike you down." Did the Israelites believe this Word of the LORD? Would they do this strange thing that God had commanded? Yes. The Bible records: "Then the people bowed down and worshipped. The Israelites did just what the LORD commanded . . ." By faith they kept the Passover and the sprinkling of blood, so that the destroyer of the firstborn would not touch the firstborn of Israel.

The few Egyptians, who may have seen the Israelites sprinkling their doorways with blood, must have been confused and concerned. What was this strange thing the Israelites were doing? What awful plague was this blood foretelling? The Egyptians had lately seen too many horrors to mock or beat the Israelites for what they were doing. No, as God's plagues had progressed, the Egyptians had come to view these Israelite slaves with respect and honour. Even Moses was highly regarded in Egypt by all the people. None of the Egyptians laughed or yelled at the Israelites when they were painting their houses with blood, for it filled them with fear and dread. What did it mean? What was going to happen now? Perhaps some of the Egyptians begged to know and then begged to stay the night in some poor slave's blood-splattered house. But the LORD had warned the Israelites through Moses and Aaron, that no foreigner may eat the Passover meal. God said, "Any alien living among you who wants to celebrate the LORD's Passover must have all the males in his household circumcised." It is unlikely that any Egyptians joined with the Israelites that night. More likely, the Egyptians all sought refuge in their own homes, praying to their own gods to spare them from the terrors of the coming night. The last plague was about to strike Egypt.

"At midnight the LORD struck down all the firstborn in Egypt, from the firstborn of Pharaoh, who sat on the throne, to the firstborn of the prisoner, who sat in the dungeon (and the firstborn of all the livestock as well). Pharaoh and all his officials and all the Egyptians got up during the night, and there was loud wailing in Egypt, for there was not a house without someone dead."

The hope and the strength of Egypt vanished in that night. The firstborn sons—the future Pharaoh of Egypt, the future head of every family—were gone. In these sons all Egypt hoped. But the God of Israel brought judgement on *all* the gods of Egypt, even their most precious ones. Tiny babies died in their cradles at home; little boys died in their beds; strong young men, soldiers in Pharaoh's army, died where they stood keeping watch over the land. Their shields and swords were useless against this invisible enemy that brought death at the stroke of midnight. One man stood his ground, while another fell at his side. It was not a random selection; only the firstborn sons of the Egyptians were slaughtered that all the world might know that this judgement was by the hand of Almighty God. Only the boys were struck. Only the firstborn were taken. Only the Egyptians were killed. Even in this judgement God showed mercy. The whole nation could have been swept away in God's wrath.

Meanwhile, the Israelites were safe under the roofs of their houses, safe under the blood of the lamb. They heard the awful wail that arose around them in the darkness as God executed justice. Long ago Pharaoh had commanded the death of Israel's sons; now God commanded the death of Egypt's sons. "Vengeance is mine," saith the LORD. "I will repay." The Egyptians paid dearly for their many sins. It cost them their sons. This time it was the Israelites who rejoiced and looked upon their living children with relief. Mothers must have looked at their tiny, newborn, firstborn sons sleeping peacefully in their arms, untouched by the terrors of that night. (Thank You God!) Fathers must have looked at their little boys, their firstborn sons, who drowsed happily in their houses, secure from the horrors of that night. (Thank You God!) Whole families must have looked with new wonder at the teenage boys, the firstborn sons, who still stood strong and straight, living and breathing and even smiling, while other boys in other houses in other parts of this land writhed in the agonies of death. (Thank You God!) Children are the LORD's good gift, and this night the Israelites had been given their sons anew. Their lives had been spared. They had been saved. *Thank you God!* While there was only wailing, "loud wailing," in the homes of the Egyptians, there must have been only the sounds of rejoicing, the praises of God both whispered and shouted, in the homes of the Israelites, for death had passed over their houses on that awful, wonderful night.

The Exodus

Fear and grief, terror and anguish, filled the land of Egypt and the palace of Pharaoh. The king himself had to look upon the prince of his land and pride of his heart, his own first born son, who now lay cold and still and dead. Did Pharaoh shed a tear? Did he weep for the son he could have saved? I don't know, for Pharaoh was a hard-hearted man, but something in him did break. In the middle of that dreadful night, Pharaoh summoned Moses and Aaron. When they faced each other, Pharaoh did not have them executed, as he had threatened earlier. No, Pharaoh yielded at last to them saying, "Up! Leave my people, you and the Israelites! Go! Worship the LORD as you have requested. Take your flocks and your herds, as you have said, and go. And bless me also." Yes, even Pharaoh was afraid of God, and now he wanted God's favour. Pharaoh would obey the Word of the LORD. Pharaoh would let the people go to worship their God. He would even ask Moses to bless him, the king of Egypt, when they worshipped the God of Israel. "Bless me also." begged Pharaoh. The Egyptians also, fearing that soon they all would be dead, urged their slaves to hurry and leave the country.

Thus Israel was set free from their bondage. The exodus had begun. The command had been given. After 430 years, it was time for them to leave Egypt and go to the Promised Land. Now, after waiting so long, everything was happening very quickly. They were being driven from the land in the middle of the night. They were being urged to move faster, faster. There was no time to prepare food for their journey. They could not wait for the bread to rise or even to bake, so the Israelites took dough without any yeast in it. Later they would bake it; later they would eat cakes of unleavened bread. So the Israelites left Egypt with their bread dough still in the kneading troughs, wrapped up in clothes and they carried these big troughs on their shoulders.

The Israelites also left the land of their slavery laden with silver and with gold. How did these poor slaves so suddenly become rich and free? It was all part of the miracle of that night. As surely as God set them free, He also made sure they were paid for their work. The Israelites simply did as Moses instructed them. Both men and women asked the Egyptians for articles of gold and silver, and the LORD moved the Egyptians' hearts to give them whatever they asked for! That was how the Israelites plundered the Egyptians.

The Israelites also left Egypt laden with some old bones. They were very old bones, bones that had been waiting to be buried for 400 years! Do you remember whose bones they were? and why they were waiting? and why Moses carried them out of Egypt? Long, long ago Joseph had made the sons of Israel swear an oath that they would bury his bones in the Promised Land. Joseph did not want to be buried in Egypt. He wanted to be buried in the land that God had promised his forefathers to give to their descendants. Joseph believed those promises. Joseph believed that some day God would deliver His people. Because He believed God's Word, Joseph said, "God will surely come to help you, and then you must carry my bones up with you from this place" (Genesis 50:25). Moses remembered this, so when he left Egypt, he took the bones of Joseph with him, to bury in the land of Canaan. Moses also believed the promises of God, that God would surely bring the Israelites into the land He promised to Abraham, Isaac and Jacob.

God had set His people free! When the Israelites left Egypt there were 600, 000 men on foot, as well as women and children, which would make the count over 2, 000, 000 people. They were beginning to look like a great nation, just as the LORD had promised. All Egypt's slaves marched out of the land of their bondage, boldly and freely. They walked out in full view of all the Egyptians, who were burying their firstborn sons. No one stopped them. No one hurt them. The exit from Egypt had begun, and one day their entry into Canaan would be complete. In between, there would be a long hard journey, but for now the people rejoiced in their deliverance. They were no longer slaves. They were a free people, set free by the LORD their God, who brought them out of Egypt, out of the land of slavery. This exodus of God's people was surely one of the greatest miracles in all the earth!

The teacher's guide for this lesson starts on page 212.

DO THIS IN REMEMBRANCE OF ME

- **Exodus 12:1–13:16**
- **Leviticus 23:4–8**
- **Numbers 28:16–25**
- **Deuteronomy 16:1–8**
- **Luke 22:1–20**
- **I Corinthians 5:6–8; 11:23–26**

Could the Israelites ever forget that night, the night when the LORD passed through Egypt and struck down every firstborn male in all the land, but passed over their homes, which had been sprinkled with the blood of the lamb? Could they ever forget that night when the LORD their God brought them out of Egypt, out of the land of slavery? Could they forget the sound at midnight, the loud wailing that arose all over Egypt, because there was not a single house without someone dead in it? Could they forget the sight as they left the country, of all the people burying their dead? Their last memories of Egypt must have left a deep impression upon them: a land of weeping and wailing, a land of graves and death, while they marched forth joyfully, triumphantly, to a new life. Could the Israelites ever forget that night, the night of their deliverance? Yes. They could forget. As the days and the years passed, the memory of that night would begin to fade. They might forget to recall and retell all the events of that night to their children and grandchildren. Perhaps the great-grandchildren would never hear the story at all. The details of their deliverance would disappear; it would all be forgotten; that night would vanish from their minds as if it had never happened. But The LORD wanted the Israelites to remember that night—forever! To help them remember their great deliverance, God instituted three lasting ordinances, that they were to keep for the generations to come:

1. The Celebration of the Passover

God said, "This is a day you are to commemorate; for the generations to come you shall celebrate it as a festival to the LORD—a lasting ordinance." They could never forget what day it was because God began a new calendar for them at that time, a sacred calendar for a holy people. Just before they left Egypt, the LORD said to Moses and Aaron, "This month is to be for you the first month, the first month of your year!" The Israelites' New Year would not begin on the first day of January, as ours does. Their New Year would begin on the first day of Abib. "Praise be to the name of God forever and ever . . . He changes times and seasons" (Daniel 2:20, 21). This new first month was called Abib, which means "sprouting or budding," because their new life and their new year was just beginning. God commanded the Israelites, "Observe the month of Abib and celebrate the Passover of the LORD your God, because in the month of Abib, He brought you out of Egypt by night" (Deuteronomy 16:1).

Every year, on the tenth day of the first month, the month of Abib, the whole community of Israel was to prepare for the LORD's Passover. Each man was to select a lamb for his family. The animal chosen must be a year-old male without defect. God said to take care of this special lamb until the fourteenth day of the month. At twilight, on the fourteenth day of the first month, the LORD's Passover would begin. All the people of the community of Israel must slaughter their lambs at twilight. Not one of the bones of the Passover lamb was to be broken. That same night the members of each family must eat the meat of the lamb which was roasted whole over a fire. None of the meat was to be leftover until the morning. If there was, it must be burned. They must also eat this special meal with bitter herbs and unleavened bread. This was the Passover meal.

Before the first Passover, Moses commanded the Israelites, "Obey these instructions as a lasting ordinance for you and your descendants. When you enter the land that the LORD will give you as He promised, observe this ceremony. And when your children ask you, 'What does this ceremony mean to you?' then tell them, 'It is the Passover sacrifice to the LORD, who passed over the houses of the Israelites in Egypt and spared our homes when He struck down the Egyptians.' " Every year there would be an anniversary of that night, where the children would be taught, for hundreds and thousands of years, what the LORD had done, so they would not forget. In this way the memory of that night would be kept alive. "Because the LORD kept vigil that night to bring them out of Egypt, on this night, [Passover Night, the four-teenth night of the month of Abib,] all the Israelites are to keep vigil to ho-nour the LORD for the generations to come." Even the little children would be staying up late that night to honour the LORD, for it was a very special night, a night to remember!

God commanded the Israelites to keep the Passover celebration, so that they would *remember* what God had done, how God had brought them out of Egypt, out of the land of slavery. Their exodus was a great deliverance — and they must always honour God by remembering it — but God had an-other reason for giving them this yearly holiday. *The Passover Celebration was to help the Israelites look forward to a greater deliverance.* They must re-member the Passover, not only because of what God had done in the past, but because of what God would do in the future.

One day, thousands of years later, a Man would come, who would be the final Passover Lamb. Who was He? It says in the New Testament that "Christ, our Passover Lamb, has been sacrificed" (I Corinthians 5:7). He was a male lamb, without defect, without sin. He was "holy, blameless, pure, set apart from sinners . . ." (Hebrews 7:26). Before the appointed night of the Passover, Jesus rode into Jerusalem, the appointed place of the Passover, and He was acclaimed by the whole congregation of Israel. Later He was examined in three separate courts, but no defect was found in this Lamb. Jesus stood trial before the Jews. "At daybreak, the council of the elders of the people, both the chief priests and the teachers of the law, met together, and Jesus was led before them" (Luke 22:66). Did they find any sin or any crime in this Man? The Scriptures record, "The chief priests and the whole Sanhedrin were looking for evidence against Jesus so that they could put Him to death, but they did not find any" (Mark 14:55). He was the male lamb, without defect, and they took Him away to be executed; "the whole assembly arose and led Him off to Pilate" (Luke 23:1). The Roman gover-nor, Pontius Pilate, also found no defect and announced, "I find no basis for a charge against this man." However, the Roman governor sent him to the Jewish king to be examined. King Herod sent him back to governor Pilate, who again declared, "I have examined Him in your presence and have found no basis for your charges against Him. Neither has Herod, for he sent Him back to us; as you can see He has done nothing deserving of death." But the whole assembly of Israel shouted, "Crucify Him! Crucify Him!" The Scriptures record that for the third time Pilate said to them, "Why? What crime has this man committed? I have found in Him no grounds for the death penalty" (Luke 23:4, 15, 22). But with loud shouts the crowd insistently demanded that He be crucified, and their shouts prevailed. Thus the final Passover Lamb was chosen by all the people of the community of Israel. And although "He had done no violence, nor was any deceit in his mouth . . . it was the LORD's will to crush Him and cause Him to suffer" (Isaiah 53:9, 10). Christ, the spotless, sinless Lamb of God, was sacrificed on Passover night. "The next day was to be a special Sabbath. Because the Jews did not want the bodies left on the crosses during the Sabbath, they asked Pilate to have the legs broken and the bodies taken down. The soldiers therefore came and broke the legs of the first man who had been crucified with Jesus, and then those of the other. But when they came to Jesus and found that He was already dead, they did not break his legs . . . These things happened so that the Scripture would be fulfilled: Not one of His bones will be broken" (John 19:31–33, 36). God commanded it long ago, back in the land of Egypt, back in the book of Exodus: "Do not break any of its bones." The Passover Lamb must have no bones broken, for that would be an important sign in the future, a sign that people might believe that Jesus was the Christ, the Son of God, and that by believing they might have life in His name. There was a man who stood by the cross and witnessed these things with his own eyes. He testified that these things really happened. The Bible says, "His testimony is true. He knows that he tells the truth, and he testifies so that you also may believe" (John 19:35).

By His death on the cross, Christ accomplished a greater deliverance for God's people. At the first Passover, the LORD delivered His people from Egypt, from the land of slavery, which foreshadowed the last Passover, when the LORD delivered His people from the bondage of sin and the domain of death and the horror of hell. Christ died, that "by His death, He might destroy him who holds the power of death—that is, the devil—and free those who all their lives were held in slavery by their fear of death" (Hebrews 2:14,

15). The blood of God's Passover lamb was poured out, so that death might pass over all who sought shelter under the blood of the lamb of God, even Jesus Christ our Lord. Death would forever pass over all who received that sprinkling of blood and that cleansing by faith. How can we escape if we neglect so great a salvation?

On the night when He was betrayed, Jesus Himself said that He was the fulfilment of the Passover. While he sat with His disciples in Jerusalem, eating the Passover meal, Jesus said, "I have eagerly desired to eat this Passover with you before I suffer. For I tell you, I will not eat it again until it finds fulfilment in the Kingdom of God" (Luke 22:15, 16). Later He said, "What is written about Me is reaching its fulfilment" (Luke 22:37). That last night Jesus changed the Passover meal. From that night on, it became known as "The Lord's Supper." Jesus took the unleavened bread, gave thanks, broke it, and gave it to them saying, "This is My body, given for you. Do this in remembrance of Me." In the same way, after the supper, He took the cup saying, "This cup is the new covenant in My blood, which is poured out for you." From that night on, the Passover was to be celebrated in a new way. God's people were to remember a greater deliverance, a greater Passover. They were to remember Jesus, the Passover lamb, whose body was broken, whose blood was poured out, to save them from sin and death and hell. The Passover meal had found its fulfilment in Christ. Now it was to be celebrated honouring and remembering and proclaiming Jesus' death until the day when He would return.

2. The Feast of Unleavened Bread

Back in Egypt, before the exodus, God commanded, "Celebrate the Feast of Unleavened Bread, because it was on this very day that I brought your divisions out of Egypt. Celebrate this day as a lasting ordinance for the generations to come. In the first month [the month of Abib] you are to eat bread made without yeast, from the evening of the fourteenth day [which was the night they slaughtered the Passover lamb] until the evening of the twenty-first day. For seven days no yeast is to be found in your houses. And whoever eats anything with yeast in it must be cut off from the community of Israel . . . Eat nothing made with yeast. Wherever you live, you must eat unleavened bread." Why? Why did God command the Israelites to eat unleavened bread for a whole week? God commanded them to do this so that they would remember. They must never forget the exodus. Later Moses said, "For seven days eat unleavened bread, the bread of affliction, because you left Egypt in haste—so that all the days of your life you may remember the time of your departure from Egypt" (Deuteronomy 16:3). They must always remember the night they left Egypt, when they left so quickly that there was no time to prepare food for their journey. There was not even time to let the bread rise or to let the bread bake. They left Egypt carrying the raw bread dough in big bowls on their shoulders. When they finally had a chance to bake it, the bread was not fluffy, but flat, because there was no yeast in it to make it rise. For the first part of their journey, the Israelites ate little cakes of unleavened bread.

As they travelled out of Egypt, God said to Moses and Moses said to the people, "Commemorate this day, the day you came out of Egypt, out of the land of slavery, because the LORD brought you out with a mighty hand. Eat nothing containing yeast. Today, in the month of Abib, you are leaving. When the LORD brings you into the land of the Canaanites . . . the land He swore to your forefathers to give you, a land flowing with milk and honey— you are to observe this ceremony in this month. For seven days eat bread made without yeast and on the seventh day hold a festival to the LORD. Eat unleavened bread during those seven days; nothing with yeast in it is to be [even] seen among you, nor shall any yeast be seen anywhere within your borders. On that day tell your child, 'I do this because of what the LORD did for me when I came out of Egypt.' This observance will be like a sign on your hand and a reminder on your forehead that the Law of the LORD is to be on your lips, for the LORD brought you out of Egypt with His Mighty hand. You must keep this ordinance at the appointed time, year after year." For a whole week each year, every time the Israelites sat down to a meal, there would be a sign. There would be a reminder, that they must obey God; they must obey the Law of the LORD, because He had delivered them from the land of their slavery. They were no longer slaves of Pharaoh, but now they must be servants of the Most High God. They must be a holy people. The unleavened bread would remind them of this. They must be without sin, just as this bread was without yeast. They must be a holy people, because they belonged to a Holy God.

The Feast of the Unleavened Bread was to help God's people *remember* their great deliverance from Egypt, but it was also a pointer to the future. *The Feast of Unleavened Bread was to help the Israelites look forward to a greater deliverance.* This feast also found its fulfilment in Christ. The bread without yeast was a picture of the Christ without sin.

It is very interesting to examine what Jesus taught about Himself during the Feast of Unleavened Bread:

1) "The Jewish Passover Feast was near . . . Jesus said to them . . . 'It is My Father who gives you the true bread from heaven. For the bread of God is He who comes down from heaven and gives life to the world.' Then Jesus declared, 'I am the bread of life. He who comes to Me will never go hungry, and he who believes in Me will never be thirsty . . . For My Father's will is that everyone who looks to the Son and believes in Him shall have eternal life, and I will raise him up at the last day.' Jesus said, 'I tell you the truth: He who believes has everlasting life. I am the bread of life. Your forefathers ate the manna in the desert, yet they died. But here is the bread that comes down from heaven, which a man may eat and not die. I am the living bread that came down from heaven. If anyone eats this bread, he will live forever. This bread is My flesh, which I will give for the life of the world.' Jesus said, 'I tell you the truth: Unless you eat the flesh of the Son of Man and drink His blood, you have no life in you. Whoever eats My flesh and drinks My blood has eternal life, and I will raise him up at the last day. For My flesh is real food and My blood is real drink. Whoever eats My flesh and drinks My blood remains in Me, and I in him. Just as the living Father sent Me and I live because of the Father, so the one who feeds on Me will live because of Me. This is the bread that came down from heaven. Your forefathers ate manna and died, but he who feeds on this bread will live forever' " (John 6:4, 32–58).

2) At the last supper, at the Passover meal, which was the beginning of the Feast of Unleavened Bread, Jesus took the unleavened bread, blessed it, broke it, and gave it to his disciples saying, "Take and eat; this is My body." Then He took the cup, gave thanks and offered it to them, saying, "Drink from it, all of you. This is My blood of the covenant, which is poured out for many for the forgiveness of sins" (Matthew 26:26–28).

The Jews still celebrate this Feast of Unleavened Bread, though thousands of years have passed. When I was a little girl, I had a Jewish friend. During this week-long festival, if I was staying at her house for lunch, we would have peanutbutter sandwiches made on big, flat, dry, crackers—the unleavened bread, the Passover matzos. The Jews still celebrate this feast and so must we. It says in the New Testament: "For Christ our Passover lamb, has been sacrificed. Therefore let us keep the Feast, not with the old yeast, the yeast of malice and wickedness, but with bread without yeast, the bread of sincerity and truth" (I Corinthians 5:7, 8). The way we keep the Feast of Unleavened Bread, is not by eating matzos for a week, but by living every day of our lives righteously before God, because Christ sacrificed Himself for us. He paid dearly for our sins. He gave His body and His blood for us. In gratitude we must live holy lives before Him, in remembrance of Him and His death upon the cross for us.

3. The Consecration of the Firstborn

The LORD said to Moses, "Consecrate to Me, [or set apart for Me,] every firstborn male. The firstborn offspring of every womb among the Israelites belongs to Me, whether man or animal." They belonged to God because, when God went through the land of Egypt destroying all the firstborn males, He spared the firstborn of the Israelites. Now they belonged to Him. Moses told the people, "After the LORD brings you into the land of the Canaanites and gives it to you, (as He promised on oath to you and your forefathers,) you are to give over to the LORD the first offspring of every womb." What did this mean?

1) The firstborn males of all the clean animals, (from their flocks of sheep and herds of cattle,) were to be set apart for sacrifice to the LORD. They belonged to God. The Israelites were not to use these consecrated animals for their own benefit; they were to be set apart for sacrifice to the LORD. Later, Moses instructed the people, "Set apart for the LORD your God every firstborn male from your herds and flocks. Do not put the firstborn of your oxen to work, and do not shear the firstborn of your sheep. Each year you and your family are to eat them in the presence of the LORD your God at the place He will choose" (Deuteronomy 15:19, 20). Every year, the Israelites were to take these firstborn animals and sacrifice them to the LORD at the temple in Jerusalem. There they would partake of the sacrifice; there they would eat their allotted portion of the burnt offering; there they would worship, rejoicing and praising the LORD their God.

2) The firstborn males of all the unclean animals also belonged to God. The firstborn of their donkeys and horses and camels were set apart for God, but the unclean animals could not be used for sacrifice in the worship of

God. What would happen to them? They must be redeemed or bought back from God. A certain price had to be paid to God for these unclean animals. For example, a firstborn donkey colt could be redeemed or bought back with a lamb, which would then be sacrificed to the LORD. If they did not want to pay the price for the unclean animal, then it must be killed. They could not just keep it for themselves.

3) The firstborn sons of the Israelites also belonged to God. God did not require the firstborn sons to be sacrificed. No. The killing of children was an abomination to God. The firstborn sons must not be killed, but they must be redeemed. A price had to be paid for them, to buy back their lives.

Why? Why did God command the Israelites to practice such strange customs? God wanted them to remember the night of their exodus from Egypt. In future generations, the children would wonder why this was being done. Why were the firstborn lambs and bulls always set apart for sacrifice? Why did their firstborn donkeys and camels have to be bought back with a price? Didn't these animals belong to them? The answer was "No, they belonged to God." Why? Moses said, "In days to come, when your child asks you, 'What does this mean?' say to him, 'With a mighty hand the LORD brought us out of Egypt, out of the land of slavery. When Pharaoh stubbornly refused to let us go, the LORD killed every firstborn in Egypt, both man and animal. This is why I sacrifice to the LORD the first male offspring of every womb and redeem each of my firstborn sons.' And it will be like a sign on your hand and a symbol on your forehead that the LORD brought us out of Egypt with His mighty hand." They must never forget what happened that night. They must keep that memory alive throughout the generations, for hundreds and thousands of years. They must honour the LORD and remember the LORD and worship the LORD all the days of their lives, because the LORD had set them free! They must never forget God's LOVE! "It was because the LORD loved you . . . that He brought you out with a mighty hand and redeemed you from the land of slavery, from the power of Pharaoh king of Egypt" (Deuteronomy 7:8).

The consecration of the firstborn son was to help the Israelites *remember* the night of their deliverance in the past, but it was also to point them to a time in the future. *The consecration of the firstborn son was to help the Israelites look forward to a greater deliverance,* when a firstborn son would be sacrificed to free them from the power of the devil. The life of this Son would not be spared. Death would not pass over Him. This firstborn son, God's only Son, would give His life as a ransom for many. By the sacrifice of Himself, this Son of Israel, would redeem or buy back all the sons and daughters of God. It would be an awful price that He would pay. The Bible says, "It was not with perishable things such as silver or gold that you were redeemed [or bought back] . . . but with the precious blood of Christ, a lamb without blemish or defect" (I Peter 1:18, 19). But it was for this task that the Son of God came into the world. He was named Jesus, *the LORD saves*, because He was the one sent into the world to save His people from their sins. Forever and ever this Lamb of God would be praised:

> *You are worthy . . . because You were slain,*
> *and with Your blood You purchased people for God*
> *from every tribe and language and people and nation . . .*
> *Worthy is the Lamb, who was slain,*
> *to receive power and wealth and wisdom and strength*
> *and honour and glory and praise!*
> *To Him who sits on the throne and to the Lamb*
> *be praise and honour and glory and power,*
> *for ever and ever!*
> *Amen.*

Revelation 5:9–14

The teacher's guide for this lesson starts on page 218.

GOD WITH US
DAY AND NIGHT

- Exodus 13:17–22
- Psalm 121
- Isaiah 4:5, 6

T he Lord had accomplished what He had promised. The Lord had said, "I will free you from being slaves . . ." and now the Israelites were free indeed. They were not escaping Egypt as runaway slaves by slipping out of the country one by one, sneaking across the border, hiding in the darkness. No. Scripture records that "they marched out boldly in full view of all the Egyptians" (Numbers 33:3), in broad daylight—a proud people, a mighty army, a great nation. Just as God had promised Abraham so long ago, "I will make you into a great nation" (Genesis 12:2). The Israelites were now numbered in the millions. The Bible records that there was an army of 600, 000 men, who left Egypt "armed for battle." Where did these slaves get weapons? Perhaps they made them, by beating their "ploughshares into swords" and their "pruning hooks into spears" (Joel 3:10). Perhaps they stole them during the plagues, when the country was in total chaos. Perhaps they simply asked for swords and spears from their neighbours, collecting them with the rest of the plunder. These slaves marched out of Egypt armed for battle, but were they ready for battle? God knew they were not. When Pharaoh let the people go, God did not lead them on the road straight to the Promised Land. They could have been there in a few days. There was a short fast route to get to Canaan, through the Philistine country, but God did not lead them along that ancient expressway. Instead, He took them by a back route through the desert. Why? Was that the scenic route? No, there were other reasons. God did not want his people facing war immediately. God said, "If they face war, they might change their minds and return to Egypt." They must not return to the land of slavery. They must go forward by faith, but God knew that their faith was not strong. God would not test them beyond what they were able to endure. God would not tempt them to go back to Egypt, by allowing them to face situations too difficult for them at this time. They were not yet ready to conquer kingdoms by faith. Canaan must be won "not by might, nor by strength, but by My Spirit" says the LORD Almighty (Zechariah 4:6). The Israelites must gain the Promised Land by faith, and their faith was not strong enough yet. Let them see God destroy a mighty enemy army, while they stood still, without raising a single sword. Let them learn to trust in God to fight for them. One day they must be able to sing that it was God's LOVE, not their 600, 000-man army, that secured the Promised Land for them. "It was not by their sword that they won the land, nor did their arm bring them victory;" it was God's right hand, God's arm and the light of God's face, *"because he loved them"* (Psalm 44:3). They must enter the Promised Land by faith, not trusting in their own weapons, but saying within their hearts, "I do not trust in my bow; my sword does not bring me victory, but You [O LORD] give us victory over our enemies . . . In God we make our boast all day long, and we will praise Your name forever" (Psalm 44:6–8).

The Israelites had left Egypt. However, did they know where they were going? Yes, they knew they were going to the Promised Land. They knew that somewhere ahead of them, somewhere beyond the borders of Egypt, was a land flowing with milk and honey. None of them, however, had ever been there, including Moses, the man who was leading them. These people had lived in Egypt all their lives. So had their parents and grandparents and great-grandparents. Egypt was the land where they had all been born. Egypt was their homeland, the only home and land they had ever known, and now, after so many generations, the Israelites were leaving and going to a place that lay before them like some distant dream. But did anyone know how to reach that dream? Did anyone know the right road to take or the safe route to march? Which way should they go? God knew. The LORD Himself would show them the way.

God was going to take the Israelites on an incredible journey through a howling wilderness. Imagine 600,000 families setting out on an arduous, dangerous journey that would take forty years to complete. At the LORD's command Moses kept a record of the stages of that journey. (See Numbers 33:1–50.) Moses also wrote the entire account of that journey from Egypt to Canaan. (It is found in these books of the Bible: Exodus, Leviticus, Numbers and Deuteronomy). God did not take His people along the fastest, easiest, shortest, happiest route, but He took them along the best route, where they would learn to trust in God. They must learn to trust God to proceed before them through a remote area, where there were no roads, no maps, no signs, no guides. They must learn to trust God to provide for them in a barren wasteland, where there was no food or water, certainly not enough for a multitude of millions. They must learn to trust God to protect them in a hostile region, where enemy armies hid in the hills all around them. If the Israelites had taken the shortcut, there would have been no opportunity for them — or for us — to learn about trusting in God in that wilderness. You see, what happened to the Israelites on that journey and what was written about them, was recorded for our instruction. "These things happened to them as examples and were written down as warnings for us" (I Corinthians 10:11). This journal of Moses in the Word of God was written to help God's people in every place in every age on their own journey to the promised land. What happened to the Israelites will help each one of us on our own pilgrimage through this life, as we press onward to heaven. So let us pay careful attention to all the stages of Israel's journey through the wilderness and to all that happened along the way.

After leaving Rameses in the province of Goshen in the land of Egypt, the Israelites camped at a place called Succoth. There they pitched their tents; there they built campfires and baked flat cakes of unleavened bread with the dough they had brought from Egypt. There they rested and there, after the campfires burned low, they sat under the twinkling stars and glowing moon in the vast, dark, desert sky. But there was something else, something very strange, that shone before them in the heavens that night. What was it? There was a pillar of cloud that burned in the darkness in front of the camp of Israel. What was this strange phenomenon? No other people on the face of the earth had seen such a sight. For an instant some people have seen balls of fire as they flash through the night sky — meteorites — a natural, though unusual phenomena in earth's atmosphere. But what was this? This was a pillar of fire that burned all through the night. What was it? It was the LORD! He was appearing to all Israel in the burning cloud, just as He had appeared to Moses in the burning bush. What comfort that must have given Israel's camp, as they sat by their tents in the cold, dark, wild desert. God was with them. They could actually see with their own eyes that God was there, that the great God above all gods was there, guarding them all through the night. They could see that God was there, giving them the light and warmth of His Presence. If the cheery little flames of a campfire bring such comfort to people on a cold, dark, wild night, imagine the effect of these glorious flames burning with the majesty of Almighty God. That night the Israelites could sleep peacefully in their tents, fearing nothing, for they knew, by sight, that the LORD was with them.

In the morning when they awoke, the people saw that the pillar of cloud was still there, but it was no longer burning. Now it was a cloud to shade the Israelites from the hot desert sun. The Israelites could actually see with their own eyes that they lived in the shadow of the Almighty. The LORD's LOVE was like a canopy over them wherever they were, shielding them from all harm.

This was how the LORD led Israel. By day the LORD went ahead of them in a pillar of cloud to guide them and shield them on their way. By night the LORD went ahead of them in a pillar of fire to give them light. In this way the Israelites could travel by day or by night. The sun would not be too hot for them by day, nor would the way be too dark for them by night. When the pillar of God's presence moved forward, that was the signal for God's people to follow. When the pillar stopped, that was how God showed them when to stop and where to camp. God was their guide and their guard through the wilderness. The LORD would safely bring His people to the promised land.

The LORD did not abandon His people in the wilderness. God kept His covenant of LOVE with them. The LORD showed that He was with them, day and night. The pillar of cloud by day and the pillar of fire by night were visible demonstrations of God's great LOVE for them. Throughout all their wanderings in the wilderness, "the pillar of cloud never ceased to guide them on their path by day, nor did the pillar of fire cease to shine on the way they were to take by night" (Nehemiah 9:19). God even "spoke to them from the pillar" (Psalm 99:7). Yes, the LORD was surely with them.

The teacher's guide for this lesson starts on page 222.

THROUGH THE RED SEA... BY FAITH!

- **Exodus 14, 15:1–21**
- **Psalm 77:13–20; 106:6–12**
- **I Corinthians 10:1, 2**
- **Hebrews 11:29**

The LORD continued to lead the Israelites southward. They left Succoth and camped at a place called Etham on the edge of the desert. There the LORD spoke to Moses, because He was going to lead them next in a very strange direction. Perhaps the people wouldn't follow the cloud, if it started to go backwards. So God told Moses, "Tell the Israelites to turn back." First they had come south; now God wanted them to backtrack and go north. Why? Were they lost? Didn't God know the way? Had He made a mistake? No, the LORD was setting a trap for the Egyptians. It was very important that the people follow the LORD and obey His Word. God pinpointed for the Israelites exactly where to camp. It was a place beside the Red Sea.

God was leading the Israelites back and forth to trap Pharaoh. God explained to Moses, "Pharaoh will think, 'The Israelites are wandering around the land in confusion, trapped by the desert.' " But God was setting the trap for Pharaoh. The LORD said, "And I will harden Pharaoh's heart, and he will pursue them. But I will gain glory for Myself through Pharaoh and all his army, and the Egyptians will know that I am the LORD." God did not explain to Moses or the people exactly how He was going to gain glory for Himself, but the people believed the Word of the LORD and they obeyed the Word of the LORD. The Israelites went back north and camped by the edge of the Red Sea.

Pharaoh had sent spies to watch every move the Israelites made. It was reported to the king of Egypt that, although the Israelites had fled from Egypt, they could not find their way out of the desert. Their God seemed to have left them to wander around aimlessly, looking for a way to escape. Their mighty power seemed to have vanished, and now they were camped by the Red Sea. Their way was blocked by the Red Sea. It was not too late for Pharaoh to capture his runaway slaves.

When Pharaoh and his officials heard this report, they said, "What have we done? We have lost our slaves! Why did we let the Israelites go?" Had they really so quickly forgotten why they had let the Israelites go? Surely they were still mourning, surely their hearts were still aching, over their first-born sons. Surely the weeping and wailing could still be heard in Egypt. But the LORD had hardened Pharaoh's heart, so nothing could penetrate it; nothing could soften it, not even his grief over the lost sons of Egypt. Pharaoh would not stop fighting against God, even now. Once again Pharaoh changed his mind. One last time Pharaoh declared that he would not let the Israelites go.

Pharaoh had his personal chariot made ready to lead 600 of his champion chariots into battle, along with all the other chariots of Egypt. The whole Egyptian army was also ordered to join in the chase, for God hardened the heart and darkened the mind of Pharaoh, so that he would pursue the Israelites with the entire force of Egypt. Hundreds of thousands of troops marched out of Egypt after the Israelites. They also galloped out on their horses and thundered out in their chariots. Pharaoh must have laughed as he raced after his runaway slaves. It would not be hard to over-take Israel's pathetic "army" of slaves, plodding along nowhere. It would not be hard to over-run the "ranks" of Israel's armed men, for among them were tottering old people, weary pregnant women, mothers carrying tiny infants, and lots of little children running around everywhere. There were flocks of sheep and herds of cows grazing along the way. How fast could this army of Israel go? How far could they get? How well could they fight? "Ha-ha!" laughed Pharaoh. "They have no chance at all of escaping from the fast horses and strong soldiers of Egypt!" Pharaoh was sure of capturing his run away slaves.

The Israelites could see the army of Egypt marching after them in the distance . . . and they were terrified. What would the Egyptians do to them? If the Egyptians showed no mercy to their slaves who had served them faithfully, what would they do to their slaves, who had served them treacherously? These Israelites were runaway slaves, armed with Egyptian weapons, laden with Egyptian gold. They could expect no mercy from their cruel masters. If none was shown when their masters carried whips, what could they expect when they carried spears and swords? The worst—they could expect the worst! The Egyptians were bloodthirsty now, craving Israel's blood to quench their thirst for revenge. The firstborn sons of Egypt were in their graves because of these wretched slaves, and they would exact a harsh vengeance upon them. Surely there was going to be a Jewish bloodbath by the Red Sea, for the people were trapped. There was nowhere they could hide, nowhere they could run. Before them were the waters of the Red Sea. They were camped right on the edge of it, so close that in the stillness of the night they could hear the waves lapping upon the shore. But behind them was another sound, the distant roar of a great wave rolling towards them, the sound of a vast army of wicked men moving closer and closer to the kill. They were about to be slaughtered and the Israelites were terrified!

In their fear, some of the people cried out to the LORD in prayer and in faith, but others forgot God's miracles and "rebelled by the sea, the Red Sea" (Psalm 106:7). They did not believe that the LORD would deliver them and they spoke against God, by speaking against God's servant. They said to Moses, "Was it because there were no graves in Egypt that you brought us to the desert to die? What have you done to us by bringing us out of Egypt? Didn't we say to you in Egypt, 'Leave us alone! Let us serve the Egyptians'? It would have been better for us to serve the Egyptians than to die in the desert!" (This marked the first time that Israel rebelled against the LORD). But Moses answered the people's fear with faith. Moses said, "Do not be afraid. Stand firm and you will see the deliverance the LORD will bring you today. The Egyptians you see today you will never see again. The LORD will fight for you; you need only to be still." It was the Egyptians who were galloping full-speed to their own graves.

Then Moses cried out to the LORD for help, and God was merciful to His people, though they had rebelled against Him. The LORD said to Moses, "Why are you crying out to me? Tell the Israelites to go forward." But where could they go? The army of the enemy was pressing behind them and the waters of the sea stretched before them. How could they go forward? How could they obey God? The LORD told Moses how: "Raise your staff and stretch out your hand over the sea to divide the water, so that the Israelites can go through the sea on dry ground."

Then the angel of God, who had been travelling in front of Israel's army, withdrew and went behind them. The Angel of the LORD stood between the Israelites and the Egyptians to protect them. Not even one of God's people would be touched by the enemy. The pillar of cloud also moved from in front and stood behind them, forming a barrier between the armies of Egypt and Israel. No one could cross that barrier. Throughout the night the cloud brought darkness to one side, but light to the other side. Once again the LORD was making a separation between Egypt and Israel, bringing light and life to His people, but the darkness of death to His enemies.

Then Moses stretched out his hand over the sea, as God had commanded, and a strong wind began to blow. All that night the LORD drove the sea in the wind storm. The waters saw God and they writhed. The very depths of the sea were convulsed. The clouds poured down water in the storm. The skies resounded with thunder and lightning flashed back and forth upon the churning seas. There was a roaring tornado, a howling whirlwind that whipped the water into obedience. That night there were also earth tremors, when the ground shook and quaked. The Egyptians could hear and feel and see the storm, but in the blackness they could not see what God was doing. They waited for the light of dawn and for the storm to calm, before they punished their slaves. After all, how could their slaves escape? But the Israelites, with the light of God's presence in the pillar if fire, could see exactly what God was doing. The LORD was working a wonder with those waters. God was dividing the sea. With the whirlwind, God was a blowing a path for them, an escape route, right through the waters of the Red Sea!

God's way was a terrifying way. It was through the mighty waters. They must follow God by faith, though His footprints were not seen. One by one, the Israelites had to step out by faith, trusting their God to save them. Hundreds by hundreds, the people had to step down into the seabed by faith, with walls of water towering and quivering on both sides of them. Thousands by thousands the Israelites had to march forward on that fearful freeway by faith, where the huge waves stood in a strange suspension over them, held back only by the wind and the unseen hand of God. They went through the sea on dry ground, but a salt spray sprinkled them as they passed through the walls of water.

It was Israel's baptism. "They were all baptized into Moses . . . in the sea" (I Corinthians 10:2).

Throughout the night God rescued His people. He delivered them from death, from the waters threatening to engulf them and from the army threatening to slaughter them. Through most of the night God held the Egyptians back, but just before dawn, during the last watch of the night, the LORD let them loose. He let the Egyptians see that their slaves were escaping through the waters of the sea. God had told Moses, "I will harden the hearts of the Egyptians, so that they will go in after them," and they did. The Egyptians rushed into God's trap full speed! The horses and chariots charged into the Red Sea after the children of Israel. If this roadway through the sea was safe for the Israelites, it was safe for them too, thought the foolish Egyptians. The enemy boasted, "I will pursue. I will overtake them. I will divide the spoils. I will gorge myself on them. I will draw my sword and my hand will destroy them," but God's Hand protected them. God would not allow even one of His children, not even the least or the last of them, to be touched by an Egyptian soldier. The LORD looked down from the pillar of cloud and fire, and He threw the Egyptian army into confusion. God jammed the wheels of their chariots, so they had difficulty driving. Some of the wheels fell off, blocking the chariots behind them. The mighty army of Egypt came to a halt in the middle of the Red Sea. Then they realized, too late, that Israel's God was still with them. "Let's get out of here," they shouted. "Let's get away from the Israelites. The LORD is fighting for them against Egypt!" But even as they were speaking, even as they were turning back, even as they were racing to the other shore, the LORD said to Moses, "Stretch out your hand over the sea, so that the waters will flow back over the Egyptians, over all their chariots and horsemen." If any of them were watching, they would have seen Moses lift his hand, silhouetted by the sunrise behind him. That was the last thing they would have seen, before total chaos and terror crashed upon them. Just as the day was breaking, as Moses stretched out his hand over the sea, those great walls of water crashed down upon the entire army of Egypt and covered them. The LORD blew with His breath, and the sea covered them. They sank like lead in the mighty waters. The deep waters covered them and they sank to the depths like a stone. Not one of them survived. The whole army of Egypt drowned. The power and glory of Pharaoh, the splendour and vigour of Egypt, was destroyed in a breath. All that remained were a few bodies, floating on the waves.

That day, in the early light of dawn, the Israelites saw the majestic power of God. They saw God save them from their enemies. They saw all that was left of the great army of Egypt—dead bodies washed up along the seashore. They also saw their own families, standing safely beside them. When the Israelites saw this, when they saw the great power of the LORD displayed before them, the people feared the LORD and put their trust in Him. They also trusted God's servant, Moses. Although they had rebelled against the LORD by the Red Sea, yet God saved them for His name's sake, to make His mighty power known. God had said, "I will gain glory through Pharaoh and all his army . . . The Egyptians will know that I am the LORD." God saved His people from the hands of their enemies, and the people rejoiced in their God. Now "they believed His Promises and sang His Praise" (Psalm 106:12).

This was the song that Moses and all the Israelites sang:

I will sing to the LORD, for He is highly exalted.
The horse and the rider, He has hurled into the sea.
The LORD is my strength and my song; He also has
      become my salvation.
He is my God, and I will praise Him, my father's God,
      and I will exalt Him.
The LORD is a Warrior; The LORD is His Name.
Pharaoh's chariots and his army He has hurled into the sea.
The best of Pharaoh's officers are drowned in the Red Sea.
The deep waters have covered them; they sank to the
      depths like a stone . . .

Miriam, the prophetess, the sister of Moses, took a tambourine in her hand, and all the women followed her with the jingling of their tambourines and the singing of their voices and the dancing of their feet. Miriam sang to them:

Sing to the LORD, for He is highly exalted.
The horse and its rider, He has hurled into the sea.

The teacher's guide for this lesson starts on page 224.

BITTERNESS TO BLESSEDNESS

- **Exodus 15:22–27**
- **Psalm 103**

The Israelites rejoiced in the LORD on the eastern shore of the Red Sea. Perhaps that day it was "from the dawn to setting sun" that they "praised the LORD, the Mighty One" (Psalm 113:3). Perhaps that day it was from daybreak, when the walls of water crashed over their enemies, until twilight, when the surface of the sea reflected the glory of the western sky, that they sang and danced before the LORD. But all too soon the time came to pack away their tambourines and timbrels and press on towards the Promised Land. They could continue praising God with lips and hearts; in fact, they should rejoice in the LORD always, but now it was time to go forward.

Moses led the Israelites away from the Red Sea. What faced them was not a pleasant place. They would be trudging through a wasteland, known as the Desert of Shur. What is always a difficulty in the desert? Water! Where would they find water enough for millions of people, plus flocks and herds of animals? Where would they find any water at all? One day passed, then another, and another. The Israelites travelled three full days in that desert without finding any water, and what they carried with them was soon gone. Children were whining and crying because they were thirsty, and animals were bawling and bleating for water. Then the cloud of God stopped at a place called Marah, and there they saw a beautiful sight—sunlight sparkling on a pool of water! It was not a mirage shimmering in the desert heat. It really was water. The people must have rushed to the edge of the pond and dipped their hands into the cool water for a drink, but what a disappointment. As they wet their parched lips, they had to spit it out . . . quickly. It tasted awful! What was wrong with that water? Was it contaminated? Would it make them sick? They certainly couldn't drink the water here, for it was bitter. That was why this place was called Marah. The word meant *bitter.*

Then the people began to grumble against Moses. Why had he led them here? Why had God brought them to such a bitter place? God had promised them a land flowing with the richness of milk and the sweetness of honey, but all He had given them was bitterness. Who could drink the bitter water of Marah? (This was the second time that the people rebelled against the LORD). And they shouted at Moses, "What are we to drink?"

Then poor Moses cried out to the LORD. He prayed to God and God answered his prayer. God's answer was a strange one. The LORD showed Moses a piece of wood. Moses then took the piece of wood and threw it into the water, and it became sweet. So the Israelites had water to drink in the desert—safe water, good water, sweet water.

At that place called Marah or bitter, the LORD tested the Israelites. Do you think they passed the test? No, God tried their faith, testing them with bitter waters, to see if His people would trust in His LOVE, but immediately they grumbled against Moses, and so against God. "How often they rebelled against Him in the desert and grieved Him in the wasteland. Again and again they put God to the test. They vexed the Holy One of Israel. They did not remember His power" (Psalm 78:40–42). The Israelites tested God, but God also tested them, and they failed that test miserably. But perhaps that test, that trial, would teach the Israelites to trust God in whatever bitter troubles that they faced.

Then the LORD made a law for the Israelites at that place. God told them something very important: "If you listen carefully to the voice of the LORD your God and do what is right in His eyes, if you pay attention to His commands and keep all His decrees, I will not bring on you any of the diseases I brought on the Egyptians, for *I am the* LORD, *who heals you."* In Egypt the Israelites had seen the LORD change good water into bad; they had seen the rivers and reservoirs, the drinking wells and watering holes, turn into blood. They had seen the LORD bring all manner of plagues and ills upon the Egyptians. Before their very eyes they had witnessed a nation flourish, then shrivel and wither under the judgements of God. They had seen green lush fields become brown and bare. They had seen food crops crushed and livestock killed. They had seen children die and soldiers drown, all by the hand of their God. But now they were seeing something else: They were seeing a healing hand, a hand that could change bitter water into blessed water. Now they were hearing something else: "I am the LORD who heals you." God could destroy; that they knew. But now they learned that God could also restore. He could change crying into laughing and turn tears into a song. He could change crippling into healing and certain death into everlasting life. Blessedness, not bitterness, could be what the Israelites received from God, but they must believe Him and obey Him.

After the people had been refreshed not only with the sweetness of the water but also with the sweetness of God's Word and God's LOVE, the LORD then led His people southward to Elim, which means Palm Trees. Elim was an island of green in the desert. Seventy palm trees grew in that oasis, and there were twelve springs of water, one for each of the twelve tribes of Israel. There was an abundance of good drinking water at Elim. There was also a river. It was a beautiful pleasant place for the Israelites to pitch their tents. God had brought them from the place called bitterness to a place of blessedness.

The teacher's guide for this lesson starts on page 226.

THE BREAD OF ANGELS

T he Israelites enjoyed the campground at Elim with its twelve sparkling water springs and its seventy shady palm trees, but one day the pillar of cloud began to move onward. The pillar of God's presence was showing the Israelites that it was time to go, so they packed up their tents and followed. They continued southward, entering a desolate region, so bare and barren that it was named the Desert of Sin. It seemed to be a God-forsaken landscape, a wasteland so wild and wicked that even God would not walk there, but that was precisely the place where the LORD led His people.

Why did God lead them there? Where would they find food and water? They had been travelling for one full month. Didn't God know that their supplies were almost gone, that many families were already without food? They were all going to starve in this wasteland. Didn't God know, or didn't He care? Perhaps it was not God who had led them to this place. Perhaps there was no God at all! Thus the people began to doubt. "They did not believe in God or trust in His deliverance" (Psalm 78:22).

How quickly they had forgotten the faithful words they had sung by the Red Sea. How quickly they had forgotten the song where they praised God for leading them in His "unfailing LOVE." But it was not God's LOVE that had failed; it was Israel's faith that had faltered and failed. Instead of trusting God, instead of praying earnestly and waiting patiently for God's deliverance, the Israelites began complaining and rebelling. (This was their third rebellion against God on their journey).

In the Desert of Sin the whole community of Israel grumbled against Moses and Aaron, blaming them for the trouble they now faced. They shouted at Moses and Aaron, "We wish we had died in Egypt! At least we had food there . . . we sat around pots of meat and ate all the food we wanted, but you have brought us into this desert to starve the entire assembly to death." What dreadful lies the Israelites spoke about their leaders. How could they suspect them and accuse them of such a horrible crime? But most shocking of all was their unbelief. Did they not yet have faith in God? Did they not yet believe that it was the LORD their God who brought them out of Egypt? Did they not know that it was God who also led them to this desert? Did they not yet trust God and His LOVE to provide for them? Did they not yet fear God and His wrath to punish them? Moses must have been utterly distressed and dismayed by the Israelites' unbelief. They were not just rebelling against Moses. They were rebelling against God!

But the LORD spoke to Moses and told him what He would do. God promised that He would provide food for the Israelites. God said, "I will rain down bread from heaven for you." God also was going to give something else to the Israelites—a test. God said, "I will test them and see whether they will follow my instructions." These were God's instructions:

PART ONE OF GOD'S TEST: "The people are to go out each day and gather enough [just enough] for that day." It was a test of faith. Would they trust God to provide their daily bread? Would they obey God's Word? Would the Israelites pass God's test?

PART TWO OF GOD'S TEST: "On the sixth day they are to prepare what they bring in, and that is to be twice as much as they gather on the other days." This too was a test of faith. Would they trust God to provide food for them if they kept the Sabbath Day as a day of rest? Would they obey God's Word? Would the Israelites pass God's test?

After Moses listened to God's plan, he and his brother spoke to the Israelites, saying, "In the evening *you will know* that it was the LORD who brought you out of Egypt, and in the morning *you will see* the glory of the LORD." They must not be unbelieving, but believing! They also said, "The LORD has heard your grumbling against Him. Who are we, that you should grumble against us?" It was not Moses who had brought the Israelites out of Egypt, but God. Moses said, "You will know that it was the LORD when He gives you meat to eat in the evening and all the bread you want in the morning, because He has heard your grumbling against Him! Who are we? You are not grumbling against us, but against the LORD."

Then Moses through Aaron commanded the entire Israelite community: "Come before the LORD, for He has heard your grumbling." Were they not afraid now? The Israelites assembled before the LORD, and when they looked toward the desert, behold, there was the glory of the LORD appearing in the cloud. How they must have trembled before the splendour of His Majesty! The LORD spoke to Moses, "I have heard the grumbling of the Israelites. Tell them: 'At twilight you will eat meat, and in the morning you will be filled with bread. *Then you will know that I am the LORD your God.'*"

The people must have wondered: How could God provide bread and meat for millions of people? Where could God find food for so many people in this wilderness? They would find out very soon. That evening God ordered meat for His people. The same God who commanded locusts to swarm over Egypt's fields to devour their crops, now commanded birds to flock over Israel's camp to provide them food. Hundreds of thousands of small wild chickens, known as quail, covered Israel's camp. "He rained meat down on them like dust, flying birds like sand on the seashore. He made them come down inside their camp, all around their tents." Even the children were able to catch these plump little birds. That night the people sat by their tents with pots of meat stewing over the fires and spits of meat roasting over the flames. It was a delicious meal and all the people ate till they were full. "They had more than enough" (Psalm 78:27–29).

That night the Israelites did not go to bed hungry, and they dreamed of the bread that would be waiting for their breakfast, for God said, "I will rain down bread from heaven for you, and in the morning you will be filled with bread." The same God who commanded hailstones to fall on the fields of Egypt to destroy their crops, would now command bread to rain from heaven to feed His people. But when the Israelites awoke in the morning, what a disappointment! There was no bread for breakfast. There was only dew on the ground. However, as the warm sun rose and the dew disappeared, the people noticed something else on the ground. What was it? It looked as if frost, thin flakes of frost, had formed on the floor of the desert, but it was too warm for frost. "What is it?" the Israelites asked each other, for they did not know what it was. (The way you say "what is it" in Hebrew is: "manna"). All over the Israelites' campground thousands upon thousands of people were murmuring, "Manna? Manna? What is it? What is it?" Moses answered them, "It is the bread the LORD has given you to eat." The Israelites called this sweet white bread "manna." The manna tasted like wafers made with honey. It was delicious! It could be boiled to make a sweet porridge for breakfast or it could be baked to make a sweet bread for supper.

Then Moses gave the Israelites —

PART ONE OF GOD'S TEST: He said, "This is what the LORD has commanded: 'Each one is to gather as much as he needs. Take an omer [that is, about two litres,] for each person you have in your tent.' " The Israelites did as they were told; some gathered much, some little. And when they measured it by the omer, he who gathered much did not have too much, and he who gathered little did not have too little. Each one gathered as much as he needed. Then Moses said to the people, "No one is to keep any of it until morning." This time some of the Israelites paid no attention to Moses. They disregarded God's command. They failed God's test. They decided to keep some of the manna until morning — just in case — just in case there was no more bread. They didn't trust God to provide for them each day their daily bread. When they awoke the following morning, however, they discovered that their breakfast of unbelief was not fit to eat. The manna was wormy and smelly and had to be disposed of quickly. Moses was very angry with these people.

All through the work week, the people gathered the manna. Each morning everyone gathered as much as he needed for the day. When the sun grew hot, the manna melted away. But day by day, one day at a time, God in His great LOVE provided food for His people. "He gave a command to the skies above and opened the doors of the heavens; He rained down manna for the people to eat; He gave them the grain of heaven. Men ate the bread of angels. God sent them all the food they could eat" (Psalm 78:23–25).

Then Moses gave the Israelites —

PART TWO OF GOD'S TEST: On the sixth day the people gathered twice as much food, two omers (that is, about 4 litres,) for each person. Moses said, "This is what the LORD has commanded: 'Tomorrow is to be a day of rest, a holy Sabbath to the LORD. So bake what you want to bake and boil what you want to boil. Save whatever is left and keep it until morning.' " They must prepare for the Sabbath Day. The sixth day would be the preparation day for the seventh day, the Sabbath Day. On the sixth day they must do all their work. They must gather and prepare all their food on the day before the Sabbath. Most of the people did as they were told. They saved some manna until morning, as Moses commanded, and it was fine. On the LORD's Day the manna had no worms crawling in it, nor did it have a sickening stench to it. Moses said, "Eat it today, because today is a Sabbath to the LORD. You will not find any of it on the ground today. Six days you are to gather it, but on the seventh day, the Sabbath, there will not be any." This was God's Law from the beginning: Six days you shall labour and do all your work, but the seventh day is a Sabbath to the LORD your God. Did the people pass this part of God's test? Sadly, no, they did not. They did not keep God's ancient law or recent Word to them. Some of the people ignored the Sabbath. They went outside on the seventh day hoping to work and looking for food, but they found none. Not only did these people go hungry that day, but a much worse thing happened. They caused the Israelites to fail God's test. The LORD was angry and said to Moses, "How long will you people refuse to keep My commands?. . . Bear in mind that the LORD has given you the Sabbath; that is why on the sixth day He gives you bread for two days. Everyone is to stay where he is on the seventh day; no one is to go out."

So the people rested on the seventh day. The Israelites learned that lesson, before they received God's Law on the tablets of stone. Keeping the fourth commandment was already part of their way of life, a holy habit God forced upon them. God made His people remember the Sabbath in the wilderness. If they didn't, they went hungry. As the Israelites rested in their tents on the Sabbath Day, they could say, "The LORD is my Shepherd; I shall not want. He makes me to lie down" (Psalm 23:1, 2).

God wanted the Israelites to remember the manna. When they came to the Promised Land, a land flowing with streams and rippling with wheat, a land where bread would not be scarce, where they would have butter and honey and an abundance of every good thing, then they would no longer need the manna. The day the Israelites entered the Promised Land, the manna would disappear from the earth. It would not be seen on the ground again. The LORD wanted the Israelites to remember the bread they ate in the desert, so the LORD commanded them to save some of the manna in a sealed jar. God said, "Take an omer of manna [that is, the portion for one person,] and keep it for the generations to come, so they can see the bread I gave you to eat in the desert when I brought you out of Egypt." So Moses said to Aaron, "Take a jar and put an omer of manna in it. Then place it before the LORD to be kept for the generations to come." The manna was put in a gold jar; later the jar was put in a gold chest called the ark of the covenant, which stood inside the Holy of Holies, which was the Most Holy Place in God's tabernacle and God's temple.

God had many reasons why He led His people into that dreadful desert and why He provided food for them the way He did:

1) God led them there to humble them. Later Moses wrote, "God humbled you, causing you to hunger and then feeding you with manna" (Deuteronomy 8:3). The LORD did this to teach the Israelites to rely on Him, to rest in Him, to believe in Him, to trust in Him. God's people must learn to live by faith, not just once, but day after day after day, until they die.

2) God led them there to discipline them. Later Moses wrote, "Know then in your heart that . . . the LORD your God disciplines you" (Deuteronomy 8:5). They must be taught that man does not live by bread alone, but on every Word that comes from the mouth of the LORD. God's people must learn to obey the commands of the LORD their God, "walking in His ways and revering Him" (Deuteronomy 8:6). "God disciplines us for our good, that we may share in His holiness. No discipline seems pleasant at the time, but painful. Later on, however, it produces a harvest of righteousness and peace for those who have been trained by it" (Hebrews 12:10, 11). God's plan was to reap a harvest in the wilderness—a harvest of righteousness and holiness in the hearts of His people. The desert was their training ground.

3) God led them there to test them. Later Moses wrote, "God led you all the way in the desert . . . to test you in order to know what was in your heart, whether or not you would keep His commands" (Deuteronomy 8:2).

4) The manna in the wilderness was to point to the Messiah in the world. God wanted the Israelites to remember the manna, so they would recognize the Messiah. One day, God would send to Israel the true bread from heaven. One day the bread of God would come down from heaven to give life to the world. One day Jesus would say to the Jews, "I tell you the truth: He who believes has everlasting life. I am the bread of life. Your forefathers

ate manna in the desert, yet they died. But here is the bread that comes down from heaven, which a man may eat and not die. I am the living bread that came down from heaven. If anyone eats of this bread, he will live forever. This bread is my flesh, which I will give for the life of the world" (John 6:47–51).

5) To those who persevere in their faith to the end, the risen Christ has made this promise: "To him who overcomes, I will give some of the hidden manna" (Revelation 2:17). There is a manna hidden for us in heaven, sweeter than any manna that was ever gathered upon this earth. All who trust in Christ will taste that manna, that grain from heaven, that bread of angels.

The teacher's guide for this lesson starts on page 228.

THE LORD IS MY ROCK!

- **Exodus 17:1–7**
- **Psalms 95;**
  78:15–16; 105:41;
  114:7–8
- **John 4:14**
- **John 7:37–39**
- **I Corinthians**
  10:1–5

The LORD led the Israelites out of the Desert of Sin. He led them southward and upward through a high rocky mountainous region. The people camped from place to place in these lonely highlands, wherever the LORD commanded. Then God led them to a place called Rephidim, and here the people faced trouble: There was no water for them to drink.

Surely the Israelites knew by now that the LORD could be trusted to provide water for his people. Surely by now they had faith in God. Surely by now they believed in the power of God and the LOVE of God to supply all the water they needed to sustain life in this remote region. How sad and how wrong was the Israelites' response to their need. Instead of believing, instead of praying, instead of living by faith and dying to sin, the Israelites chose to begin quarrelling. They quarrelled again with Moses and with God (which was the fourth time that they rebelled against the LORD in the wilderness).

The people shouted at Moses, "Give us water to drink!" What could Moses do? Was he Moses the magician, who could just snap his fingers and make water appear from nowhere? Moses could not give them water to drink, but he could give them food for thought. Moses said, "Why do you quarrel with me? Why do you test the LORD?" Did they have any reason to respond this way? Had not God blessed them again and again? Had not Moses blessed them too?

But the people refused to listen to reason. They refused to respond to the present difficulty with trust in God. They did not set the LORD before their faces, nor did they focus their hearts and minds on the promises of God. What they looked at instead were the visions of their own fears. What they saw were their own bodies lying dead in the desert, with their little children lying lifeless beside them. The Israelites allowed themselves to be ruled by fear, rather than by faith, and because they could not quench their thirst, they would not quench their sin. They continued to grumble against Moses. "Why did you bring us out of Egypt?" they asked. "Was it to make us and our children and our livestock die of thirst?" The people knew it was the LORD their God who brought them out of Egypt—to give them life and life abundantly! How could they say such wicked things? How could they accuse Moses of leading them here to kill them? Moses had been a prince in Egypt, but he forsook all the pleasures and treasures of Egypt to suffer with the people of God and to lead them to the Promised Land. How could they turn against such a righteous man? How could they now say Moses brought them out of Egypt, not to free them, but to kill them?

The people persisted in their lies and anger and unbelief. The crowd around Moses grew larger and their voices grew louder. Some of them were shouting and shaking their fists. Others were picking up stones. Moses was afraid that this angry mob was going to kill him. Moses cried out to the LORD, "What am I to do with these people? They are almost ready to stone me."

The LORD did not forsake Moses to the wrath of this angry crowd. The LORD answered his prayer and said to him, "Walk on ahead of the people. Take with you some of the elders of Israel and take in your hand the staff, with which you struck the Nile, and go. I will stand there before you by the rock at Horeb. Strike the rock, and water will come out of it for the people to drink."

So Moses did as the LORD commanded. He walked through the midst of the angry people who wanted to stone him, but no one laid a hand upon him. He walked ahead to the great rock by Mount Horeb (which was the mountain where Moses saw the burning bush). He went to the rock and there, in the sight of the elders of Israel, Moses struck the rock with his staff. The elders of Israel witnessed a miracle. Water gushed forth from the rock! Yes, from solid rock, God brought forth liquid life. A waterfall in the wilderness was created by the Word of the LORD. It ran like a river down the mountainside and branched into streams through Israel's campground and flowed into hollows to form ponds. Hard dry holes became deep clear pools. With the staff, with Moses' hand, God "split the rocks in the desert and gave them water as abundant as the seas; He brought streams out of a rocky crag and made water flow down like rivers" (Psalm 78:15, 16). God "opened the rock, and water gushed out; like a river it flowed in the desert" (Psalm 105:41).

How the people must have cheered when they saw the rivers of flowing water. It might have been better, however, if they had trembled because of their sin. "Tremble, O earth, at the presence of the LORD, at the presence of the God of Jacob, who turned the rock into a pool, the hard rock into springs of water" (Psalm 114:7, 8). This was the good God, whom they had doubted. This was the great God, whom they had tested. This was the LORD who had promised to be with them, whose Holy Word they had not believed. They doubted and tested God by their wicked words: "Is the LORD among us or not?" Moses left a memorial of the Israelites' sin at that place. He called that place Massah (which means "testing") and Merribah (which means "quarrelling"). Perhaps those names would warn the Israelites from sin. Never again must they harden their hearts against God!

Why did God lead the Israelites to a place without water?

1. God did this to test the Israelites' faith, and the Israelites failed the test—again.

2. God did this to teach the Israelites: *God was with them!* He would provide all their daily needs, not just their daily bread, but their daily drink too. They must learn this lesson. They must believe in God. They must trust their loving heavenly Father to take care of them.

3. Most importantly, God wanted to point his people to the Messiah. This was another sign, pointing to the Christ.

That rock, which gushed forth water, was a type of Christ. The Israelites drank a "spiritual drink . . . from the spiritual rock that accompanied them, and that rock was Christ!" (I Corinthians 10:4). Jesus is the Rock of our salvation. The Lord Jesus Christ, when He walked upon this earth, said, "Whoever drinks the water I give him will never thirst. Indeed, the water I give him will become in him a spring of water welling up to eternal life" (John 4:13, 14). Another time Jesus stood teaching at the temple and said in a loud voice, "If anyone is thirsty, let him come to me and drink. Whoever believes in Me, as the Scripture has said, streams of living water will flow from within him" (John 7:37, 38). What was that living water? Jesus meant the Holy Spirit, who would be given to all who believed in Jesus. The Old Testament prophets also spoke about this promise of the Holy Spirit: "Listen, O Jacob, my servant, Israel whom I have chosen. This is what the LORD says . . . 'Do not be afraid . . . for I will pour water on the thirsty land and streams on the dry ground; I will pour out My Spirit on your offspring, and my blessing on your descendants' " (Isaiah 44:1–3). Christ was "The rock of our salvation," from whom flowed the rivers of living water, even the Holy Spirit of God, the spirit of life. If the Spirit of God, "who raised Jesus from the dead, is living in you, He who raised Christ from the dead will also give life to your mortal bodies through His Spirit, who lives in you" (Romans 8:11). How does a person receive this living water that Christ offered? How does a person receive the Holy Spirit? It is by faith, by believing in Jesus. "Whoever believes in Him shall not perish, but have eternal life" (John 3:16).

That miracle in the mountains, when Moses struck the rock and water gushed forth to give life, was a great miracle, but it pointed to a greater miracle—the life that Christ would give to the world. What God did for the Israelites in the wilderness that day was a sign of His Great LOVE for them, but one day there would be a greater LOVE demonstrated to the world.

> This is LOVE: not that we loved God,
> but that He loved us and sent His Son
> as an atoning sacrifice for our sins
>
> (I John 4:10).

The teacher's guide for this lesson starts on page 230.

THE LORD IS
MY BANNER

- Exodus 17:8–16
- Deuteronomy 25:17–19
- Isaiah 11:10, 12

As the Israelites continued their journey through that rough and rocky region near Rephidim, they faced more trouble. Rephidim was a place of double trouble. There the people of Israel had been thirsty for water; there another people were thirsty for blood. The LORD was watching over his people at Rephidim, but there were other eyes watching them too, enemy eyes that watched them from hidden haunts among the rocks, enemy eyes that watched them from dark shadows and secret spots. Whose eyes were these, that looked at the Israelites with envy and mockery and hatred? These eyes belonged to the people who had made these mountains their home, the Amalekites.

What did those wicked eyes see? They saw a weary, worn-out band of people wandering through *their* wilderness. They saw a crowd of teary, tired-out travellers trudging through *their* mountains. These Amalekites had no pity for these poor people, and they offered them no help on their way. What they offered them was war. "Come," they said, "let us destroy them as a nation. Let the name of Israel be no more" (Psalm 83:4). Without any reason, other than their own wickedness, they attacked the Israelites. In their greediness, they thought they could steal the flocks and herds, the silver and gold, that belonged to the Israelites. In their ruthlessness, they thought they could spill innocent blood—and laugh. The Amalekites had no fear of God. What they did was totally wicked. Without any provocation, they attacked, and their targets were the weakest members of Israel's number, the few feeble ones who lagged behind. The Amalekites cut down the old and the sick with their swords. They shot arrows at the unsuspecting stragglers of Israel.

What did those wicked eyes not see? They did not see the LORD, the God of Israel, the invisible and invincible one, who would fight for the people He loved. The Israelites were about to fight their first battle! This time the Israelites were not to stand still and see God's deliverance; this time they were to fight and see God's deliverance. Moses chose a man to lead Israel's army, a man who was both strong in faith and wise in war. This man's name was Joshua. Moses told him the battle plan: "Choose some of our men and go out to fight the Amalekites. Tomorrow I will stand on top of the hill with the staff of God in my hands." So the next day Joshua went out with his men to fight the Amalekites and Moses went up with his men (Aaron and Hur) to watch and to pray. Moses stood on top of the hill, where the soldiers of Israel could see him, and he lifted his staff over them, as he held his hands up to God in prayer. As long as Moses held up his hands with the staff of God, the Israelites were winning, but whenever he lowered his hands, the Amalekites were winning. The three men on top of the hill quickly realized that to win this war, Moses must not lower his hands. He must keep his hands lifted high to God and to the throne of God's Grace. But Moses was an old man and his arms grew tired, very tired. How long could an old man keep his arms lifted up? One hour? Two hours? The war could not be won in such a short time. Perhaps if he sat down it would be easier. So Aaron and Hur brought a stone for Moses and he sat on it. Later they held up his arms for him too, one on one side, one on the other side, so that his hands remained steady until sunset.

For an entire day Moses' hands had been lifted high in prayer. On the battlefield below, the soldiers of Israel must have taken courage from the sight of Moses and his staff lifted above them. They all knew that staff. It was a constant reminder for them of mighty miracles and glorious victories. That staff was a reminder to them that the LORD was on their side, fighting for them!

Down on the battlefield, what did the Amalekites see? All they saw was an old man, who couldn't even keep his arms lifted by himself, and an old stick, an old shepherd's crook, in his hands. They must have wondered scornfully: Don't the Israelites even have a flag to fly? Doesn't Israel even have a banner for their troops? But when the sun set, it was the flagless army of Israel that cheered. It was the faithful hands of Joshua and his men, who overcame the Amalekite army with the power of the sword, and it was the faithful hands of Moses and his men, who overcame the Amalekite enemy with the power of prayer.

Then the LORD said to Moses, "Write this on a scroll as something to be remembered and make sure that Joshua hears it, because I will completely blot out the memory of Amalek from under heaven." Moses said, "The LORD will be at war against the Amalekites from generation to generation." What they had planned to do to the Israelites, God would do to them. One day, God was going to end *their* nation.

Moses built an altar to the LORD, to worship God with thanksgiving for their deliverance. Moses named this altar, "The LORD is my Banner," because hands were lifted up to the throne of the LORD.

Many centuries later the LORD promised that, in the fullness of time, He would lift up a banner for the whole world. The LORD will "raise a banner for the nations and gather the exiles of Israel." This banner would be a man, a Saviour, who would "stand as a banner for the peoples; the nations will rally to Him, and His place of rest will be glorious" (Isaiah 11:12, 10). Who was that man? It was Jesus Christ! "The Son of Man must be lifted up, that everyone who believes in Him may have eternal life. For God so loved the world that He gave His one and only Son, that whoever believes in Him shall not perish, but have eternal life" (John 3:15, 16).

The teacher's guide for this lesson starts on page 232.

THE VOICE OF GOD

T hree months after the Israelites left Egypt, on the very day of the three-month anniversary of the exodus, the Israelites arrived at Mount Sinai, the "mountain of God," the same mountain where God spoke to Moses from the burning bush and sent him to bring the people out of Egypt. At that time God promised Moses, "I will be with you. And this will be the sign to you that it is I who have sent you: when you have brought the people out of Egypt, you will worship God on this mountain" (Exodus 3:12). And now they had arrived. God had kept his promise. What a wonderful sign it must have been for Moses to see the tents of Israel—hundreds of thousands of tents—pitched at the foot of Mount Sinai. The Israelites camped there in the Desert of Sinai in front of the mountain for almost a year.

Why had God brought them to this mountain in the desert? They had come here to worship the LORD! When they were in Egypt, again and again Moses declared to Pharaoh the reason the Israelites must be set free. Many times he said to Pharaoh, "Thus says the LORD: Let my people go so that they may *worship* me." Moses said to Pharaoh, "We must take a three-day journey into the desert to offer sacrifices to the LORD our God" (Exodus 8:27). It had taken a little longer than three days. It turned out to be a three-month journey through the desert, but their purpose remained the same. God's purpose for them had not wavered as they wandered that long way through the wilderness. What was it? Why had they come here to this mountain? They had come to worship the LORD! They had faced many difficulties along the way, the worst one being their own sins, which so easily entangled them, but at last they had arrived. They had come to this place in the wilderness, away from all the distractions of the world, for one great purpose, the purpose for which all people were created—to glorify God! The Israelites would spend almost a year by this mountain, learning how to worship the LORD.

When they arrived at Mount Sinai, Moses went up to God and the LORD called to him from the mountain, saying, "This is what you are to say to the house of Jacob and what you are to tell the people of Israel: 'You yourselves have seen what I did to the Egypt, and how I carried you on eagles' wings and brought you to myself. Now, If you obey Me fully and keep My covenant, then out of all nations you will be My treasured possession. Although the whole earth is mine, you will be for Me a kingdom of priests and a holy nation.' These are the words you are to speak to the Israelites."

They were such important words for everyone to understand. God was the one who had rescued them; God was the one who had carried them; and God was the one who had brought them—where? To the middle of a wilderness? In the world's estimation, Israel had just arrived at the pinnacle of nowhere. Mount Sinai? There was nothing here. There was nothing to buy, nothing to see, nothing to do. It was a wilderness! There were no buildings, no cities, no centres of civilization, nothing except the most important thing of all. God! The LORD said He had brought the Israelites to Himself. There was no better place in all the world, than to be with God. There was no greater gift in all the earth, than to have the LORD Himself. At Mount Sinai the Israelites would see and hear things which no other people on earth would ever see or hear again. Soon Mount Sinai would be an amazing place to be because God Himself was going to descend upon that mountain.

God was going to make a *covenant* with Israel. Long ago God had made a covenant with Abraham, Isaac and Jacob, and now God was going to make a covenant with all their descendants at Mount Sinai. Out of all the nations

on earth God had chosen these people, the Israelites, to be in covenant relationship to Him. These were God's covenant promises to Israel:

1. You will be my treasured possession,

2. You will be for me a kingdom of priests,

3. You will be a holy nation.

What was Israel's part in the covenant? Obedience! They must obey
God's Word. They must keep God's Law. The LORD said, "Obey Me fully
and keep My Covenant." Would the Israelites agree to do this? Would they
enter into this covenant "agreement" with God? Would they whole-heartedly
accept this relationship with God? Would they gratefully and joyfully say
"yes" to God's gracious offer? Did they want to be God's possession? Did
they want to be God's nation? Did they want to be God's priests? Were they
willing to enter into God's service to obey Him fully? Were they willing to
be holy, because the LORD their God was holy? Moses went down the mountain to Israel's camp, where he summoned the elders of the people and set
before them all the words the LORD had commanded him to speak. And the
people said "yes" to God. They all responded together, "We will do everything the LORD has said." Then Moses brought their answer back to God.

Then the LORD told Moses that in three days He would meet with the
people. God said, "I am going to come to you in a dense cloud, so that the
people will hear me speaking with you and will always put their trust in
you." The people must be ready to hear the word and the voice of the LORD.
God said, "Go to the people and consecrate them . . . Be ready by the third
day, because on that day the LORD will come down on Mount Sinai in the
sight of all the people." Surely then, when they heard with their own ears
and saw with their own eyes, the people would not rebel. Surely then they
would fear and trust God and so follow Moses. God warned Moses to put
limits around the mountain and set it apart as holy. Moses must warn the
people not to touch the mountain: "Be careful that you do not go up the
mountain or touch the foot of it. Whoever touches the mountain shall surely
be put to death . . . He shall not be permitted to live." Only when the ram's
horn sounded a long blast were they allowed to approach the mountain.

After Moses had gone down the mountain, he prepared the people to
meet with God. They had two days to get ready for this meeting. Moses consecrated the people and they all washed their clothes, just as God com-

manded. They must be a holy people, to meet with the Most Holy God. They must be pure and clean, not only on the outside, but also on the inside, in the very depths of their hearts. Not only their clothes, but also their hearts, must be prepared to worship the LORD. Holy, holy, holy is the LORD God Almighty. Limits were placed all around the mountain, and warnings were made, so that neither man nor beast touched the mountain. This mountain was set apart as holy, because God Himself was going to descend on Mount Sinai in the sight of all the people and speak to them.

What an amazing day that was going to be. Never had a congregation of so many people gathered together in one place to worship the LORD. The members of the congregation were numbered in the millions, as they stood before a pulpit, which was a mountain, and a preacher, who was God Himself. How the people must have looked forward to that day of worship, but when it dawned, it came with terror:

On the morning of the third day there were flashes of lightening and crashes of thunder all around. When the people looked toward the mountain, it was covered with a thick dark cloud. Something far more frightening than a storm was brewing. Gloom and dread enveloped everything. Suddenly a trumpet blasted from the top of the mountain. The sound struck alarm in every heart and set every body shaking. Even Moses said, "I am trembling with fear" (Hebrews 12:21). But the signal had been sounded. The time had come. In spite of the paralysing terror, Moses led the people out of the camp to stand at the foot of the mountain, where they would meet with God. Then the LORD descended to the top of the mountain in fire. The people saw it blaze up with flames to the very heavens, while thick smoke and black clouds and deep darkness billowed up from it. Then not only the people trembled; even the mountains trembled before the LORD. They could feel the ground shaking beneath their feet and they could see the mount quaking before their eyes. The very earth trembled at the presence of the LORD. The sound of the trumpet, blaring from the mountain-top, grew louder and *louder* and **louder!** Who was blowing it? The Scriptures record that thousands upon thousands of angels attended God when His glory and majesty blazed from the summit of the mountain. "The LORD came from Sinai . . . He shone forth . . . He came with myriads of holy ones" (Deuteronomy 33:2). God often calls his angels to sound his trumpets. (See Revelation 8:6.) As the sound of the trumpet grew louder, the fear of the people grew deeper. And then the most terrifying thing of all happened. The LORD spoke.

"The God of glory thunders . . . The voice of the LORD is powerful. The voice of the LORD is majestic . . . The voice of the LORD strikes with flashes of lightening . . . The voice of the LORD shakes the desert." Like a roaring tornado, ripping up the trees in its path, "the voice of the LORD breaks in pieces the cedars . . . the voice of the LORD twists the oaks and strips the forests bare" (Psalm 29:3–9). Like a roaring waterfall, like the sound of rushing waters, the voice of the LORD spoke to his people. From out of the fire, from the burning mountain, the LORD's voice came. The people "heard the sound of words, but they saw no form; there was only a voice." (Deuteronomy 4:12). It was the voice of God!

What did God say to the people? The voice of the LORD declared to them His covenant—the Ten Commandments.

The teacher's guide for this lesson starts on page 234.

THE TEN COMMANDMENTS

- **Exodus 20:1–17**
- **Deuteronomy 5:1–22**
- **Psalms 19:7–11; 119**
- **Matthew 5:17–48; 7:12; 22:36–40**
- **Romans 3:21–31; 5:20–21; 7:7–25**
- **Galatians 2:15–3:25; 5:4–6, 14**

When the LORD descended upon Mount Sinai, the Israelites came near and stood at the foot of the mountain, while it blazed with fire to the very heavens, with black clouds and deep darkness surrounding it. The LORD spoke to them out of the fire. They heard the sound of words, but saw no form. There was only a voice. Then God declared His covenant—the Ten Commandments:

"I am the LORD your God, who brought you out of Egypt, out of the land of slavery.

1. *You shall have no other gods before me.*

2. *You shall not make for yourself an idol* in the form of anything in heaven above or on the earth beneath or in the waters below. *You shall not bow down to them or worship them*; for I, the LORD your God, am a jealous God, punishing the children for the sin of the fathers to the third and fourth generation of those who hate Me, but showing LOVE to a thousand generations of those who love Me and keep My commandments.

3. *You shall not misuse the name of the Lord your God*, for the LORD will not hold anyone guiltless who misuses His name.

4. *Remember the sabbath day by keeping it holy.* Six days you shall labour and do all your work, but the seventh day is a Sabbath to the LORD your God. On it you shall not do any work, neither you, nor your son or daughter, nor your manservant or maidservant, nor your animals, nor the alien within your gates. For in six days the LORD made the heavens and the earth, the sea, and all that is in them, but He rested on the seventh day. Therefore the LORD blessed the Sabbath Day and made it holy.

5. *Honour your father and your mother,* so that you may live long in the land the LORD your God is giving you.

6. *You shall not murder.*

7. *You shall not commit adultery.*

8. *You shall not steal.*

9. *You shall not give false testimony against your neighbour.*

10. *You shall not covet* your neighbour's house. You shall not covet your neighbour's wife, or his manservant or maidservant, his ox or donkey, or anything that belongs to your neighbour."

This is the Law of God! It must be obeyed — by everyone! The Israelites had to obey God's Law then, and we must obey God's Law now. There are many reasons why we must obey this Law.

1) *We must obey this Law because* . . . It is the Law of the LORD. The "Lord God Almighty reigns" (Revelation 19:6). All people must obey God's Law because "the earth is the LORD's, and everything in it, the world, and all who live in it" (Psalm 24:1). The LORD is the great God, the great King above all gods" (Psalm 95:3). He is the *"King of kings and Lord of lords"* (Revelation 19:16). "God is the King of all the earth . . . God rules the nations; God sits on His throne of holiness . . . The kings of the earth belong to God. He is highly exalted" (Psalm 47:7–9). No one is exempt from this Law. Everyone — even rulers who themselves establish laws — are under God's rule and God's Law. We must obey the Ten Commandments because "the LORD Almighty — He is the King of Glory" (Psalm 24:10).

2) *We must obey this Law because* . . . It is a Law of LOVE. When the Son of God walked and talked upon this earth, He was asked: "Which is the greatest commandment in the Law?" Jesus replied: "Love the LORD your

God with all your heart and with all your soul and with all your mind. This is the first and greatest commandment. And the second is like it: Love your neighbour as yourself. All the Law and the Prophets hang on these two commandments" (Matthew 22:36–40). "The entire Law is summed up in a single command: "Love your neighbour as yourself" (Galatians 5:14), which is the "royal law" found in Scripture (James 2:8). The Ten Commandments can be condensed into two great commandments: Love God and love other people. It is a Law of LOVE! God is LOVE and God has demonstrated His LOVE to us. "This is LOVE: not that we loved God, but that He loved us, and sent His Son as an atoning sacrifice for our sins" (I John 4:10).

God both made us and saved us. Because we owe Him our very lives, we also owe Him love and loyalty. We show our allegiance to God by obedience to His Law. "We love, because He first loved us . . . This is love for God: to obey His commands. And His commands are not burdensome . . . This is love: that we walk in obedience to His commands" (I John 4:19;5:3 & II John 6). Jesus said, "If you love Me, keep My commandments." Again Jesus said, "Whoever has my commands and obeys them, he is the one who loves Me." A third time Jesus said, "If anyone loves Me, he will obey My teaching" (John 14:15, 21, 23). Jesus summarized the Ten Commandments into one all-encompassing command. He said, "A new command I give you: *love one another.* As I have loved you, so you must love one another." Again Jesus said, "My command is this: Love each other as I have loved you." A third time Jesus said, "This is My command: Love each other" (John 13:34, 15:12, 15:17). We must "live a life of love, just as Christ loved us and gave Himself up for us . . ." (Ephesians 5:2).

3) *We must obey this Law because* . . . It is an everlasting Law. It applies to us now, just as it applied to the Israelites then. God's Law has not been repealed; it has not been replaced. "Your Word, O LORD, is eternal; it stands firm in the heavens . . . Your Laws endure to this day . . . You established them to last forever . . . All Your Words are true; all Your Righteous Laws are eternal" (Psalm 119:89, 91, 152, 160). "All His commandments are sure. They stand fast for ever and ever . . . He ordained His covenant forever" (Psalm 111:7–9). Jesus Himself said, "Do not think that I have come to abolish the Law or the Prophets; I have not come to abolish them, but to fulfil them. I tell you the truth, until heaven and earth disappear, not the smallest letter, not the least stroke of a pen, will by any means disappear from the Law until everything is accomplished" (Matthew 5:17, 18).

4) *We must obey this Law because* . . . It is a holy Law, a perfect Law. We read in the New Testament that "the law is holy and the commandment is

holy, righteous and good" (Romans 7:12). Again and again the Bible declares that God's laws are right and good and true. "O LORD . . . I will praise You with an upright heart as I learn Your righteous laws . . . Your laws are good . . . I know, O LORD, that Your laws are righteous . . . Righteous are You, O LORD, and Your laws are right. The statutes You have laid down are righteous; they are fully trustworthy . . . Your righteousness is everlasting and Your law is true . . . Your statutes are forever right . . . All Your commands are true . . . All Your commands are righteous . . . All Your commands are trustworthy" (Psalm 119:7, 39, 75, 137, 138, 142, 144, 151, 172, 86). God's commandments are wonderful. They are boundless in perfection! "Therefore I obey them" (Psalm 119:96, 129). "The Law of the LORD is perfect" (Psalm 19:7).

5) *We must obey this Law because* . . . It is a Spiritual Law. "We know that the Law is spiritual" (Romans 7:14), "reviving the soul" (Psalm 19:7), "preserving life" (Psalm 119:93).

Can we be saved then by God's Law? Are we made righteous by keeping the Ten Commandments? Can we work our way into heaven by obeying God's Law? Are the Ten Commandments the way of our salvation? No! We are saved by the LOVE and mercy and grace of God. We were dead in our sins, unable to keep God's Law, unable to save ourselves. "But because of His great LOVE for us, God, who is rich in mercy, made us alive with Christ, even when we were dead in transgressions . . . It is by grace you have been saved, through faith—and this not from yourselves, it is the gift of God—not by works, so that no one can boast" (Ephesians 2:4, 5,8, 9). All people have broken God's Law and disobeyed His commandments. "There is no one righteous, not even one" (Romans 3:10). If that was the way of salvation, heaven would be empty of human beings, for no one could be saved. "No one will be declared righteous in [God's] sight by observing the Law; rather, through the Law we become conscious of sin" (Romans 3:20); through the Law we are convicted of sin and condemned to death. "But now a righteousness from God, apart from the Law, has been made known . . . This righteousness from God comes *through faith in Jesus Christ to all who believe* . . . All have sinned and fall short of the glory of God, and are justified freely by His grace through the redemption that came by Christ Jesus . . . A man is justified by faith" (Romans 3:21, 22, 23). "Clearly no one is justified before God by the law, because 'The righteous will live by faith' " (Galatians 3:11). "Law brings wrath" (Romans 4:15), God's wrath upon sin, but "since we have been justified *through faith*, we have peace with God through our Lord Jesus Christ" (Romans 5:1).

If we cannot be saved by obeying God's Law, if we cannot be made righteous or holy by observing His commandments, if our good works cannot gain for us heaven or eternal life or everlasting glory, is there any reason for us to obey God's Laws? Do they grant to us any benefit at all? Yes! Many and great are the benefits for those who keep God's Law:

1) *God's Law is a blessing.* All who keep God's Law are blessed! *"Blessed* are they whose ways are blameless, who walk according to the Law of the LORD. *Blessed* are they who keep His Commandments and seek Him with all their heart" (Psalm 119:1, 2). *"Blessed* is the man . . . whose delight is in the Law of the LORD and on [God's] Law he meditates day and night" (Psalm 1:1, 2). *"Blessed* is the man you train, O LORD, the man you teach from Your Law" (Psalm 94:12). *"Blessed* is the man who fears the LORD, who finds great delight in His Commandments" (Psalm 112:1).

2) *God's Law gives us peace.* "Great peace have they who love Your Law . . . O LORD" (Psalm 119:165).

3) *God's Law gives us comfort.* "I remember your ancient laws, O LORD, and I find comfort in them" (Psalm 119:52).

4) *God's Law gives us wisdom and insight* (Psalm 119:98–104).

5) *God's Law gives us joy.* His commandments are "the joy of my heart" (Psalm 119:111) and they are a source of delight to the one who loves them: "O LORD . . . I delight in Your commands, because I love them" (Psalm 119:47). "O LORD . . . direct me in the path of Your commands, for there I find delight . . . Your commands are my delight . . . I long for your salvation, O LORD, and your Law is my delight" (Psalm 119:35, 143, 174).

6) *God's Law is precious.* It is a source of great wealth to all who treasure it. "O LORD . . . the Law from your mouth is more precious to me than thousands of pieces of silver and gold" (Psalm 119:72). The commandments of the LORD are "more precious than gold, than much pure gold . . . In keeping them there is great reward" (Psalm 19:10, 11).

7) *God's Law is sweet,* like honey for our hearts. The commands of the LORD are "sweeter than honey" (Psalm 19:10).

8) *God's Law is bright.* "The commands of the LORD are radiant, giving light to the eyes" (Psalm 19:8). "O LORD . . . Your Word is a light to my feet and a light for my path" (Psalm 119:105).

9) *God's Law gives us freedom* (Psalm 119:45), in that it keeps us from the snares of sin. It is "the perfect law that gives freedom" (James 1:25).

10) *God's Law points us, leads us, drives us to Christ.* God's Law convicts us of sin and condemns us to death, making us aware of our desperate need for a Saviour. "If a law had been given that could impart life, then righteousness would certainly have come by the law. But the Scripture declares that the whole world is a prisoner of sin, so that what was promised, being given through faith in Jesus Christ, might be given to those who believe . . . The law was put in charge to lead us to Christ that we might be justified by faith" (Galatians 3:21–24). There is no greater blessing in this life than to be saved by faith in Jesus Christ! The Law of the LORD leads us to that ultimate blessing.

What then should be our response to God's Law?

1) *We should believe God's Law.* "O LORD . . . I believe in Your commands" (Psalm 119:66).

2) *We should obey God's Law.* "O LORD . . . I will obey Your Word . . . I will keep Your Law . . . I will hasten and not delay to obey your commandments . . . I will keep your precepts with all my heart . . . I will follow your righteous laws . . . I will always obey your Law for ever and ever . . . I wait for your Salvation, O LORD, and I follow your Commands . . . My heart is set on keeping your decrees to the very end" (Psalm 119:17, 55, 60, 69, 106, 44, 166, 112).

3) *We should be thankful for God's Law.* We should sing of God's Word, our lips overflowing with praise, because all God's commands are righteous (Psalm 119:171, 172). "O LORD . . . I will praise you with an upright heart as I learn your righteous laws . . . At midnight I will rise to give you thanks for your righteous laws . . . Seven times a day I will praise you for your righteous laws (Psalm 119:7, 62, 164)!

4) *We should long for God's Law.* "O LORD . . . My soul is consumed with longing for your laws at all times . . . I open my mouth and pant, longing for your commandments (Psalm 119:20, 131).

5) *We should love God's Law.* "Oh, how I love your Law! I meditate on it all day long . . . I love your Law . . . I love your commandments more than gold, more than pure gold . . . I delight in your commandments because I love them . . . I lift up my hands to your commandments, which I love . . .

I obey your statutes, for I love them greatly (Psalm 119:97, 113, 127, 47, 48, 167).

6) *We should study God's Law.* "Blessed is the man . . . whose delight is in the Law of the LORD, and on His Law he meditates day and night" (Psalm 1:1, 2). We should think about God's Law and meditate on God's Word "all day long" (Psalm 119:97).

7) *We should speak about God's Law.* "O LORD . . . with my lips I recount all the laws that come from your mouth" (Psalm 119:13).

8) *We should remember God's Law.* We should never forget it, neglect it or forsake it. "I remember your ancient laws, O LORD . . . I will not neglect your Word . . . I will not forget your Law . . . I will never forget your precepts . . . I have not forgotten your commandments . . . I have not departed from your laws, for you yourself have taught me" (Psalm 119:52, 16, 61, 93, 176, 102).

9) *We should rejoice in God's Law.* "O LORD . . . I rejoice in following your statutes as one rejoices in great riches . . . I delight in your decrees . . . I delight in your Law . . . I delight in your commands" (Psalm 119:14, 16, 20, 47).

10) *We should respect God's Law.* "O LORD . . . I will always have regard for your decrees . . . My heart trembles at your Word . . . My flesh trembles in fear of you; I stand in awe of your laws" (Psalm 119:117, 161, 120).

Jesus once said, "I know that [my Father's] command leads to eternal life" (John 12:50). Which of God's commands leads to eternal life? "Believe in the Lord Jesus, and you will be saved" (Acts 16:31). "This is [God's] command: to believe in the name of His Son Jesus Christ, and to love one another as He commanded us" (I John 3:23). "The only thing that counts is faith, expressing itself through love" (Galatians 5:6), for "faith without works is dead" (James 2:26).

The teacher's guide for this lesson starts on page 236.

WORSHIP THE LORD YOUR GOD

- Exodus 20:18–26
- Exodus 23:20–33
- Deuteronomy 5, 7

When the Israelites were all assembled at the foot of Mount Sinai, they saw the blazing fire and the smoking mountain; they heard the crashing of the thunder and the blaring of the trumpet; they felt the earth quaking violently and their hearts beating wildly and their bodies trembling uncontrollably with fear. Then the LORD spoke, and the voice of God was so terrifying that the people thought they would die. They pleaded with Moses, "Speak to us yourself and we will listen. But do not have God speak to us or we will die." All the leaders and elders of the tribes of Israel came to Moses begging that no further word be spoken to them directly by God. They said, "The LORD our God has shown us His glory and His majesty, and we have heard His voice from the fire. Today we have seen that a man can live even if God speaks with him. But now, why should we die? This great fire will consume us, and we will die if we hear the voice of the LORD our God any longer. For what mortal man has ever heard the voice of the living God speaking out of fire, as we have, and survived? Go near and listen to all that the LORD our God says. Then tell us whatever the LORD our God tells you. We will listen and obey." God heard what the Israelites were saying to Moses. Do you think God was pleased with them? Was it good what they were saying? The LORD said to Moses, "I have heard what this people said to you. Everything they said was good. Oh, that their hearts would be inclined to fear Me always and that they would keep all My commandments, so that it might go well with them and their children forever." Then the LORD said to Moses, "Go, tell them to return to their tents. But you stay here with Me, so that I may give you all the commands, decrees, and laws that you are to teach them to follow in the land I am giving them to possess" (Deuteronomy 5:22–31). So Moses sent the people back to their tents. He reassured them, saying, "Don't be afraid." God had not come to them to kill them. God had come to test them, so that the fear of God would be with them to keep them from sinning. It was good that they were afraid of God. Oh, that they would always fear God and so keep His Commandments. Thus the people returned to their tents and remained at a distance, while Moses alone approached the thick darkness where God was.

What did God say to Moses? The LORD told Moses in great detail how the people were to keep the Ten Commandments. God began with the most important thing they must do. What was that? *Worship the LORD your God and serve him only.* (Deuteronomy 6:13; Matthew 4:10). The first four commandments were concerned with the worship of God, and now the LORD said to Moses, "Tell the Israelites this: You have seen for yourselves that I have spoken to you from heaven. Do not make any gods to be alongside Me. Do not make for yourselves gods of silver or gods of gold." But there was something they must make for worship. What was it? They must not make idols for themselves, but they could make altars for God. The LORD said, "Make an altar of earth for Me [or an altar of stones] and sacrifice on it your burnt offerings and your peace offerings your sheep and goats and cattle." In this manner—through sacrifice for sin—were God's people to call upon the name of the LORD. With such worship God's name would be glorified. And the LORD promised Moses, "Wherever I cause My name to be honoured, I will come to you and bless you." There was *great blessing* in worshipping God. That was the LORD's promise: "I will come to you and I will bless you."

When Moses was with God in the deep darkness on Mount Sinai, the LORD gave the Israelites another very gracious promise. God said, "See, I am sending an angel ahead of you to guard you along the way and to bring you to the place I have prepared." Who was this angel, whom God would send to guard and guide the Israelites on their way to the Promised Land? It was probably the "angel of the LORD," the eternal Son of God Himself. When Jesus walked upon this earth, the voice of God came from the cloud on another mountain and said, "This is My Son, whom I love. Listen to Him" (Mark 9:7). Now, thousands of years earlier, God's Voice spoke of this "angel" to Moses. The LORD said, "Pay attention to Him and listen to what He says. Do not rebel against Him. He will not forgive your rebellion, since My name is in Him."

The Promised Land lay ahead of the Israelites, but it could not be won without war, because that land was already occupied by several different nations. That land belonged to other peoples—the Amorites, Hittites, Perizzites, Canaanites, Hivites, Girgashites and Jebusites—who were not about to happily hand over their homes and towns, their fields and farms, their lakes and streams, their entire country just because the Israelites said that their God had promised it all to them. No, the Israelites would have many hard battles ahead of them to gain the Promised Land. But before even one sword flashed in that war, the LORD promised, "If you listen carefully to what [My angel] says and do all that I say, I will be an enemy to your enemies and I will oppose those who oppose you. My angel will go ahead of you and bring you into the land . . . and I will wipe them out . . . I will send My terror ahead of you and throw into confusion every nation you encounter. I will make all your enemies turn their backs and run. I will send the hornet ahead of you to drive [your enemies] out of your way. But I will not drive them out in a single year, because the land would become desolate and the wild animals too numerous for you. Little by little I will drive them out before you, until you have increased enough to take possession of the land." God promised his people victory! They knew beforehand that they would win the war because the Word of the LORD never fails.

God also said, "I will establish your borders." He was the one who would make the boundaries of their land. God promised that one day Israel would extend as far south as the Red Sea, as far west as the Mediterranean Sea, as far east as the Arabian Desert, and as far north as the Euphrates River. The Israelites would have to fight for this territory, but God said, "I will hand over to you the people who live in the land and you will drive them out before you." Little by little, battle by battle, over the next few hundred years, God would give the Israelites the good land He had promised to their forefathers. Slowly . . . but surely . . . God's promise would be fulfilled.

The Promised Land was a land flowing with milk and honey. The people must have imagined that beautiful land; in their minds they must have seen the sun sparkling on streams of clear water, bees buzzing in fields of wild flowers, sheep grazing on hills of green pastures. But there was something else in the Promised Land, something evil, something ugly. Do you know what filled the land? Idols! There were idols everywhere. On every high hill, under every spreading tree, the wicked peoples who owned the land had set up their false gods. The LORD warned the Israelites that they must rid the land of these idols. God said, "Do not bow down before their gods or worship them or follow their practices. You must demolish them and break their sacred stones to pieces." Later Moses warned the people, "Break down their altars, smash their sacred stones, cut down their Asherah poles and burn their idols in the fire. For you are a people holy to the LORD your God . . . The images of their gods you are to burn in the fire. Do not covet the silver and gold on them, and do not take it for yourselves, or you will be ensnared by it, for it is detestable to the LORD your God . . . Utterly abhor and detest it, for it is set apart for destruction" (Deuteronomy 7:5, 6,25, 26). God commanded the Israelites, "*worship the LORD your God!*" If they worshipped the LORD, God promised that His *blessing* would be upon them.

God also warned the Israelites to rid the land of the people who worshipped these idols. They were not to make peace treaties with them when they were conquered. God said, "Do not make a covenant with them or with their gods. Do not let them live in your land, or they will cause you to sin against Me, because the worship of their gods will certainly be a snare to you." Later Moses warned the people, "When the LORD your God brings you into the land you are entering to possess and drives out before you many nations (the Hittites, Girgashites, Amorites, Canaanites, Perizzites, Hivites and Jebusites—seven nations larger and stronger than you), and when the LORD your God has delivered them over to you and you have defeated them, then you must destroy them totally. Make no treaty with them and show them no mercy. Do not intermarry with them, for they will turn your sons away from following Me to serve other gods, and the LORD's anger will burn against you and will quickly destroy you" (Deuteronomy 7:1–4).

If the people worshipped the LORD, if they obeyed God's commands, they could expect the *blessing* of life. If the people did not worship the LORD, if they did not obey God's commands, they could expect the cursing of death. The Israelites had a choice. What would they choose? Moses went back to the people and told them all the LORD's words and laws, and they responded with one voice: "Everything the LORD has said we will do."

Moses then wrote down everything the LORD had said, so that God's people would never forget the words and laws of the LORD. Thousands and thousands of years have passed, but we still study this Word of God, written so long ago by the hand of Moses. Although these words have often been ignored, they have never been destroyed. They have been preserved through the generations of God's people, century after century, because they were put in writing. We read them now in the Bible, in the Book of Exodus, which the LORD had Moses write for the Israelites—and for us! In every age God's people must remember: *worship the LORD your God!*

The teacher's guide for this lesson starts on page 238.

THE BLOOD OF
THE COVENANT

- **Exodus 24**
- **Hebrews 9:11–28**

The LORD commanded Moses what to make to worship God. The LORD said, "Make an altar of earth [or stones] for Me and sacrifice on it" (Exodus 20:24). Moses wasted no time in obeying that command. He got up early the next morning and built an altar at the foot of the mountain. Moses also set up twelve stone pillars, representing the twelve tribes of Israel. Then he sent young Israelite men to sacrifice offerings to the LORD. Next Moses took half the blood from these sacrifices and put it in bowls; the other half he sprinkled on the altar. Then Moses took the Book of the Covenant, in which he had written all the LORD's words and laws, and he read it to the people. Again the people responded, "We will do everything the LORD has said. We will obey." This was the third time that the people had promised to keep the LORD's commandments. (See Exodus 19:8; 24:3; 24:7.) Finally, Moses took the blood of the sacrifice and he sprinkled it on the people, saying, "This is the *blood of the covenant* that the LORD has made with you in accordance with all these words."

Do you remember what a covenant is? It is a relationship between two parties, based upon solemn promises. This covenant, this relationship between God and the Israelites, was an agreement based upon promises and confirmed with blood. The Israelites made covenant promises to God in response to God's covenant promises made to them. What did the Israelites promise? They promised to obey all God's commandments. They promised that the LORD would be their God and that they would have no other gods except Him. What did God promise? He promised that He would be their God and they would be His people. The LORD said, "If you obey Me fully and keep My covenant, then out of all nations you will be My treasured possession. Although the whole earth is Mine, you will be for Me a kingdom of priests and a holy nation" (Exodus 19:5, 6). These covenant promises, both by God and by the people, were sealed in blood. The sight of that sprinkled blood proclaimed to the people that God would surely keep His promises to them and that they must surely keep their promises to Him.

God's covenant was put into effect with blood. Why? Why was there the shedding of blood? Why was there the sprinkling of blood? It was necessary because of sin. Holy, holy, holy is the LORD God Almighty, but in the entire human race, there was no one righteous, no, not one. Could anything evil come near to God? Could a Holy God dwell in the midst of a wicked people? Could a wicked people live in the Presence of a Holy God? Surely the fire of God's holiness would consume them and destroy them! Could a Holy God enter into a covenant relationship with sinful creatures? Could His holiness unite Himself to their wickedness? Could a Holy God join Himself by covenant to an evil race? Absolutely not. The people had to be purified from the filth of their sin in order to come near to the Most Holy God. "Without the shedding of blood there is no forgiveness" (Hebrews 9:22). Without the sprinkling of blood, there is no cleansing from sin.

There was only one way for people to be acceptable to God: They must be purified from sin by the blood of the sacrifice.

But could the blood of some animals sprinkled on the people really cleanse them from their sins? Could the blood of some animals really be so vital in confirming the covenant and securing the promises between God and His people? No, the blood of these animals could do nothing. The blood of these animals had no value, no meaning, no power, except that it represented the blood of another sacrifice, a greater sacrifice. The blood sprinkled on the people at Mount Sinai was but a shadow, pointing to the blood of the Son of God, poured out for God's people on the cross to cleanse them from their sins. The blood of an animal, even the blood of another human, could save no one. Only the blood of God Himself could cleanse a person from his sin and save him from death.

But long ago, when Moses stood on Mount Sinai, sprinkling the people with a branch of hyssop dipped in the blood of the sacrificed animals, and proclaiming, "This is the blood of the covenant . . ." the fullness of time had not yet come. That was the first covenant, the Old Covenant, and Jesus, the mediator of the New Covenant, had not yet come. That day when Moses stood on Mount Sinai was thousands of years before the Son of God would be born and then die upon this earth. The blood of Jesus had not yet been formed or spilled. It was thousands of years before Jesus would say, "This is My blood of the covenant, poured out for many for the forgiveness of sins" (Matthew 26:28). Moses and the Israelites only had the shadow of better things to come. They only had the blood of bulls and sheep and goats. Would it be enough? Could the blood of animals cleanse them from their sin? Would God accept them? Could they stand in the presence of the most holy God—and live?

Yes. God commanded Moses and Aaron, Nadab and Abihu (Aaron's oldest sons) and seventy of Israel's elders to come up to the LORD. God said, "You are to worship at a distance." So they went, and the Bible records that they "saw the God of Israel." They did not see any form, for no one can see God and live, but they saw God's glory! They saw under His feet something like a pavement made of sapphire, clear as the sky itself. In the presence of the most holy God, these men probably fell facedown on the ground, as though dead. When they dared to open their eyes, they probably did not raise them above that holy ground, from where they caught a glimpse of the glory of the LORD. "It is a dreadful thing to fall into the hands of the living God" (Hebrews 10:31), but God did not raise His hand against these leaders of the Israelites. They saw God and they survived. Not only did they survive; they rejoiced and feasted in the Presence of the LORD, by God's Grace and by the blood of the covenant.

The teacher's guide for this lesson starts on page 240.

MOSES ON THE MOUNTAIN

- Exodus 24:12–18; 25–31
- Deuteronomy 9:7–11

The leaders and elders of Israel "saw the God of Israel" (Exodus 24:10). They caught a glimpse of God's glory under His feet like a pavement of sapphire, clear as the sky itself, but they worshipped God at a distance. Then the LORD said to Moses, "Come up to Me on the mountain." Only Moses was allowed to approach the LORD, for God said, "The others must not come near" (Exodus 24:2). God said to Moses alone, "Come up to Me on the mountain and stay here, and I will give you the tablets of stone, with the law and commands I have written for their instruction." The Israelites had heard God's own voice speak the Ten Commandments to them, but now God's own finger would write these commandments on tablets of stone for them. (God's finger could easily write upon hard stone, the way your finger can write upon wet sand or soft snow). These two tablets of stone were known as the "Tablets of Testimony." It was a very gracious gift God was giving to His people. This good Law was an expression of His great LOVE for them. What other nation on earth was given such a gift? All nations are governed by laws, some good laws, some bad laws, but they are all laws made by men. The Israelites were given the Law of God to govern them. The law of the LORD was not only good and fair and just. God's law was holy and righteous . . . and perfect. It was written in stone by the hand of Almighty God Himself, that it might be kept from generation to generation, that it might last forever.

So Moses went up the mountain of God to receive the LORD's gift for Israel—the two stone tablets, the "Tablets of Testimony." Joshua went with him, but the rest of Israel's leaders and elders remained at the foot of the mountain, where they could continue to govern the people. When Moses went up on the mountain, the cloud covered it and the glory of the LORD settled on Mount Sinai. For six days the cloud covered the mountain, while Moses continued to climb. On the seventh day, the Sabbath Day, the LORD called to Moses from within the cloud. To the Israelites far below, the glory of the LORD looked like a consuming fire on top of the mountain. But when God called Moses, he went forward by faith. He entered the cloud and continued climbing, drawing nearer and nearer to that terrifying fire.

When Moses entered the cloud of God's presence, he disappeared from sight. Moses was gone for forty days and forty nights. What did Moses do there during that long time? He was with the LORD and that was enough. The presence of the living God filled his days and nights. Moses also fasted during that long time, eating nothing and drinking nothing. He said, "I stayed on the mountain forty days and forty nights; I ate no bread and drank no water" (Deuteronomy 9:9). How could that be possible? Why did he not slowly starve to death or quickly die of thirst? In God we live and move and have our being, and Moses was with God. In God is *life*. It is not food and water that keeps us alive but God. Moses was with the LORD and the LORD spoke to Moses during that time. Man shall not live by bread alone, but by every Word that proceeds from the mouth of God. Moses had no need to eat or drink because, in a miraculous way, God's Word nourished him and sustained him on the mountain.

What did God say to Moses during those forty days and forty nights? We will never know everything that God spoke to Moses, but during that time God gave to Moses some very special plans. This was what God was going to do: God was going to have the Israelites make a tent for Him, a tent where they could meet with God, called the "Tent of Meeting." The Israelites were living in tents in the wilderness and God wanted a tent for Himself, where the people could come to worship Him. God said, "Have them make a sanctuary for Me, and I will dwell among them" (Exodus 25:8). So great was God's LOVE for Israel, that He would dwell in a tent, pitched in the midst of His people. The LORD, Who sits enthroned in the heavens, whose footstool is the earth, who dwells in unapproachable light, who is clothed in majesty, glory and might, who is attended by myriads of angels, whose being is perfect holiness, this great God above all gods was willing to humble Himself and live in a tent and dwell among sinful human beings. Why? Because "God is LOVE." God was drawing near to His people, that they might draw near to Him. That was the reason God was going to have a tent or a tabernacle made for Himself.

One day, thousands of years later, God would humble Himself even further and draw even nearer to mankind. The eternal Son of God, would become a man and dwell in the midst of men; He would become flesh and "tabernacle" among us. Jesus Christ, "who being in the form of God, did not consider equality with God something to be grasped, but made Himself nothing, taking the very form of a servant, being made in human likeness. And being found in appearance as a man, he humbled Himself and became obedient to death—even death on a cross!" (Philippians 2:6–8). That is how far God would go to bring men near to Him. This is LOVE! God loved us so much that He sent His Son as an atoning sacrifice for our sins that we might dwell forever with God and He with us.

But thousands of years before the time of Christ, during those forty days and forty nights on Mount Sinai, the LORD said to Moses, "Tell the Israelites to bring Me an offering . . . Then have them make a sanctuary for Me, and I will dwell among them. Make this tabernacle and all its furnishings exactly like the pattern I will show you" (Exodus 25:1–9). God gave Moses very detailed plans about how His tabernacle was to be made. (These plans are recorded in the Bible—Exodus 25, 26, 27, 28, 29, 30, and 31). Again and again the LORD impressed upon Moses that this tabernacle must be made exactly according to God's plans. The LORD said, "See that you make [everything] according to the pattern shown you on the mountain" (Exodus 25:40). "[The tabernacle] is to be made just as you were shown on the mountain" (Exodus 27:8). God's tabernacle on earth would be patterned after the tabernacle in heaven, "the true tabernacle set up by the LORD, not by man." The Israelites must make God's sanctuary exactly according to God's commands, because it was "a copy and shadow of what was in heaven" (Hebrews 8:2, 5). In the book of Revelation, where we are given glimpses of heaven, we see that indeed there is a tabernacle in heaven. The Apostle John writes what he witnessed there: "I looked, and in heaven the temple, that is, the tabernacle of the Testimony, was opened" (Revelation 15:5). He saw angels coming out of this tabernacle and "the temple was filled with smoke from the glory of God and from his power . . ." (Revelation 15:8). Again and again the apostle John writes about this tabernacle or temple in heaven, after which God's tabernacle on earth was patterned. (See Revelation 7:15, 11:1, 19; 14:15, 17; 16:1, 17; etc.) It was very important that the Israelites make God's tabernacle exactly according to the pattern shown to Moses on the mountain.

When the tabernacle was built according to God's instructions, and the people came to God according to his directions, God promised to meet with them there. That was why the tabernacle would also be called the "Tent of Meeting." God promised Moses, "There I will meet you and speak to you; there also I will meet with the Israelites, and the place will be consecrated by My glory. So I will consecrate the Tent of Meeting . . . Then I will dwell among the Israelites and be their God. They will know that I am the LORD their God, who brought them out of Egypt, so that I might dwell among them. I am the LORD their God" (Exodus 29:42–46).

When God finished speaking to Moses on Mount Sinai, when He had finished telling him exactly how and where and when the Israelites were to worship the LORD, then God gave Moses the two tablets of the testimony, the tablets of stone inscribed by the finger of God.

The teacher's guide for this lesson starts on page 242.

ISRAEL MAKES AN IDOL

- **Exodus 32:1–10**
- **Deuteronomy 9:7–14**
- **Psalm 106:19–23; 115**
- **Romans 1:18–25**
- **I Corinthians 10:6–7**

T he LORD had delivered the Israelites from their cruel bondage in Egypt. The LORD had proceeded them and provided for them and protected them as they travelled through the wilderness. The LORD had saved them from death, not once, but many times. He had brought them to Horeb, to the "Mountain of God," to worship Him . . . just as He had promised Moses. There at the foot of Mount Sinai, the people had heard the voice of God, speaking to them the Ten Commandments. There the LORD proclaimed to them: *You shall have no other gods before me. You shall not make for yourself an idol in the form of anything . . . you shall not bow down to them or worship them.* Those words had been impressed upon them at Mount Sinai by the blazing fire, the billowing smoke, the roaring thunder, the blaring trumpet, the trembling mountain and the terrifying voice of the LORD. Then the people had heard these commandments spoken to them again—and again—by the voice of Moses. Three times the Israelites had heard God's law and three times they had promised, "We will do everything the LORD has said; we will obey." At Mount

Sinai the Israelites had received instructions how they were to worship God—
with an altar, sacrifice and blood—nothing more, nothing less. There, at
the foot of the mountain, they had been sprinkled with the blood of the
covenant. It was also at Mount Sinai that the leaders and elders of Israel had
been given a glimpse of the glory of God. They had seen the God of Israel,
and they had lived to tell about it, being eye-witnesses to testify to all Israel
that the holy God of heaven was in truth with them.

Yet, in spite of all these merciful demonstrations of God's Love for them
and all these powerful declarations of God's Law to them, it was there, at
that same mountain, that the people made for themselves an idol. While
the glory of the Lord still burned on the mountaintop in their sight, they
exchanged the glory of the immortal and invisible God, for the glitter of gold
in the image of an animal. They exchanged the truth of God for a lie, and
worshipped and served the creature, rather than the Creator, who is blessed
forever. Almighty God had revealed Himself to Israel, but now they chose
for themselves another god: a stupid dirty animal! They knew that when
God spoke to them they saw no form; they only heard a voice, but now they
made a god for themselves in the form of a filthy beast, a grass-chewing,
plough-pulling beast of burden, an ordinary bull-calf that went galloping and
bellowing among their herds of cattle. This was the form the Israelites chose
for their god, which they fashioned for themselves out of gold at the foot of
the sacred mountain. They had become fools. What they did was not only
wicked; it was stupid! The Bible says, "At Horeb they made a calf and worshipped an idol cast from metal. They exchanged their Glory for the image
of a bull, which eats grass. They forgot the God who saved them" (Psalm
106:19–21). They were without excuse. They knew God's Love and they
knew God's Law, but they forgot and forsook the God who saved them.

This was not Israel's first rebellion against God (and against Moses) in
the wilderness, but it was their worst one! Here is the tragic account of Israel's fifth rebellion:

Moses entered the cloud and vanished from sight on the mountain. He
was gone for such a long time (forty days and forty nights) that the Israelites
began to wonder what had happened to him. Where was he? Why hadn't
he returned? Was he still alive? Perhaps he had been burned to death by
the fire or choked to death by the smoke on the top of the mountain. Maybe
he had starved to death up there. Or perhaps he had run away. Now, who
would lead them into the Promised Land? In their distress at Moses' disap-

pearance, the Israelites did not turn to God for help. No, once again, they faced trouble by forgetting and forsaking God. They gathered around Aaron and demanded, "Make us a god who will go before us. As for this fellow Moses, who brought us up out of Egypt, we don't know what has happened to him."

Aaron did what the people said. He obeyed the people's demands, rather than God's commands. He gathered their golden earrings and melted the precious metal into an idol, which he then cast in the shape of a calf and carved with a tool. He engraved onto its horned head eyes and ears and a mouth, but it was still a dead god, a lifeless image, which would never see or hear or speak. Aaron also fashioned little hooves onto the golden calf's legs, although it would never walk or move. When the Israelites saw this golden "god," glittering in the sunshine, they bowed down before it and uttered the most stupid, ungrateful, wicked, and blasphemous words that are recorded anywhere in Scripture. They praised their idol, proclaiming, "This is your god, O Israel, who brought you up out of Egypt." Now, when Aaron saw that the people were actually worshipping the golden calf, what did he do? What did he say? Did he repent? Did he suddenly realize what his own two hands had done? Did he rip his robes and tear his hair in anguish? Did he weep and pray for his sin and the sins of the people? Did he rebuke Israel for breaking God's Covenant? Aaron was a powerful preacher. Did he remind the people of God's Law? *You shall have no other gods before me. You shall not make for yourself an idol in the form of anything. You shall not bow down to them or worship them.* Aaron was a beautiful speaker. Did he remind the people of God's LOVE? God Himself had said about Aaron "I know that he can speak well" (Exodus 4:14). God had given him that gift. Would Aaron use that gift to glorify God? Alas, alas! Aaron's speech was used by Satan to lead Israel even deeper into sin. When Aaron saw the people bowing down before the idol he had made, he built an altar, but not to the LORD and not for their sin. Aaron built an altar to Israel's new god—the golden calf! Aaron built an altar in front of the idol and announced, "Tomorrow there will be a festival to the LORD." What was Aaron doing? Did he think that the only God of Israel, the true God, would be pleased because he had built an altar? Did Aaron think that God would be pleased with a celebration in his honour that was shared with an idol? Did Aaron think that somehow they could worship the true and living God through an idol? Was Aaron even thinking of the LORD? Was he thinking at all? Or was he just stupidly being swept away in a whirlwind of sin that was howling from the very pits of hell? By faith, Aaron could have stood firm. He could have anchored his heart and mind and soul to the Word of God and the Law of God, while this storm of sin raged and roared all around him. He could have led the children of Israel to safety, by resisting the devil and fleeing from sin. But Aaron led them even deeper into sin. Aaron himself broke another of God's commandments. By calling this idol "The LORD," Aaron was also breaking the third commandment: *You shall not misuse the name of the Lord your God, for the Lord will not hold anyone guiltless who misuses his name.* Aaron was guilty of terrible sins in the sight of God. This was the man whom God had chosen to be the high priest for his people.

While all this was happening at the foot of the mountain, what was happening on the top of the mountain? God was speaking to Moses and telling him that Aaron and his sons were to serve the LORD as his priests. God said, "Have Aaron your brother brought to you from among the Israelites, along with his sons . . . so they may serve Me as priests." "Aaron is to bear the names [of the sons of Israel] on his shoulders as a memorial before the Lord." "Whenever Aaron enters the Holy Place, he will bear the names of the sons of Israel over his heart . . . as a continuing memorial before the LORD" (Exodus 28:1, 12, 29). While Aaron and the Israelites were forgetting God, God was remembering them. While Aaron was dishonouring God, God was honouring him. While they were breaking their covenant promises to the LORD, God was keeping His covenant promise to them. At the top of the mountain, while God was instructing Moses in true worship of the one true God and giving him the heavenly pattern for earthly worship, at the bottom of the mountain, the Israelites were indulging in idolatry, the false worship of a false god.

The Israelites were eager to do this. The Bible records that the people rose "early" the next morning to engage in their idolatry and revelry. They sacrificed offerings to their golden god. There was a great feast in honour of their idol. There was eating and drinking, singing and dancing, laughing and shouting. People were staggering around drunk; others were falling down before the golden calf (either in ecstatic fervour or lethargic stupor). But their god of gold could not hear one praise sung in his honour; their lifeless idol could not see one knee bend before him; their divine statue could not smell the aroma of sizzling meat burning on the altar. But the one true living God was not like their false dead one. The LORD saw everything they did; He heard every blasphemous word they spoke; and the smoke from their burnt offerings was a stench in His nostrils! The idol the Israelites had made, the golden god they had claimed for themselves, was utterly life-less and powerless, either to rescue them or destroy them, but not so the Lord, the mighty Lord! Many times He had saved them and now He de-clared that He was going to kill them. The Lord said to Moses on top of the mountain, "Go down, because your people, whom you brought up out of Egypt, have become corrupt. They have been quick to turn away from what I commanded them and have made themselves an idol cast in the shape of a calf. They have bowed down to it and sacrificed to it and said, 'This is your god, O Israel, who brought you up out of Egypt.'" Moses must have been appalled. He had no idea what was going on below him, beyond the cloud of God's glory, at the foot of the mountain. Had they really made for themselves an idol? Had they really been bowing down to it and wor-shipping it? Could it be possible that so soon, before they had even left Mount Sinai, they had broken God's commandments? The Lord said to Moses, "I have seen these people. They are a stiff-necked people. Now leave Me alone, so that My anger may burn against them and that I may destroy them!" In an instant, God could annihilate the entire nation. They had bro-ken God's holy law. They had aroused God's righteous anger. The Lord had commanded, "You shall not make for yourself an idol . . . You shall not bow down to them or worship them; for I, the Lord your God, am a jealous God, punishing . . . those who hate me." The Israelites had shown that they hated God. If they loved Him, they would have kept His commandments. Now they faced the wrath of Almighty God, and who now could rescue them from the hands of an angry God? If God was against them, who in all the world could be for them? Who could save them from God's destruction?

The teacher's guide for this lesson starts on page 244.

PRESERVED BY THE POWER OF PRAYER.

- **Exodus 32:11–14**
- **Deuteronomy 9:7–29**
- **Psalm 106:19–23**

The Israelites broke their covenant promises. They were quick to turn away from God and break the Ten Commandments. They chose for themselves another god, by making for themselves an idol—the golden calf. They bowed before it and worshipped it and sacrificed to it. They called it the LORD and claimed this was the god that had delivered them from Egypt. So God's anger burned against Israel. God said to Moses, "Leave Me alone, so that My anger may burn against them and that I may destroy them." God said, "Let Me alone, so that I may destroy them and blot out their name from under heaven" (Deuteronomy 9:14). Who now could rescue them from the wrath of God?

If God destroyed Israel, what would happen to the Promises of God? Long ago the LORD had promised Abraham, "I will make you into a great nation" (Genesis 12:2), but now that nation was about to be destroyed by God Himself. Would God's promise then fail? No, for the LORD was going to make another promise; God was going to make a new nation, through one of Abraham's descendants—Moses. The LORD said to Moses. "Then

I will make you into a great nation." God said, "I will make you into a nation stronger and more numerous than they" (Deuteronomy 9:14).

But Moses sought the favour of the LORD his God, not for himself, but for Israel. Truly Moses was a good shepherd and a great leader of these people, although they had rebelled against him many times too. Moses thought of their safety, rather than his own glory. Moses thought of what was good for them, rather than what was great for him. Although God said he would make Moses into a great nation, Moses pleaded for the nation that was already there—Israel. Moses prayed for Israel. He pleaded with God to spare the life of Israel. This was the case that Moses presented and argued before the LORD, the judge of all the earth:

1) Moses said, "O LORD, why should your anger burn against your people, whom you brought out of Egypt with great power and a mighty hand?" Moses reminded God that these people were God's own people, the ones whom God Himself had saved. Don't destroy them now, not after such a mighty deliverance. These people had been saved by the hand of God, touched by the LOVE of God. Please, don't destroy them!

2) Moses said, "Why should the Egyptians say, 'It was with evil intent that He brought them out, to kill them in the mountains and to wipe them off the face of the earth'?" The whole world was watching. Imagine what God's enemies would say. The name of the LORD would be maligned in all the earth. The God of Israel would be known as an evil God and an impotent God. They would say, 'Because the LORD was not able to take them into the land He had promised them, and because He hated them, He brought them out to put them to death in the desert" (Deuteronomy 9:28). Such lies would be spoken about the LORD in all the earth. People would not believe in God's Might—or God's LOVE. For the sake of God's holy name, Moses pleaded, "Turn from your fierce anger. Relent, and do not bring disaster on Your people."

3) Moses reminded God of the promises He made to Abraham, Isaac and Jacob. The Word of the LORD must endure forever. The promises of God must never fail. Moses said, "Remember your servants Abraham, Isaac and Israel, to whom you swore by your own self: 'I will make your descendants as numerous as the stars in the sky . . .'" And there they were at the foot of the mountain, the children of Israel, as numerous as the stars in the sky.

Would God now destroy them, the fulfilment of His promise? God also promised that He would give them the promised land as an inheritance forever. They were on their way to that promised land! They were half-way there. Would God now kill them on the way? Remember your servants. Remember your promises. For the sake of Your holy Word, turn from your fierce anger! "O LORD," pleaded Moses, "Overlook the stubbornness of this people, their wickedness and their sin" (Deuteronomy 9:27).

God listened to the prayer of Moses. Yes, on that day, thousands of years ago, on the top of Mount Sinai, the Almighty God listened to the words of a mere man, and God did as Moses asked. The LORD relented and did not bring on His people the disaster He had threatened. Israel would be preserved by the power of prayer.

This account in the Bible teaches us many important truths:

1) God is merciful. He pities our weakness, overlooks our faults, forgives our sin and preserves our lives. "The LORD, the LORD, the compassionate and gracious God, slow to anger, abounding in LOVE and faithfulness, maintaining LOVE to thousands, and forgiving wickedness, rebellion and sin . . ." (Exodus 34: 6). "The LORD is compassionate and gracious, slow to anger, abounding in LOVE. He will not always accuse, nor will He harbour His anger forever. He does not treat us as our sins deserve or repay us according to our iniquities" (Psalm 103:8–10). "If we confess our sins, He is faithful and just and will forgive us our sins and purify us from all unrighteousness" (I John 1:9).

2) God listens to our prayers, and He answers them. "The prayer of a righteous man [or woman or child] is powerful and effective" (James 5:16). Our prayers can accomplish so much good. Moses was only human, as we are, but this one man saved an entire nation by his prayer. God commands us to be "faithful in prayer" and to "devote ourselves to prayer" (Romans 12:12 & Colossians 4:2). God urges that "prayers . . . be made for everyone" (I Timothy 2:1). We must "pray in the Spirit on all occasions with all kinds of prayers and requests" (Ephesians 6:18). God commands His people "Pray continually. Pray without ceasing" (I Thessalonians 5:17). "Dear friends, build yourselves up in your most holy faith and *pray* in the Holy Spirit. Keep yourselves in God's LOVE as you wait for the mercy of our Lord Jesus Christ to bring you to eternal life" (Jude 20).

3) Moses was a faithful shepherd, whose prayer preserved the people, but we have someone greater than Moses praying for us. If God answered the prayers of Moses, will He not answer the prayers of His own beloved Son? Jesus Christ, the great shepherd of the sheep, ever lives to make intercession for us. We can be certain and have comfort that the prayers of the Son of God are answered. "During the days of Jesus life on earth, He offered up prayers and petitions with loud cries and tears" (Hebrews 5:7), not only for Himself, but for His people. Jesus prayed for the protection of His disciples: "Holy Father, protect them by the power of your name . . . My prayer is not that you take them out of the world, but that you protect them from the evil one" (John 17:11, 15). At that time Jesus prayed for us too, saying, "My prayer is not for them alone. I pray also for those who will believe in Me through their message . . ." (John 17:20). It is amazing to think that Jesus, on the eve of His crucifixion, was praying for you and for me. Now Christ is alive forevermore, praying for us in heaven. How secure is our salvation! "Christ Jesus, who died—more than that, who was raised to life—is at the right hand of God and is also interceding for us" (Romans 8:34). Nothing can separate us from the LOVE of God that is in Christ Jesus our Lord. "He is able to save completely those who come to God through Him, because He always lives to intercede for them" (Hebrews 7:25).

The teacher's guide for this lesson starts on page 246.

SEVEN SORROWS FROM ISRAEL'S SIN

- Exodus 32:15–35; 33:1–6
- Deuteronomy 9:17–21 & 25–29
- Jude 5

T he Israelites broke God's covenant by making for themselves an idol and worshipping it. God's anger burned against Israel, enough to destroy the entire nation, but Moses interceded for them. The LORD listened to Moses' prayer and did not bring on Israel the disaster He had threatened. "The LORD, the LORD, the compassionate God, slow to anger, abounding in LOVE and faithfulness, maintaining LOVE to thousands, and forgiving wickedness, rebellion and sin. *Yet He does not leave the guilty unpunished . . .*" (Exodus 34:6, 7). Although God did not destroy Israel, there were direct consequences and terrible punishments for their sin of idolatry:

1. The Stone Tablets were Smashed

Moses left the glory of God at the top of the mountain and began his journey downward, descending to the evil of men at the base of the mountain. In his hands Moses carried a very great treasure, two stones worth more than the most precious stones or gems or jewels in all the world. Moses cradled in his arms two stones, more valuable than the largest diamond or brightest emerald on earth. Moses carried the two tablets of testimony—the Ten Commandments—which were God's gift to Israel. Those stone tablets were inscribed with the Law of the LORD. They were the work of God. The writing was the writing of God, engraved upon the stones. It was a very great gift, a national treasure, which was going to be destroyed before their very eyes.

As Moses climbed down the mountainside, along with Joshua, they heard a noise in the distance. There was some sort of commotion in Israel's camp. Joshua, the captain of Israel's army, was alarmed. When he heard the noise of people shouting, he feared that war had broken out while he was away. Joshua said to Moses, "There is the sound of war in the camp." But Moses knew what had happened. He knew that something far worse than a war had occurred. Moses said to Joshua, "It is not the sound of victory; it is not the sound of defeat. It is the sound of singing that I hear." Singing? Yes, the Israelites were raising their voices in song, singing praises to their god of gold, like a mighty choir conducted from the pits of hell. To the ears of Moses, that singing was a sound more hideous than the shrieking of demons or the wailing of devils. God's own people were worshipping an idol!

As they drew nearer, Moses and Joshua soon saw the stupid wicked object of Israel's praise. There in the midst of the camp, encircled by their dancing, stood the idol. When Moses saw their disgusting god of gold and their degrading dance of praise, he burned with anger. Just as the LORD's anger burned against Israel, so Moses' anger burned against them too. He threw the stone tablets out of his hands and broke them to pieces at the foot of the mountain. The tablets that were the work of God, the writing that was the writing of God—smashed! God's gift to them and to their children for a thousand generations lay in shattered pieces at the foot of the mountain. They had broken God's Law, and now God's Law lay broken before them at the foot of the mountain. What greater disaster could befall a nation than to lose the Law of the LORD? It was a terrible punishment upon Israel.

2. Their Gold was Gone

The Israelites had given their gold, their precious gold, to make this idol. It was the gold they had taken out of Egypt, the gold God had given them on the night of the exodus. Now they were going to lose that reward from the LORD. They would never see their gold or their "god" again. Moses showed them how vain it was to worship an idol. He showed them how their idol was helpless and useless and worthless. Moses took the "god" they had made and burned it in the fire. Then he ground it into powder, scattered it on the water, and made the Israelites drink it. They were made to devour their god and their gold. They were made to drink the dust of their defilement. Perhaps such bitter medicine would cure them of idolatry. Their god of gold was gone, and there would be no glittering remains to comfort them. No nuggets could be found in the stream; no gold dust could be found on the ground. It was gone. All that remained was a bitter taste in their mouths. Perhaps by losing their gold, they would learn what was of true value. The Laws of the LORD, "they are more precious than gold, than much pure gold" (Psalm 19:10).

3. Their High Priest was Shamed

Next Moses confronted Aaron with his sin. Aaron had been left in charge of the people, but they were running around wildly and wickedly. Aaron had let the people get out of control, and worse; he was the one who had led them in this sin of idolatry. Moses questioned Aaron. What had happened? How had he led them into such a great sin? Moses held Aaron responsible for the corruption of the nation. Aaron pleaded with Moses not to be angry; Aaron blamed the people; Aaron lied about what happened, but Aaron did not confess his sins. Aaron said to Moses, "Do not be angry, my lord. You know how prone these people are to evil. [It was their fault.] They said to me, 'Make us a god . . .' Then they gave me the gold, and I threw it into the fire, but out came this calf! [I didn't make this idol. The golden calf just appeared out of the flames, all by itself.]" Aaron lied. His lips did not confess the sin that his own hands had made this idol, but Moses was not fooled. Aaron's sins were not forgotten. What he did and what he said were recorded in Scripture, to the disgrace of Aaron throughout the generations. The Bible records that it was Aaron's own hands that took the gold and "made it into an idol, cast in the shape of a calf, fashioning it with a tool" (Exodus 32:3). Four thousand years later, we are still appalled and ashamed as we read about the words and deeds of the first high priest, Aaron.

4. Their Leaders were Killed

Israel's camp was in total chaos. The people were completely out of control. Law and order had to be restored to Israel—God's good law, God's holy order. Those who had led in the rebellion against the LORD must be put to death, but who would do it? Who would be willing to kill their own brothers and friends and neighbours? The Law of the LORD demanded that any such rebel "be put to death, because he preached rebellion against the LORD your God . . . He has tried to turn you from the way the LORD your God commanded you to follow. You must purge the evil from among you. If your very own brother, or your son or daughter, or the wife you love, or your closest friend secretly entices you, saying, 'Let us go and worship other gods' . . . do not yield to him or listen to him. Show him no pity. Do not spare him or shield him. You must certainly put him to death. Your hand must be the first in putting him to death . . . because he tried to turn you away from the LORD your God" (Deuteronomy 13:1–11). Moses knew that the leaders in this rebellion against God must be executed. So he stood at the entrance to the camp and said, "Whoever is for the LORD, come to me." All the Levites rallied to Moses to fight on God's side. Yes, the men of Moses' tribe, the tribe of Levi, were willing to fight for the LORD. Then Moses said to them, "This is what the LORD, the God of Israel, says: "Each man strap a sword to his side. Go back and forth through the camp, killing . . ." They were to kill everyone—friends, neighbours, relatives—who had led the people into idolatry. The Levites did as Moses commanded, and at the end of the day about three thousand of the people lay dead. What a terrible punishment that was for Israel's sin. Israelite blood shed by Israelite hands! What a terrible price they had to pay for their idolatry! Three thousand people lay dead in the camp, but the men of the tribe of Levi, who loved the LORD more than their own families, they were blessed for their loyalty to God. Moses said to the Levites, "You have been set apart to the LORD today, for you were against your own sons and brothers, and He has blessed you this day."

5. Their Names were Blotted Out of God's Book

The next day Moses said to the people, "You have committed a great sin. But now I will go up to the LORD. Perhaps I can make atonement for your sin." So Moses went back to the LORD. Once again he fell prostrate before the LORD for forty days and forty nights, eating no bread and drinking no water, because of all the sin Israel had committed, doing what was evil in the LORD's sight and so provoking Him to anger. Moses feared the anger and wrath of the LORD, for He was angry enough to destroy Israel, but again the LORD listened to Moses' prayer. Moses confessed the people's sin. He prayed, "Oh, what a great sin these people have committed! They have made for themselves gods of gold. But now, please, forgive their sin—but if not, then blot me out of the book You have written." The LORD answered Moses, "Whoever has sinned against Me I will blot out of my book." God would not destroy the entire nation of Israel, but not a single individual would be overlooked. No one could hide in the crowd of millions. No one's sin was hidden. God knew the heart of each and every person, whether it contained belief or unbelief, devotion or rebellion. God knew every knee that bowed before the idol and every knee that bowed before the LORD alone. He knew which voices sang praises to Him and which voices honoured other gods. There was nothing hidden from the LORD. He knew which names were recorded in the Book of Life, and which names would be blotted out forever. Though many unbelieving rebels were spared from the sword that executed punishment, they would not be spared from eternal judgement. God's Word declared it: "Whoever has sinned against Me, I will blot out of my book."

6. They Were Struck with A Plague

God said to Moses, "When the time comes for Me to punish, I will punish them for their sin." And the LORD struck the people with a plague, because of what they did, worshipping the calf that Aaron made. In Egypt, the plague of death passed over them, but this time, it was Israel that God struck with a plague.

7. God Said, "I Will Not Go With You"

There was one final punishment worse than all the rest. God said to Moses, "Leave this place . . . and go up to the land I promised . . . I will send an angel before you . . . Go up to the land flowing with milk and honey. But *I will not go with you*, because you are a stiff-necked people and I might destroy you on the way." God was no longer going to go with them. God was no longer going to dwell with them. When the people heard these distressing words, they began to mourn and grieve. They did not want to be abandoned by God. To be forsaken by God, to be separated from God, was worse than anything—even death. It seems that, after all, Israel did want the LORD to be their God.

The teacher's guide for this lesson starts on page 248.

ALL GOD'S GOODNESS

- Exodus 33, 34
- I Corinthians 13:12
- II Corinthians 3:7–18

The LORD said to Moses, "Go up to the land I promised . . . but I will not go with you." When the people heard these distressing words, they began to mourn. At last they saw what their sin had done. Their sin had made a separation between them and their God. The LORD would no longer be with them.

Moses knew that he must speak to God again. He must have a meeting with the LORD, beseeching Him to go with the Israelites to the promised land. Moses had pitched a tent outside the camp some distance away, where he used to go to meet with God, calling it the "tent of meeting." Whenever Moses walked to this tent, all the people rose in respect and stood at the entrances to their tents, watching Moses until he entered it. The pillar of cloud would descend and stay at the entrance to the tent, while the LORD spoke with Moses. Whenever the people saw the pillar of cloud standing at the entrance to the tent, they all stood and worshipped, each at the entrance of his own tent. But what would happen this time? Would God even meet with Moses anymore? Had God already abandoned them? It was with hope restored and joy renewed, that the people saw the pillar of cloud descending as Moses entered the tent. The people knew then that God by His grace had condescended to meet with Moses. All the people stood by their own tents worshipping the LORD, while Moses spoke with God. It was a very important meeting. The very life of Israel depended upon the outcome of that meeting! No doubt, the people's worship included weeping and mourning for their sins, thanking and praising God for His LOVE and grace, praying and pleading with God that He would continue to be with them.

In that "Tent of Meeting," the LORD spoke with Moses directly, just as any one of us would speak face to face with a friend, and Moses *was* God's friend. The LORD called Moses by name, for Moses had found favour with the LORD. God knew Moses and God was pleased with Moses. Nor was Moses afraid or ashamed to open his heart and pour out his grief to the One who loved him. The amazing truth was this: The LORD God Almighty and this mere man, communicated with each other in a close and deep relationship. Moses was God's friend, and God was Moses' Friend.

On this day, when Moses knelt down in that "Tent of Meeting," his heart was heavy. Moses had some very serious concerns to discuss with the LORD. God wanted Moses to lead these people, but God was not going to go with them anymore. Moses' heart was filled with grief. He did not want to be separated from God. Moses wanted their relationship to continue. He wanted to know God more clearly; he wanted to walk with God more closely. Moses said, "If you are pleased with me, teach me your Way so I may know you and continue to find favour with you." Moses did not want to be abandoned by God. He did not want to lead God's people by himself, without God's presence. Moses was doing this work of leading these people, because these were God's people. "Remember that this nation is Your people," said Moses. All Moses wanted was to be near God, because he loved God.

The LORD answered Moses' prayer graciously and speedily. God said, "My presence will go with you, and I will give you rest." Moses would not have to bear this burden alone. God would be with him and Moses could rest in the LORD and count on His LOVE.

But Moses had more to say. If God was not with them, there was no reason to go to the promised land and there was no reason to be a great nation. There was no reason to be a nation at all. The only thing that made Israel a special people was the fact that God was with them. There was no point in being a people or possessing the land without God. The LORD alone was their reason for existence. Moses said, "If Your presence does not go with us, do not send us up from here." It would be better to die in the desert, than to go forth without God. What joy could they have in the land, if they had not the joy of the LORD? They had been set free to worship God. The reason for their journey was not so much to possess the land, but to possess God. That was God's greatest Promise to them: *I will be their God and they will be my people.* Moses asked, "How will anyone know that you are pleased with me and with your people, unless You go with us? What else will distinguish me and your people from all the other people on the face of the earth?"

Again God assured Moses of His unfailing LOVE. The LORD said to Moses, "I will do the very thing you have asked, because I am pleased with you and I know you by name." God would be with Israel and go with Israel, because God was pleased with Moses.

How grateful Moses must have been to hear this gracious answer. Now Moses wanted to know God even better. He wanted to come even closer to this LORD of LOVE. So Moses said to God, "Show me Your glory." Moses asked to see what no man on earth had ever seen. He asked to behold on earth, what is reserved for us in heaven—the glory of the LORD! What we see now is just a poor reflection of God's glory, as if we were looking at a dim reflection in a dark mirror. On earth no man has seen what Moses asked to see, for here we live by faith, not by sight, with the hope that one day "we shall see Him as He is" (I John 3:3). That day awaits us in heaven. Then "we shall see face to face;" then we shall know fully (I Corinthians 13:12). But Moses said, "Now, show me your glory." God answered, "I will show you My goodness." The LORD said, "I will cause all My goodness to pass in front of you, and I will proclaim My name, the LORD, in your presence. I will have mercy on whom I will have mercy, and I will have compassion on whom I will have compassion. But you cannot see My face, for no one may see Me and live." God would reveal to Moses what he could bear, which was the glory of His goodness, rather than the glory of His greatness. God would reveal Himself in a way that was safe for Moses. The LORD said, "There is a place near Me, where you may stand on a rock. When My glory passes by, I will put you in a cleft in the rock and cover you with My hand, until I have passed by. Then I will remove My hand and you will see My back; but My face must not be seen."

Then the LORD said to Moses, "Chisel out two stone tablets like the first ones, and I will write on them the words that were on the first tablets, which you broke. Be ready in the morning, and then come up on Mount Sinai. Present yourself to Me there, on top of the mountain. No one is to come with you or be seen anywhere on the mountain; not even the flocks and herds may graze in front of the mountain." So Moses did as the LORD commanded. Early the next morning, Moses could be seen climbing up the mountainside by himself, carrying two new, blank, stone tablets in his hands.

Then the LORD came down in the cloud and stood there with him and proclaimed His name, the LORD. While Moses was sheltered in the cleft in the rock and covered by the Hand of God, the LORD passed in front of Moses, proclaiming: "The LORD, the LORD, the compassionate and gracious God, slow to anger, abounding in LOVE and faithfulness, maintaining LOVE to thousands, and forgiving wickedness, rebellion and sin. Yet He does not leave the guilty unpunished; He punishes the children and their children for the sin of the fathers to the third and fourth generation."

Moses bowed down to the ground at once and worshipped. He had not seen the glory of God's majesty, but he had heard the glory of God's mercy, and Moses was overwhelmed by all God's goodness, which had passed before him. With his face on the ground, but emboldened by this revelation of God's goodness, Moses again interceded for the people of Israel, who were surely guilty and who justly deserved to be punished. Moses prayed, "O LORD, if I have found favour in your eyes, then let the LORD go with us. Although this is a stiff-necked people, forgive our wickedness and our sin, and take us as your inheritance." The LORD answered Moses' prayer. The LORD, the compassionate and gracious God, extended His LOVE once again to the countless thousands of Israel and forgave their sin, their wickedness and their rebellion.

God also renewed His covenant with Israel. The LORD said, "I am making a covenant with you. Before all your people I will do wonders never before done in any nation in all the world. The people you live among will see how awesome is the work that I, the LORD, will do for you . . ." God promised that He would be with Israel. The LORD Himself would work for them and fight for them in the promised land. God would perform great wonders and awesome miracles before the eyes of Israel and all the world. That was what God promised to do for His people that day on Mount Sinai. And what must His people do? They must be faithful to God. They must obey the commands of God. The LORD said, "Obey what I command you today . . . Do not worship any other god, for the LORD, whose name is jealous, is a jealous God." Again the LORD warned the Israelites about making treaties with the people in the land. They must not allow these wicked people or false gods to remain in the land. They must drive out these nations and destroy their gods. They must smash their sacred idols and altars, lest they ensnare Israel in idolatry again. They must not intermarry with these people, lest they ensnare Israel in idolatry again. How quickly and easily Israel had fallen into this sin at the first opportunity. They must be on their guard against idolatry. Israel had the LORD; they must worship Him alone. Israel had holy festivals and sacred ceremonies commanded by God; they must celebrate them alone. Israel had sacrifices that were to be made to God alone. Israel must worship the LORD their God and serve Him only. The LORD commanded Moses: "Write down these words, for in accordance with these words I have made a covenant with you and with Israel."

Again Moses was on top of the mountain for forty days and forty nights, neither eating nor drinking, but communing with the LORD. Moses wrote on the new tablets the words of the covenant—the Ten Commandments. Again Moses descended from the mountain-top, carrying the two tablets of testimony in his hands. What would be waiting for him this time at the foot of the mountain? He had been away for a long time, for forty days and nights, like the last time. Had Israel remained faithful during his absence?

When Aaron and all the Israelites saw Moses again, they were afraid to come near him. Why? Moses himself did not know the reason. He did not realize that his face was radiant, shining with the glory of the LORD, because he had been speaking with God. Even that small pale reflection of God's glory in Moses' face terrified the people. Just as you cannot look at the brightness of the sun, "the Israelites could not look steadily at the face of Moses because of its glory" (II Corinthians 3:8). So Moses called to them. Aaron and the elders came back to him, and Moses spoke to them. Later, all the Israelites came near Moses and he gave them all the commands the LORD had given him on Mount Sinai.

When Moses finished speaking to them, he "put a veil over his face to keep the Israelites from gazing at it while the radiance was fading away" (II Corinthians 3:12). Moses did not want the people to stare at the glory of God fading from his face. But whenever Moses entered the LORD's presence to speak with Him, he removed the veil, so that when he came out and told the Israelites what had been commanded, they saw that his face was radiant again. Thus Israel was given yet another assurance that God was with them. They saw the glory of the LORD reflected in the face of this man, and it was a sign for them to listen to the words of Moses, because it was the Word of God. Moses shining face was a constant testimony to them that the Holy God of heaven really was with them!

All God's goodness. God surely was good to Israel, even after they committed such a terrible sin against the LORD, the sin of worshipping an idol. Behold all God's goodness to Israel:

1. The LORD met with Moses at the tent of meeting. The pillar of cloud descended and God promised: "My presence will go with you, and I will give you rest."

2. God met with Moses on the top of Mount Sinai. The LORD came down in the cloud and stood there with him.

3. The LORD passed in front of Moses, proclaiming His Name: The LORD, the LORD!

4. God revealed to Moses who He was, that He was a just God, punishing the guilty, but He was also a compassionate and gracious God, slow to anger, abounding in LOVE and faithfulness, maintaining LOVE to thousands, and forgiving wickedness, rebellion and sin. It is one of the clearest declarations of the LOVE and mercy and compassion of God found anywhere in the Bible. What an encouragement to the Israel of God!

5. God graciously renewed His covenant with Israel.

6. God gave the Israelites two new stone tablets, to replace the ones that were broken. Once again they had the Law of God. The Ten Commandments were their great national treasure.

7. God gave the Israelites a sign of His presence. They saw the glory of God reflected in the radiant face of Moses!

The teacher's guide for this lesson starts on page 250.

THE SURPASSING GLORY

A Superior Covenant

At Mount Sinai God made a covenant with the nation of Israel. All the people heard the voice of the LORD speak the words of the covenant—the Ten Commandments. They also heard the voice of Moses tell them all the LORD's words and laws. Together, with one voice, the people responded, "Everything the LORD has said we will do." Moses also took the Book of the Covenant and read to the people all God's Law. Again the people responded, "We will do everything the LORD has said. We will obey." God also gave the Israelites the two tablets of the testimony, the Ten Commandments, inscribed by the finger of God. The words of the covenant were engraved in stone for them. The writing was the writing of God. The words were the Word of God. The laws were the Law of God. But in spite of all this, how quickly the Israelites turned away from God. How quickly they disobeyed God's Law. How quickly they broke God's Covenant.

What does this show us? First of all, it shows us how deceitful and desperately wicked the human heart is. Although these people promised to keep God's Law, they did not do it. Within a few days of their covenant promise, their own hearts led them into the worst of sins, in which they broke the first and foremost of God's commandments. Although God's own voice spoke this Law to them, although God's own hand wrote this Law for them, they broke it. This also shows us something about God's Law. Although the Law of God is holy and righteous and perfect, it is unable to change a single heart or save a single soul. God's Law is not able to sanctify; nor is it able to justify. God's Law can only condemn us. God's Law can only give us the knowledge of sin; it cannot give us the rescue from sin. God's Law tells us what is wrong, but it cannot make us right. The Law of God makes us aware of our desperate need. We need someone to save us from our sin and from the curse of the law, which condemns us. We need a Saviour. God's Law then is a teacher, that points us to Christ.

God made a covenant with Israel at Mount Sinai, but "God had planned something better for us" (Hebrews 11:40). From the beginning it was God's plan to institute another covenant, a better covenant. If there had been nothing wrong with the first covenant, there would have been no need for another one, but we know that there *was* something wrong and there *was* a desperate need! Even in the Old Testament or Covenant, God spoke of the New Testament or Covenant. (See Jeremiah 31:31–34.) "The time is coming, declares the LORD, when I will make a New Covenant with the house of Israel . . . It will not be like the covenant I made with their forefathers . . . because they did not remain faithful to My covenant, and I turned away from them, declares the LORD. This is the covenant I will make with the house of Israel after that time, declares the LORD: I will put my laws in their minds and write them on their hearts. I will be their God and they will be my people . . . They will all know Me, from the least of them to the greatest. For I will forgive their wickedness and will remember their sins no more" (Hebrews 8:8–12). That was God's promise. One day he would make another covenant with Israel, in which He wrote His Law, not on slabs of stone, but in the hearts and minds of His people by the Holy Spirit of the living God. The ministry of the Old Covenant brought death through the Law, but the ministry of the New Covenant brought life through the Spirit.

We know that the Old Covenant came with glory. How do we know this? How do we know that the giving of God's Law came with glory? Moses face shone with the radiance of the glory of God. "Now if the ministry that brought death, which was engraved in letters on stone, came with glory, so that the Israelites could not look steadily at the face of Moses because of its glory, fading though it was, will not the ministry of the Spirit be even more glorious? If the ministry that condemns men is glorious, how much more glorious is the ministry that brings righteousness! For what was glorious [then] has no glory now in comparison with the surpassing glory. If what was fading away came with glory, how much greater is the glory of that which endures" (II Corinthians 3:7–11).

A Superior High Priest

A better priest than Aaron (or his sons) was needed. There is no doubt in our minds that Aaron, the first high priest, was a sinner, a man who was as weak and wicked as we are (maybe worse). We know that Aaron broke God's Law in a most grievous way, making an idol, worshipping it and leading Israel astray. What greater sin could he have committed? Even we have not sinned like that. Nonetheless, on Mount Sinai God appointed Aaron as high priest. God also appointed his sons and grandsons to be high priests after him, throughout the generations. The Law appointed as high priests men who were weak, but from the beginning God had someone better planned. Even in the Old Testament/Covenant God swore an oath to appoint another High Priest in another order of priests. "The LORD has sworn and will not change his mind: You are a priest forever, in the order of Melchizedek" (Psalm 110:4). This priest would not be a son of Aaron from the tribe of Levi. No, this priest would be from the tribe of Judah, and He would be the Son of God Himself! When God spoke in the Old Testament, "You are a priest forever . . ." He was speaking of Jesus Christ.

What makes Jesus, the Son of God, a superior high priest?

1) *Jesus is sinless.* Because Jesus was flesh and blood like us, sharing in our humanity, and because He himself suffered when He was tempted, Jesus is able to help us in our time of need. (See Hebrews 2:14–18.) "We do not have a High Priest who is unable to sympathize with our weakness, but we have one who has been tempted in every way, just as we are—yet was *without sin*" (Hebrews 4:15). Unlike Aaron and his descendants, Jesus did not sin. "Such a high priest meets our need—one who is holy, blameless, pure, set apart from sinners, exalted above the heavens. Unlike the other high priests, He does not need to offer sacrifices day after day, first for his own sins, and then for the sins of the people. He sacrificed for their sins once for all when He offered Himself. For the Law appoints as high priests men who

are weak; but the oath, which came after the Law, appointed the Son, Who has been made *perfect* forever" (Hebrews 7:26–28).

2)*Jesus lives forever.* The ministry of Aaron came to an end when he died. Death also prevented his sons from continuing in their offices as high priests. "But because Jesus lives forever, He has a *permanent* priesthood. Therefore He is able to save completely those who come to God through Him, because He *always lives* to intercede for them" (Hebrews 7:23–25). Jesus became a priest, "not on the basis of a regulation as to his ancestry, but on the basis of the power of an indestructible life" (Hebrews 7:16).

3) *Jesus enters heaven.* Aaron and his sons served at a sanctuary that was only a copy and shadow of what is in heaven. Jesus, however, serves in heaven. He is the "high priest, who sat down at the right hand of the throne of the Majesty in heaven, and who serves in the sanctuary, the true taber- nacle set up by the LORD, not by man . . . He went through the greater and more perfect tabernacle that is not man-made, that is to say, not part of this creation . . . He entered the Most Holy Place once for all by His own blood, having obtained eternal redemption . . . For Christ did not enter a man- made sanctuary that was only a copy of the true one; He entered heaven it- self, now to appear for us in God's presence" (Hebrews 8:1, 2, 12, 24).

The Bible says, that "since we have a Great High Priest who has gone through the heavens, Jesus the Son of God, let us hold firmly to the faith we profess. Let us then approach the throne of grace with confidence, so that we may receive mercy and find grace to help us in our time of need" (Hebrews 4:14, 16). "Since we have confidence to enter the Most Holy Place by the blood of Jesus . . . and since we have a Great High Priest over the house of God, let us draw near to God with a sincere heart in full as- surance of faith, having our hearts sprinkled to cleanse us from a guilty con- science . . . Let us hold unswervingly to the hope we profess, for He who promised is faithful" (Hebrews 10:19–23).

A Superior Prophet

Moses was the mediator of the Old Covenant. Moses was the one who mediated between God and the people. When they broke God's covenant and the LORD said He would destroy them, Moses "stood in the breach be- fore God, to keep His wrath from destroying them" (Psalm 106:23). Moses, by his prayers, turned God's wrath away from Israel. Moses was a great prophet, who proclaimed to the people all God's words and laws. Moses' face even reflected the glory of God, but there was one coming who would not just reflect God's glory; He would be "the radiance of God's glory and the exact representation of His being" (Hebrews 1:3). He would be "the image of the invisible God . . . for God was pleased to have all His fullness dwell in Him" (Colossians 1:15, 19). Yes, there would be a Man far greater than Moses. Moses knew this and said himself that God would raise up for them another Prophet. Moses said, "The LORD your God will raise up for you a Prophet like me from among your own brothers. You must listen to Him" because the LORD had said to Moses, "I will put My Words in his mouth, and He will tell them everything I command them" (Deuteronomy 18:18). Jesus was that prophet, the one who was greater than Moses. "Moses was faithful as a servant in all God's house, testifying to what would be said in the future, but Christ is faithful as a Son over God's house" (Hebrews 3:5, 6). Moses was the mediator of the Old Covenant, but Jesus is the mediator of a better covenant, a covenant of superior and surpassing glory, the New Covenant. Moses spoke the Word of God, but Jesus *was* the Word of God. "In the beginning was the Word, and the Word was with God, and the Word *was* God. He was with God in the beginning . . . The Word became flesh and made His dwelling among us. We have seen His Glory, the glory of the One and Only, who came from the Father, full of grace and truth . . . From the fullness of His grace we have all received blessing upon blessing. For the law was given through Moses; grace and truth came through Jesus Christ. No one has ever seen God, but God the One and Only , who is at the Father's side, has made Him known" (John 1:1, 2,14, 16–18). Moses, as a prophet of the LORD, revealed God to the people, but Jesus revealed God to man completely and perfectly. "In the past God spoke to our forefathers through the prophets at many times and in various ways, but in these last days He has spoken to us by His Son . . . the Son is the radiance of God's glory and the exact representation of His being . . ." (Hebrews 1:1–3) or "the express image of His person" (KJV). Jesus Himself said, "Anyone who has seen Me has seen the Father . . . (John 14:9).

A Superior sacrifice

"Every high priest is appointed to offer both gifts and sacrifices" but those gifts and sacrifices "were not able to clear the conscience of the worshipper" (Hebrews 8:3 & 9:9). It is impossible for the blood of bulls and goats to take away sin. Another sacrifice, a perfect sacrifice was necessary. The Law could never, "by the same sacrifices repeated endlessly year after year, make perfect those who drew near to worship. If it could, would they not have stopped being offered? For the worshippers would have been cleansed once for all, and would no longer have felt guilty for their sins. But those sacrifices were an annual reminder of sins, because it was impossible for the blood of bulls and goats to take away sins" (Hebrews 10:1–4). Day after day the priests of the Old Covenant would stand and perform their religious duties; again and again they would offer the same sacrifices, which could never take away sins. Another sacrifice was needed! Jesus Christ was the High Priest who offered Himself as the sacrifice for sin. "We have been made holy through the sacrifice of the body of Jesus Christ once for all . . . By one sacrifice He has made perfect forever those who are being made holy" (Hebrews 10:10, 14). It is the blood of Christ that cleanses us from all our sins. For this reason Christ came into the world; "He appeared once for all . . . to do away with sin by the sacrifice of Himself" (Hebrews 9:26).

The surpassing glory of Jesus Christ has been revealed to us. We have heard the good news; we have heard the gospel of salvation through faith in the Son of God. We have heard these blessed words: "For God so loved the world, that He gave His Only Begotten Son, that whoever believes in Him shall not perish, but have eternal life" (John 3:16). How then shall we escape if we neglect so great a salvation? If they did not escape when they refused him who warned them on earth, how much less will we, if we turn away from Him who warns us from heaven?" (Hebrews 12:25). "Anyone who rejected the Law of Moses died without mercy on the testimony of two or three witnesses. How much more severely do you think a man deserves to be punished who has trampled the Son of God underfoot, who has treated as an unholy thing the blood of the covenant that sanctified him, and who has insulted the Spirit of Grace? The LORD will judge His people! It is a dreadful thing to fall into the hands of the Living God" (Hebrews 10:28–31). We must obey God's New Covenant. We must believe in Christ! It is our only hope of salvation! *Believe in the Lord Jesus Christ and you will be saved.*

The teacher's guide for this lesson starts on page 154.

THE TABERNACLE

- Exodus 25–40
- Numbers 9:15–23
- Psalm 27:4–6
- Hebrews 9:1–10

When Moses descended Mount Sinai, he brought with him the Law of God for the people. He carried in his hands the Testimony, that is, the two stone tablets with the Words of the Covenant, the Ten Commandments, written upon them. But Moses also brought the Israelites something else from the LORD. Do you remember what it was? A pattern. He brought a pattern from heaven for the people to make something on earth—God's tabernacle. Yes, God really was going to go with them and be with them. God was going to dwell among His people, just as He had promised. God was going to have a special tent made for Himself, to be pitched in the midst of Israel's tents, in the very centre of Israel's campground. God would live in this tent, just as His people lived in tents. The LORD said to Moses, "Tell the Israelites to bring Me an offering . . . Then have them make a sanctuary for Me, and I will dwell among them. Make this tabernacle and all its furnishings exactly like the pattern I will show you" (Exodus 25:1, 8).

How gracious God was to His people. Although they had broken His commandments and covenant, God maintained His LOVE to them and forgave their wickedness, rebellion and sin. God would continue to be with them and dwell with them; He would even allow them to make a Tabernacle for Him. This honour God would bestow upon the Israelites. Although not so much as the colour of a single thread in God's tent would be left to human imagination, still, it was the amazing grace of God that permitted human hands to make a holy dwelling place for the Most High God.

There was much work to be done. It would take several months to complete all the work on God's tabernacle, so Moses first reminded the people of God's commandment concerning work: "For six days work is to be done, but the Seventh Day shall be your Holy Day, a Sabbath of rest to the LORD. Whoever does any work on it, must be put to death . . ." (Exodus 35:2). "You must observe My Sabbath. This will be a sign between Me and you for the generations to come, so you may know that I am the LORD, who makes you holy. Observe the Sabbath, because it is holy to you. Anyone who desecrates it must be put to death; whoever does any work on that day must be cut off from his people. For six days, work is to be done, but the Seventh Day is a Sabbath of rest, holy to the LORD. Whoever does any work on the Sabbath Day must be put to death. The Israelites are to observe the Sabbath, celebrating it for the generations to come as a lasting covenant. It will be a sign between Me and the Israelites forever, because in six days the LORD made the heavens and the earth, and on the Seventh Day He abstained from work and rested" (Exodus 31:12–18). Even work on God's tabernacle must be put aside on the Sabbath.

The first thing to be done was to find the materials needed to make the tabernacle. God's dwelling place would require gold, silver and bronze, precious jewels and costly gems, beautiful fabrics and colourful yarns, exotic skins and expensive woods, special oils and fragrant spices. Where would they find all these things in the middle of the wilderness? If God did not shower them with bread from heaven, they could not even find food for themselves in this remote place. Where could they find the things needed for God's tabernacle? Moses said God required emeralds and sapphires and amethysts. God even commanded the hides of sea cows to be used in the making of His tent. Where would they find such things? They could not hunt sea cows in a desert or on a mountain! What should they do? The LORD said to Moses, "Tell the Israelites to bring Me an offering." So Moses said to the whole community, "This is what the LORD has commanded: From what you have, take an offering for the LORD. Everyone who is willing is to bring to the LORD an offering" (Exodus 35:4, 5). It was all there. Everything necessary was already somewhere within the tents of the Israelites. One person would have one thing; another person would have something else. But would they be willing to give away their treasures to build a tabernacle for the LORD?

Moses made his appeal to the people. Then the whole Israelite community withdrew from Moses' presence. Each person went to his own tent, to search his heart and his home, to see if there was anything he/she was willing to give for the LORD's work. Then, everyone who was willing and whose heart moved him came and brought an offering to the LORD for the work on the tent of meeting. All who were willing, men and women alike, brought to the LORD their free-will offerings. Although these people had all been slaves just a short time ago, some of them had brought amazing treasures out of Egypt. The leaders gave to the LORD their precious jewels, and so a ruby, a topaz, a sapphire, an emerald, an amethyst and the other necessary gems were found. Men and women donated their gold and silver jewelry. In those days the women did not use glass mirrors, but little mirrors of polished bronze, and that was where the bronze for the tabernacle was found. The women gave away their mirrors, because the beauty of God's tent was more important to them than their own beauty. The people brought whatever they had for whatever was needed. Some people brought goat hair; others brought sheep skins; and some people even brought the hides of sea cows. The Israelites had not left Egypt empty-handed. God had provided for His people, and now they gave back to God a small portion of what He had given them. Morning after morning the people continued to bring freewill offerings to the LORD. They brought so much that Moses had to give an order for them to stop giving! He sent this word throughout the camp: "No man or woman is to make anything else as an offering for the sanctuary." (Imagine having to restrain generosity.) The people who had been slow to give, no longer had the chance to give, because they now had everything they needed to make God's Tabernacle.

They had the necessary materials, but who would do the work? The work on the tabernacle required skilled labour. Moses could not make the things that God required. Was there anyone in Israel's camp who could? These people had been slaves, who knew how to do hard, heavy work under the crack of a whip. They knew how to make bricks, but God's house could not be built with bricks. It must be made to move from place to place, as the Israelites wandered in the wilderness, and it must made beautifully, according to the pattern God showed to Moses on the mountain. Who could make God's Tabernacle? The LORD said to Moses, "I have chosen Bezalel . . . of the tribe of Judah, and I have filled him with the Spirit of God, with skill, ability and knowledge in all kinds of crafts to make artistic designs for work in gold, silver and bronze, to cut and set stones, to work in wood, and to engage in all kinds of craftsmanship. Moreover, I have appointed Oholiab . . . of the tribe of Dan, to help him. Also, I have given skill to all the craftsmen [and women] to make everything I have commanded you . . . They are to make them just as I commanded you" (Exodus 31:1–11). God also gave Bezalel and Oholiab the ability to teach others, so that many people could be trained to help with the work on the tabernacle.

So Moses summoned Bezalel and Oholiab and every skilled person to whom the LORD had given ability and who was willing to come and do the work. Soon the camp of Israel was humming with activity. Every talented person was using his/her gifts to glorify God. Carpenters, spinners, designers, jewellers, engravers, weavers, embroiderers, tailors, perfumers, etc.—they were all making the things necessary for the Tabernacle. Men were sawing wood, hammering gold, melting metal, engraving stones, mixing perfumes, etc. Women were dying wool, spinning yarn, and weaving cloth. "Every skilled woman spun with her hands and brought what she had spun . . . All the women who were willing and had the skill, spun . . ." (Exodus 35:25, 26).) And what were the children doing? Probably they were watching and waiting. They were watching their fathers and mothers (and aunts and uncles) as they worked on the Tabernacle, and they were waiting for God's beautiful tent to be set up in the middle of their campground. What a special day that would be!

What would God's tent look like? The tabernacle was made of fine linen with blue, purple and scarlet yarns, royal colours, fit for Israel's King. Angels (or cherubim) were embroidered all around it, just as God's throne in heaven is surrounded by myriads of angels. God's tent would be very beautiful, but would it be practical? Have you ever been camping? What is always a concern when you are sleeping in a tent? Rain! If you have looked at tents in a campground, you will notice that some of them have a second canopy covering the main tent. Why? If the weather is wet, rain drops never even touch the tent where the family is sleeping. Only the outer tent gets wet. God's tabernacle was made like that, except that it had three outer coverings, all of them water-proof. Over the beautiful tabernacle of fine linen, was a second tent of goat hair. Over the goat-hair tent was a covering of ram skins dyed red and over the red ram-skin tent was a covering of seacow hides. God's Tabernacle was a tent, inside a tent, inside a tent, inside a tent! Nothing could touch the inner sanctuary of God's tabernacle. Neither raindrops or hailstones or sandstorms could penetrate the three-layer covering over God's Tabernacle.

There are many concerns when you are sleeping in a tent. If there's a downpour, will the tent stay dry? If there's a snowstorm, will the tent stay up? If there's a gale wind, will the tent blow down? (One early autumn night, my daughter went camping with a group of Girl Guides. In the middle of the night there was a dumping of wet snow, and the tents all collapsed under the weight of it.) What about God's Tabernacle, would it be sturdy as well as pretty? Could it weather the desert storms in that harsh wilderness? What keeps any tent standing upright? The poles, the pegs and the ropes. They are very important parts of any tent, and God's tabernacle was no exception. Although God could have kept His tent upright by a breath or a word, God used ordinary means. God's tabernacle had tent poles, pegs and ropes to be secured by human hands. The LORD commanded that the tent poles be made of acacia wood, then covered with glistening gold, both beautiful and durable. Even the pole bases and tent pegs, were made of silver and bronze.

Special furniture also had to be made for God's tabernacle. God warned Moses, "See that you make them according to the pattern shown you on the mountain" (Exodus 25:40).

1) *The ark:* A box or a chest, also called an ark, had to be made. Why? What would be its use? The two stone tablets with the Law of God, the Ten Commandments, would be kept there. On these Tablets of Testimony were written the terms of the covenant. Hence the box or chest was called the "Ark of the covenant" or the "Ark of testimony." Bezalel made the ark just as God commanded. He made it of acacia wood and overlaid it with pure gold, both inside and outside. Four gold rings were fastened to the sides of this chest, two on each side, so that golden rods could be inserted through the rings to carry the ark—without touching it. Next Bezalel made a cover of pure gold for the ark. On this cover, at each end, he made two angels (or cherubim) from hammered gold. The two angels faced each other with their wings out-spread and up-stretched, overshadowing the cover of the ark.

This place was known as the mercy seat, for that was God's throne on earth. It was there, at the mercy seat, that the King of kings and LORD of lords would meet with His people. There, at the mercy seat, God would manifest His glory and His majesty—and His Mercy. There, at the mercy seat, the King of Israel, even the LORD of hosts, would judge and rule . . . yet it would be with LOVE and mercy and forgiveness. The LORD promised Moses, "There, above the cover, between the two cherubim that are over the ark of the Testimony, I will meet with you and give you all My commands for the Israelites" (Exodus 25:22).

2) *The table*: Bezalel also made a table, according to the pattern shown to Moses on the mountain. He made the table of acacia wood, overlaid with gold. It also had gold rings, one at each corner, through which golden rods were inserted, so that the table could be easily carried by the priests, as the Israelites travelled from place to place. The LORD's table must also be set. Dishes of pure gold were made. There were plates, bowls and jars of pure gold, not to be used for eating, but to be used for the offerings made to God. The table was also laid with twelve loaves of bread. The LORD said, "Set them before the LORD in two rows, six in each row, on the table of pure gold . . . This bread is to be set out before the LORD regularly, Sabbath after Sabbath, on behalf of the Israelites, as a lasting covenant." God said, "Put the bread of the Presence (or the shewbread) on this table before Me at all times" (Leviticus 24:6, 8; Exodus 25:30). Even when the Israelites moved from place to place, the bread had to remain on the table. (See Numbers 4:7.)

3) *The lampstand*: A lampstand of pure gold had to be hammered out by skilled workmen according to the pattern shown to Moses on the mountain. It was a beautifully ornate lampstand, like a golden tree with glistening branches and buds and blossoms. On top of the uplifting branches were placed seven golden lamps, which when lit, would cast a glow all around them. Oil for the lamps was to be pure clear olive oil. The lamps were to be kept burning continually. The priests were to tend the lamps before the LORD from evening till morning, continually, as a lasting ordinance for the generations to come. (See Exodus 27:20 & Leviticus 24:2.) God's tabernacle must never be dark.

4) *The altar of burnt offering*: This altar was made of acacia wood, overlaid with bronze. It had horns at each corner, for tying the sacrifice to the altar. All the utensils for this altar were also made of bronze. It too had rings and poles for easy transportation without touching it.

5) *The altar of incense:* This altar was made of acacia wood, overlaid with gold. A skilled workman, a perfumer, also made the pure fragrant incense, which the priest must burn on the altar every morning and every evening. The incense was a special blend, according to God's directions. It was to be salted and pure and sacred. The LORD said, "It shall be most holy to you. Do not make any incense with this formula for yourselves. Consider it holy to the LORD. Whoever makes any like it to enjoy its fragrance must be cut off from his people" (Exodus 30:36–38). Likewise, the priests must not burn any other incense to the LORD.

6) *The basin:* A large bronze basin was made for washing. Whenever the priests entered God's tabernacle or offered a sacrifice, they must wash their hands and feet, lest they die.

7) *The anointing oil:* God commanded Moses to take certain fine spices and mix them with olive oil into a holy fragrant blend, the work of a perfumer. It would be the sacred anointing oil, used for consecrating common things for a holy use. God warned the Israelites, "This is my sacred anointing oil for the generations to come. Do not pour it on men's bodies and do not make any oil with the same formula. It is sacred and you are to consider it sacred" (Exodus 30:31). It was to be used for the worship of God alone, to anoint His tabernacle and His priests.

Special clothes also had to be made for the people who would be servants in God's House. God commanded that sacred garments be made for all the priests ministering in the sanctuary. They alone could enter God's Tabernacle, and they must be dressed according to the LORD's command. On the mountain God said to Moses, "Make sacred garments for your brother Aaron, to give him dignity and honour. Tell all the skilled men to whom I have given wisdom in such matters, that they are to make garments for Aaron, for his consecration, so he may serve Me as a priest" (Exodus 28:2, 3). These were the sacred garments:

1) *An ephod:* Skilled craftsmen made a beautiful ephod that shimmered with gold, as the LORD commanded. They hammered out thin sheets of gold and then cut them into shining strands to be woven into the fine linen fabric along with blue, purple and scarlet yarn. On the shoulder pieces of the priest's ephod, jewellers mounted onyx stones in gold filigree settings. On these two stones the names of the sons of Israel were engraved in order

of their birth, six names on one stone, six names on the other. These were to be memorial stones for the sons of Israel. A great responsibility was placed on the high priest's shoulders. Aaron was to bear the names of the twelve tribes of Israel on his shoulders as a memorial before the LORD.

2) A *breastpiece:* Skilled craftsmen also made a breastpiece, of the same shimmering gold fabric, with glistening jewels added to it. Four rows of precious stones were mounted in gold filigree settings onto this breastpiece. In the first row there was a ruby, a topaz and a beryl; in the second row there was a turquoise, a sapphire and an emerald; in the third row was a jacinth, an agate and an amethyst; in the fourth row was a chrysolite, an onyx and a jasper, twelve stones altogether, one for each of the names of the sons of Israel. Each tribe had their name engraved upon a precious stone, for God's people were precious in His sight. Whenever the high priest entered the Holy Place, he always bore the names of the sons of Israel over his heart as a continual memorial to the LORD. Thus the high priest always had the people on his heart to intercede for them before the throne of grace, before the Mercy Seat, of the mighty and Holy God of heaven and earth.

3) A *robe:* Skilled weavers made the priests' robes entirely of blue cloth. They made little pomegranates of blue, purple and scarlet yarn and hung them around the hem of the robe, with little gold bells between them. As the priest ministered in the tabernacle, the little gold bells jingled. About this robe God said, "Aaron must wear it when he ministers. The sound of the bells will be heard when he enters the Holy Place before the LORD and when he comes out, so that he will not die" (Exodus 28:35).

4) A *tunic:* Fine linen tunics had to be woven for the priests, to give them dignity and honour.

5) A *turban:* The priest must also wear a turban of fine linen. Fastened to the front of the high priest's turban with a blue cord was a plate of gold, engraved with these words: HOLY TO THE LORD. It was called a "sacred diadem"; it was a holy crown for the high priest. God said, "It will be on Aaron's forehead, and he will bear the guilt involved in the sacred gifts the Israelites consecrate . . . It will be on Aaron's forehead continually, so that they will be acceptable to the LORD" (Exodus 28:38 & 39:30).

6) A *sash:* Sashes were embroidered for the priests, also to give them dignity and honour.

7) *Underwear:* God even commanded that the priests wear linen undergarments as a covering for the body. God said, "Aaron and his sons must wear them whenever they enter the Tent of Meeting or approach the altar to minister in the Holy Place, so that they will not incur guilt and die. This is to be a lasting ordinance for Aaron and his sons" (Exodus 28:42, 43).

It took the Israelites about five months to complete all the work on the tabernacle. Then they brought their work to Moses for inspection, to make sure they had made everything according to the pattern God had given Moses on the mountain. The Israelites brought to Moses the Tabernacle they had made, the tent with its coverings and curtains, pegs and poles, all the furnishings and all the garments for the priests. Moses carefully inspected all their work and he saw that it was done exactly as the LORD had commanded. So Moses blessed them.

Then the LORD spoke to Moses and told him to set up the Tabernacle, the Tent of Meeting, on the first day of the first month—New Year's Day. There must be a special day for setting up God's Tabernacle, and it must be set up according to God's commands.

The Tabernacle had three rooms:

1) COURTYARD: The outer room was a courtyard under the open sky. There, in that courtyard, the people of God, both men and women, worshipped the LORD. The bronze altar of sacrifice was placed in this courtyard, near the entrance to the Tabernacle. The bronze basin was also placed in this courtyard, between the altar and the inner rooms of God's tent.

2) HOLY PLACE: Beyond the courtyard, behind a curtain, was a room called the Holy Place. Only the priests were allowed in this room. There the priests burned incense at the golden altar; there they tended the lamps on the golden lampstand; there they ate the shewbread on the golden table.

3) MOST HOLY PLACE or HOLY OF HOLIES: Inside God's Tabernacle was a room inside a room. This inner room was separated by a thick veil or curtain, which divided the Holy Place from the Most Holy place. Only the high priest was allowed to enter this Most Holy place, and only once a year, on the Day of Atonement. Inside this room was the Ark of the Covenant, over which was the Atonement Cover or the Mercy Seat. It was there, in that room, above the Ark of the Covenant, that God met with His people, through the mediation of the high priest.

Moses did everything, just as the LORD commanded him. When New Year's Day arrived, he set up the Tabernacle. Almost a year had passed since the Israelites had left Egypt to come to this mountain to worship God. Soon, very soon, the worship of the Living God would begin in this Tabernacle.

The first thing Moses did on that New Year's Day was to set up the Tabernacle. The silver bases had to be set in place. The golden tent poles had to be inserted as frames and erected as posts. The bronze tent pegs had to be hammered into the ground. Over God's beautiful Tabernacle, the three other tents had to be pitched, to cover the Tabernacle. Moses did everything as the LORD commanded him.

The next thing Moses did was to place the two stone Tablets of Testimony, the Ten Commandments, into the golden ark. He attached the poles to the ark and put the atonement cover over it. Then he brought the ark into the Tabernacle. Moses hung the curtain to shield the ark from the eyes of Israel. Only the high priest once a year would see that beautiful golden ark, with the wings of the two golden angels spreading upwards to God's throne in heaven. This was God's throne on earth, and it was hidden now in that Most Holy place, the Holy of Holies. Moses did this, just as the LORD commanded him.

Outside the shielding curtain, in the room called the holy place, Moses placed the golden table on the north side of God's Tent. Moses also set out the twelve loaves of bread on the table before the LORD, just as the LORD commanded him.

In this room on the south side, Moses placed the golden lampstand and set up the lamps before the LORD, just as the LORD commanded him.

Then Moses placed the golden altar in front of the curtain and he burned fragrant incense upon it, just as the LORD commanded him. Then he hung another curtain, to separate this room, the Holy place, from the courtyard.

Outside the Tabernacle, Moses set up the bronze altar for the burnt offerings. He set this altar near the entrance to the Tent of Meeting and offered on it burnt offerings and grain offerings, just as the LORD commanded.

Between the Tent of Meeting and the altar, Moses set up the bronze basin and put water in it. It was ready now for washing, whenever Moses or Aaron or the other priests entered the Tent of Meeting or approached the altar, just as God commanded Moses.

The last thing to do was to set up the courtyard. The beautiful curtains, which surrounded the Tabernacle like a fence, were set in place. One final curtain was hung between the God's courtyard and the outside world. This was the entrance into the courts of the LORD. And so Moses finished the work of setting up the Tabernacle.

Was the LORD pleased with His Tent? Was the Israelites' work accepted by God? Would the LORD of Glory stoop to dwell in this Tabernacle made by human hands? Yes! The cloud covered the Tent of Meeting and the glory of the LORD filled the Tabernacle. God was pleased to come into His tent. Moses could not even enter the Tabernacle now, because of the over-whelming presence of the LORD. Moses could not enter this cloud that was within the Tabernacle.

From that New Year's Day onwards, the cloud of the LORD settled upon the Tabernacle. In all the travels of the Israelites, whenever the cloud lifted above the Tabernacle, it was God's signal to the Israelites to set out again on their journey. When it settled on the Tabernacle, it was God's signal to them that they should stop and rest until the cloud lifted again. So the cloud of the LORD was over the Tabernacle by day, and fire was in the cloud at night. This was in the sight of all the house of Israel during all their travels. The people could see that God really was dwelling among them, that He was with them wherever they went.

✳ ✳ ✳

One day, thousands of years later, God would dwell with His people in another way. God would raise up another Tabernacle in the midst of His people, a Tabernacle of flesh. It says in the New Testament that "In the beginning was the Word and the Word was with God *and the Word was God.* He was with God in the beginning . . . and the Word became flesh and made His dwelling among us, [or tabernacled among us]" (John 1:1, 2 14). Jesus was called Immanuel, which means God with us. Jesus Himself referred to His body as the temple of God. "For God was pleased to have all His full-ness dwell in Him . . . For in Christ all the fullness of Deity lives in bodily form" (Colossians 1:19; 2:9). The Tabernacle in the wilderness pointed to Christ in the world. Just as the Tabernacle was the place of cleansing and meeting with God, so it is in Christ that we are cleansed and reconciled to God.

The teacher's guide for this lesson starts on page 256.

EXODUS
TEACHER'S GUIDE

Explanation of the Teacher's Guide

I wrote this guide for the teacher who is using the lessons from *Herein Is Love: Exodus*. It can be used by any adult involved in teaching children — Sabbath School teachers, Christian School teachers, Home School teachers, Vacation Bible School teachers, camp counsellors, parents, etc. Here is how to use these lessons:

1. Prayerfully study the Scripture references given at the beginning of each lesson.
2. Then read the lesson carefully.
3. Find the visual aids you need to use for that lesson.
4. Prepare the memory work handouts.
5. Assemble any craft materials you might need.
6. Select and practice the psalms you wish to use.
7. If applicable, plan the route of your field trip.

If you have only an hour each week with your class of children (which is all most Sabbath School teachers have), you cannot possibly do everything suggested for each lesson in this teacher's manual. However, with one hour you will have time to teach the lesson which is your first priority, show and discuss the visual aids while you are teaching, test the children's memory work, sometimes do a quick craft, ask a few questions, pray, for there is always the time and the need to pray, and sing a psalm. If you have a two/three-hour block of time, the making of crafts and singing of psalms can be greatly extended. Camp counsellors and parent-teachers will find the field trip suggestions particularly useful.

Many Sabbath School teachers think that the children must have a lesson sheet to take home with them each week. Personally, I do not like those sheets. They are expensive, often uninteresting, sometimes damaging and they usually wind up in the garbage can unused anyway. I do agree that it is nice for the children to have something to take home with them, but really it need not be any more than a verse of memory work. What could be more important for the children to take away with them than a jewel from God's Word? However, if you think a parent page is necessary for a lesson review during the week, you can very simply and cheaply make your own by including:

1. The main Bible text to be read at home
2. The memory work to be learned at home
3. A craft suggestion if you didn't make one in class
4. A copy of the main Psalm to be sung daily in family worship
5. The field trip suggestion for a family outing.

Visual Aids

I am completely dissatisfied with (and sometimes utterly offended by) the illustrations found in most Bible curriculums currently available for children. The pictures that are intended to be visual aids become visual harms, because they represent the Scriptures as little more than fairy tales or comic strips. These pictures cheapen the holy Word of God. How can the children take seriously their forerunners in the faith, when they are so often represented visually as cartoon characters? I have suggested visual aids for the children, which will connect the Bible to the real world.

Use photographs. These are far more interesting for the children, impressing upon them that the study of the Scriptures is serious study. With this approach, there is no concern about pictures being current or relevant, because the pictures are of enduring significance. The wealth of visual aids that the human race has collected since the invention of the camera is overwhelming. Make use of this rich resource. Expose the children to the amazing scenes witnessed and captured by the human eye through the camera. Photography books, *National Geographic* magazines, old calendars, postcards, etc., are where you will find the necessary pictures. For example, the first lesson in Exodus deals with the Hebrew slaves in Egypt. There are books of photos showing the agonized faces and brutalized labours of the Jewish slaves in Nazi concentration camps. Use these photos to impress upon the children the cruelty of the Hebrews' bondage in Egypt. Pharaoh was the first, but not the lasts evil tyrant to cruelly oppress the Jews. Photographs can be used as powerful, visual testimony to help the children focus on and believe in the lessons you are teaching from the Scriptures.

Use maps. Whenever possible in a lesson use a map by tracing the route of Israel's journey, pointing out an important mountain or river, showing the area of a certain country, etc. Let the children see that the accounts in Scripture are historical events that happened in the real world.

Use specimens. Many of the stories in the Bible have an object in it that is central. It can be something so simple, and yet that object rivets the children's attention to the lesson. Real objects from the real world help to connect the children to the real and true stories of the Bible.

Memory Work

I always impress upon my children the need to store up God's Word like a treasure in their hearts, which can then help them in a time of need. I tell the children that the real reward is knowing God's Word, but I also give them a little incentive by making each child a memory work book. This is quite simple:

1) Make booklets by folding 8 x 12 sheets of construction paper in half. (Use the same colour with younger children to avoid squabbles). Make the front cover interesting by pasting on it a slightly smaller rectangle of some sort of picture. (Again, I always make the books identical). Sometimes I use wrapping paper. Sometimes I recycle attractive church bulletins. I usually make books to last three months for weekly lessons, changing them with the seasons. For example, the memory work book for the autumn quarter could

have a picture of brightly coloured leaves on a yellow background. Often I add a few sparkles to the front cover too. Make sure each child's name is on his/her book.

2) Type out the verse. (I use a 4 x 6 sheet of paper). Xerox copies for double the number of children in the class. One copy goes into their book (that you keep until the books are finished). The other copy is handed out to each child to learn during the week. I try to make the hand-out copies interesting: In autumn I make the children's verses in different shades of brightly coloured paper cut in the shape of leaves. That way, their weekly Bible verses can make a pretty display on their bulletin boards or refrigerators at home. In winter I hand out white "snowballs." It takes just a few extra moments to trace a circle around the verse before cutting it. In spring you can hand out diamond-shaped "kites" or petalled "flowers" in pastel hues. Be creative! There's more than one way to hand out a slip of memory work, giving the children something special to take home.

3) Buy sheets of stickers, continuing the seasonal theme. (There are usually 12 stickers per sheet, 4 sheets per package, which costs about 50 cents per quarter per child). Write each child's name on the back of their sticker sheet. For each week's memory work that is learned, they get to choose a sticker from their own sheet to put in their book. At the end of the term, collect all the unearned, unused stickers, but let all the children take their books home.

Craft

For each lesson I suggest one or more crafts that in some way deal with what you have discussed in that lesson. Many of the crafts can be easily modified to fit your required time-frame. I have not described in detail how to make each item, for this is not meant to be a step-by-step craft book. It's simply to give you some ideas.

Review Questions

For each lesson I ask a few specific review questions. However, there are two very important questions that should be asked with every lesson:

1. What does this lesson teach us about God?
2. How does this lesson help us to live our lives?

Prayer

The application of each lesson to the children's lives is found in the prayer.

Psalms to Sing

I list one psalm (or part of a psalm) that is particularly relevant to the lesson, as well as several others that are also related to it. Singing the Psalms is a crucial way, but simple way, for the children to store God's Word in their hearts. "Give thanks to the LORD; call on His Name . . . Sing to Him; sing psalms to Him" (Psalm 105:1, 2). "Let the Word of Christ dwell in you richly as you teach . . . and as you sing psalms" (Colossians 3:16). If time permits, I recommend singing the main psalm for each lesson several times, so that the children have already begun to memorize it. You could also send home a copy of the main psalm, so that the children can sing it at home during the week with their families. The Psalter I have used is *The Book of Psalms for Singing*, published by the Reformed Presbyterian Church of North America, 1973.

Field Trip

The teaching of the Word of God to our children is not meant to be confined within the four walls of our Christian churches, schools and homes. Take God's Word outside, into the fresh air and sun shine. Teach it in the open fields and the busy streets. Moses says, "Fix these words of mine in your hearts and minds . . . Teach them to your children, talking about them when you sit at home and when you walk along the road" (Deuteronomy 11:18, 19). How will God's Word be fixed in the hearts and minds of our children? It will happen, not only when we read the Scriptures around the family dinner table or when we study the Bible in our Sunday School classroom, but also it will happen when we are walking along the road, when we are looking at the world around us as we discuss the things of God. Teaching opportunities are along every ordinary road, along every little pathway in your life. For each lesson I have suggested some small outing to a place which will impress that particular Bible teaching upon your children. What a way to review a lesson. If you are setting out with that purpose in mind, "to teach your children . . . when you walk along the road" it will actually happen. You will do it—and they will be blessed!

The Jewish Problem

Exodus 1

VISUAL AIDS

Photographs of the Jewish slaves in the Nazi concentration camps would be excellent for this lesson.

MEMORY WORK

"There is no wisdom, no insight, no plan that can succeed against the LORD" (Proverbs 21:30).

CRAFT

How wrong it is to kill babies, within the womb or outside the womb. Your class could make *pro-life* posters, to display in public, or placards, to carry in a demonstration.

REVIEW QUESTIONS

1. What did God promise to Abraham, Isaac and Jacob?
2. God promised their children would be as numerous as . . . what?
3. How was God fulfilling His promise to them in Egypt?
4. Who was at war with the Word of God? Why? Who was his servant on earth?
5. What was the new Pharaoh's first solution to the Jewish problem? Did it work? Why not?
6. What was his second solution to the Jewish problem? Did it work? Why not?
7. What was Pharaoh's third solution to the Jewish problem? Do you think it would succeed? Why? Why not?

PRAYER

LORD, we thank you for delivering us from all kinds of evil. We pray that you would deliver us today and forever from the Evil One. LORD, we also pray that you would give us the strength to stand against evil and to fear you more than men. LORD, we pray that our names would be found among the righteous and courageous, among those people who have loved you more than their own lives.

PSALMS TO SING

128A . . . also 2; 3; 5AB; 52AB; 83C (1); 124AB; 127; 140AB; 144AC; 149.

FIELD TRIP

Have the children involved in an activity that helps and saves the lives of children. For example, they could raise money for an organization such as World Vision.

(This student lesson starts on page 1.)

By Faith, They Hid

Exodus 2:1–10

VISUAL AIDS

There are several photographs that would be useful:

1. Pictures of the banks of the Nile River, with crocodiles resting in the reeds.
2. Pictures of the papyrus plant, out of which Moses' basket-boat was woven.
3. Pictures of Hitler's SS men, capturing, dividing and murdering Jewish families during World War II.

Also, show the children some examples of tightly-woven baskets, especially ones with lids.

MEMORY WORK

"The LORD is faithful to all His Promises . . ." (Psalm 145:13).

CRAFT

For this lesson, try basket-weaving.

REVIEW QUESTIONS

1. The time was drawing near for God to fulfil His promise to Abraham. When did God say He would bring Abraham's descendants back to the promised land?
2. Who was born in Egypt in the fourth generation?
3. What were the names of Moses' father and mother? From which tribe did they come?
4. When their baby boy was born, why did they disobey Pharaoh?
5. Why did it require faith to hide their baby for three months?

6. Why didn't they hide him longer than that?
7. What did Moses' mother do in an attempt to save her baby and what was the amazing way that God rescued him from death?
8. Whose son did Moses' become? Who gave him that name? Why? When he grew older, where did he live?

PRAYER

LORD, we thank you for your faithfulness in fulfilling all your promises. We thank you for the amazing ways that you save your people. We thank you for the saviour you raised up for Israel and the saviour you raised up for us, even Jesus Christ, the Son of God. LORD, help us to live, not by fear, but by faith. Help us to obey your Word and your law, even when it goes against the words and laws of men.

PSALMS TO SING

71A . . . AND 27BC; 31A; 34A (1); 37AB; 111A; 112A (1, 2,4); 113AB.

FIELD TRIP

Take your children to play along the bank of a river. Notice the plant and animal life along the river's edge. Where I live, in Ottawa, Canada, we don't have to watch for crocodiles, but Moses' mother did. You can bring little basket-boats for the children to float in the water. Make sure the baskets have been waterproofed. (You can use varnish, rather than the messy tar and pitch). You could leave one basket without any water-proofing just to see what happens. If you have little girls on this expedition, they would probably like to float small dolls in their baskets. Have fun!

(This student lesson starts on page 7.)

By Faith, He Left

Exodus 2:11–25

VISUAL AIDS

Show the children an old-fashioned balance scale. Moses had to weigh the very real pleasures and treasures of this world with the disgrace of Christ and distress of God's people.

Also useful for this lesson would be pictures of the power and glory of ancient Egypt. You can find photos in *National Geographic* magazines, which show the treasures that have been found in the pyramids.

MEMORY WORK

"Blessed are you when men hate you, when they exclude you and insult you and reject your name as evil, because of the Son of Man. Rejoice in that day and leap for joy, because great is your reward in heaven" (Luke 6:22, 23).

CRAFT

Make a collage of the pleasures and treasures of our culture. What are the things that choke the Word of God from people's lives, that entice them to sin and forsake Christ? Just cut out pictures from any magazine's advertisements, pictures of flashy cars, sexy men or women, bottles of liquor, jewelry, etc. Cut out letters to read: PLEASURES OF SIN, TREASURES OF WORLD. The things of greater value are invisible: hope, faith, love, peace, joy, life—and God! Perhaps you could make a second collage with these words on it. Then tack both posters on a wall with the question in large letters: WHICH WILL YOU CHOOSE?

REVIEW QUESTIONS

1. What difficult choice did Moses have to make? What did he choose? Why? Do you think he made the right decision? Do we have to make the same choice? What will you choose? Why?
2. Which is better, to be a king in the palace of the wicked or a servant in the house of God? Why?
3. Moses wondered why God spared his life as a baby and why he made him a prince. What did Moses come to believe was the answer? Did the Israelites recognize him as their rescuer?
4. Why did Moses leave Egypt? Where did he live and what did he do for the next forty years?
5. What was the name of Moses' wife? How many children did Moses have? What were their names? What did they mean?

PRAYER

LORD, thank you for hiding us and helping us in all our difficulties. Please, LORD, grant us your grace to live by faith. Give us the strength to make the right decisions in our lives, always choosing for you and your Word and your reward.

PSALMS TO SING

37C . . . also 17ABC; 18A; 27B; 31D; 32B; 49BC; 62AB; 84ABC; 91AB; 119BI;

FIELD TRIP

Take a little detour on the LORD's Day and drive by a shopping mall or a sports arena on your way to church. Show your children the parking lots filled with cars, representing people who have made the wrong choice. These people have chosen the treasures and pleasures of this world, instead of the greater blessing of worshipping God.

(This student lesson starts on page 13.)

The Angel of the Lord...

Exodus 3:1–10

VISUAL AIDS

For this lesson you will need some photographs of forest fires showing bushes, trees and whole woods being consumed by flames of fire. It is an awesome sight to see the ordinary flames of a natural fire. Imagine what Moses saw. He saw the extraordinary flames of a supernatural fire! Show your students pictures of a "burnt-over" area: the black skeletons and stumps of trees, the bare charred remains of a once lush green forest. That is what an ordinary fire does. It consumes and destroys everything in its path. But Moses saw a bush on fire, that did not burn up.

MEMORY WORK

1. "Let us be thankful, and so worship God acceptably with reverence and awe, for our God is a consuming fire" (Hebrews 12:28, 29).
2. "Exalt the LORD our God and worship at His holy mountain, for the LORD our God is holy" (Psalm 99:9).

CRAFT

Perhaps the children could make a picture of the burning bush. First, have them use green crayons to colour the branches and leaves of the bush. Then have them paint (with water colours) red/yellow/orange flames all over the bush. Surprise! The bush will not be "consumed" by the flames.

REVIEW QUESTIONS

1. What promise did God make to Israel before they went to Egypt? Why did it seem that God had forgotten His promise to the Israelites? Had He? Was He slow in keeping it?
2. Did God have a plan and a person ready to rescue the Israelites? Who was that person? How had he been prepared?
3. What strange sight did Moses see? What strange sound did Moses hear?
4. Why did Moses hide his face?
5. What did God say that showed how much He loved the Israelites?
6. Who was the Angel of the LORD, who appeared to Moses in the flames of fire within the bush?
7. What was the name of the mountain where this happened? What did it mean? Why was the name of this mountain changed? What was its new name? What did its new name mean?

PRAYER

LORD, we thank you, that although you are a Holy God and a consuming fire, You have not consumed us or destroyed us because of our sins, but have rescued us in your Son, Jesus Christ. We thank you for LOVE and mercy and forgiveness in Christ. We thank you for your great salvation! LORD, help us to worship you in fear all the days of our lives. Amen.

PSALMS TO SING

97A . . . also 18ABGH; 50A; 99C.

FIELD TRIP

Burn a bush in a bonfire one night. Watch it shrivel and hear it crackle as the fire consumes it. Moses saw a burning bush that wasn't consumed

(This student lesson starts on page 20.)

The Name of God

Exodus 3:7–15

VISUAL AIDS

Show your students some photographs of the world's famous mountains, such as Mount Everest or Mount Fuji. Then show them a photo of Mount Horeb. What made this mountain special? It was not the highest or prettiest mountain in the world, but it was the mountain that God chose as a sign for Moses, the mountain where the people of Israel would worship the LORD.

MEMORY WORK

"We will lift up our banners in the name of our God" (Psalm 20:5).

CRAFT

Have each child make a banner to be lifted and waved in the name of our God. These banners could be made of different colours of bright felt, with the Hebrew letters for LORD/Jahweh cut in a contrasting colour of felt and glued on the banners. Attach the banners to sticks, add some ribbons, and march with shouts of joy before the LORD!

REVIEW QUESTIONS

1. How was God going to rescue His people? Whom would He use?
2. When God said to Moses, "Go! I am sending you," what did Moses say? What question did he ask?
3. Why did Moses think he was not the one to do this work?
4. What was God's answer?
5. God promised Moses, "I am with you." God also gave Moses a sign. What was it? How could Moses see this sign?

6. Moses asked a second important question. What did he want to know? Did God tell him?
7. What was God's answer? What name did God reveal? What did that name mean? Do we still call God by that name?

PRAYER

O LORD, we glorify your name. We praise you, LORD, for being with us. We thank you, LORD, for your great promise to us: "Lo, I am with you always, to the very end of the age." We ask that you would lead us all the days of our lives; lead us in the paths of righteousness for your name's sake. We ask that you would forgive all our sins in the name of our Lord Jesus. Amen.

PSALMS TO SING

66A (1–3); 68A (3); 69E (21); 72C (11, 12) . . . also 5B (5); 7B (9); 9A; 20AB; 29A (1); 34A; 54AB; 75 (1); 79B (8, 12); 86B (6); 92AC (1); 96A; 99C (1); 100ABC; 103A; 105A (1–3); 113AB; 135AB (1); 135C (4); 138AB (1–3); 145A; 145C (13); 149 (1, 2).

FIELD TRIP

Go for a walk, in city or country, and look for names. You will see names written on rural mailboxes; you will see names written on urban storefronts. You might see giant letters posted high above a factory building, but all these names will pass away. The paint will fade, the letters will fall, the people will move, the business will fail, but the Name of our God endures forever. The name of the LORD is exalted high above the heavens from one end of the earth to the other. God's name is exalted through our praises.

(This student lesson starts on page 25.)

Provisions For the Journey

Exodus 3:1–4:17

VISUAL AIDS

You need photographs of the signs in this lesson:

1) different kinds of snakes with their poisonous fangs
2) the hands of people deformed by leprosy and
3) blood.

The more frightening the pictures are, the greater the impression they will make upon the children.

MEMORY WORK

"The LORD your God is God of gods and LORD of lords, the great God, mighty and awesome . . . Fear the LORD your God and serve Him . . . He is your praise; He is your God, who performed for you those great and awesome wonders . . ." (Deuteronomy 10:17, 20, 21).

CRAFT

Three signs were given to Moses as identification, to prove that he was who he øsaid he was, a man to whom the LORD had appeared. Your children could make I.D. cards to prove who they are. The wallet-size I.D. cards should include their names, addresses, phone numbers, birthdates, photos, finger prints, signatures, etc. Cover the cards in plastic.

REVIEW QUESTIONS

1. God told Moses exactly what must be done in Egypt. What three things did God assure Moses would happen?
2. God gave Moses three signs to show the people. Why?
3. What was the first sign? What could it mean?
4. What was the second sign? What could it mean?
5. What was the third sign? What could it mean?
6. Moses protested that he had a problem. What was it? Did God see this as a problem? Why not? What did God promise to do?
7. God graciously allowed Moses to take someone with him. Who was it? How would he help? What would he do?

PRAYER

LORD, thankyou for assuring us of victory in Jesus Christ. With that knowledge, help us to go forward, by faith. Help us not to make excuses; instead, help us to say each day of our lives: "I am the LORD's servant. Thy will be done."

PSALMS TO SING

105A (1–3) . . . also 66A (1–4); 71C; 86A; 98A (1); 103A; 145A.

FIELD TRIP

You can impress upon the children that true miracles are supernatural. Attempt to do the signs that the LORD performed through Moses. Have each child throw down a stick. Does it turn into a snake? Have them put their hands inside their coats. Do they become leprous? Have them pour water on the ground. Does it turn to blood? No. Even if you pray that they will, they won't. God is not manipulated by us into performing tricks for our entertainment. However this is a good exercise for the children because it teaches them that only God performs miracles. It teaches them that they are not God. I remember my little three-year-old daughter, Shoshannah, after hearing how Christ calmed the stormy sea. She stood on the lakeshore at her grandparents' cottage, shouting to the waves: "Stop! Be still!" The waves continued to splash one after another on to her tiny bare toes. The water did not obey her. It was a good lesson.

(This student lesson starts on page 32.)

The Way Made Smooth For Moses

Exodus 4:18–31

VISUAL AIDS

You will need photos of elderly gentlemen with whitened hair, wrinkled faces, crooked backs. Hold up two of these pictures and ask some questions: "What harm could two such old men do? Could they fight against an entire nation? What good could two such old men do? Could they rescue an entire nation?"

MEMORY WORK

"For as high as the heavens are above the earth, so great is His LOVE for those who fear Him; as far as the east is from the west, so far has He removed our transgressions [sins] from us" (Psalm 103:11, 12).

CRAFT

Perhaps your students could sketch a portrait of an old man with wrinkled skin, white hair, bent back, etc.

REVIEW QUESTIONS

1. Where did Moses go when he left Mount Horeb? Why?
2. What did Moses take with him on the journey? Why?
3. Why did the LORD meet with Moses to kill him?
4. Why did the LORD leave him alone and let him go on his way?
5. Where did Moses and Aaron meet? Do you think that was a good meeting place? Why?
6. What did Moses and Aaron do when they arrived in Egypt? Why?
7. How did the elders of Israel respond to the words and the signs from God? What particularly touched their hearts?

PRAYER

LORD, thank you for your concern for us too. Thank you for seeing our misery and slavery to sin and having compassion upon us. Surely you have demonstrated your great LOVE for us: you sent your Only Son to die on the cross to rescue us from our sin. O LORD, we also worship you. As the elders of Israel bowed down to worship you, so do we. Please, accept our praise of you. Please, forgive our many sins for the sake of your Son Jesus. O LORD, help us to forsake the sins that so easily entangle us, that our lives might glorify you. Amen.

PSALMS TO SING

25C; 32C . . . also 6; 27BE; 30AB; 32ABD; 51ABDE; 71C; 92B; 103A; 130AB.

FIELD TRIP

Can you find a park where the old men sit on benches, resting their chins upon their canes? Eighty-year-old men rest at the end of their lives; their work is finished, but Moses and Aaron were just beginning their work in life.

(This student lesson starts on page 39.)

The Way Made Rough For Moses

Exodus 5:1–7:7

VISUAL AIDS

Show the children pictures of the brick-making process. There are drawings from ancient Egypt that show slaves hauling clay from the Nile River, mixing the clay with straw, molding the clay into bricks, baking the bricks in the sun, and then carrying the heavy bricks to the construction sites, all under the supervision of the Egyptian task-masters with their whips. You can also show the children photographs of the modern method of brick-making in Egypt, which is similar.

MEMORY WORK

God we will gain the victory. He will trample down our enemies" (Psalm 108:13).

CRAFT

The Israelites had to gather straw. Bring some straw and some red string for your students to make into straw stars, lovely ornaments to hang on a tree branch or in a window. You could also bring clay for the children to mold into small bricks. Bake it in a kiln and later use the bricks in a model building.

REVIEW QUESTIONS

1. Moses and Aaron went to Pharaoh with God's message: "Let My people go." Did Pharaoh listen? Why not? How did he answer?
2. What did Pharaoh do to keep the Israelites from thinking about leaving Egypt and serving God? What did he do to turn them against Moses and Aaron?
3. Pharaoh's plan seemed to be working. What did Moses do?

4. What were the three things of which God reminded Moses, to encourage his heart and strengthen his faith?
5. Can you summarize the seven-fold promise that God gave to the Israelites? Were they encouraged by this promise? Why not?
6. Why did Moses think God's plan was failing? Whom did he blame? Was it his fault? Was God's plan really failing?
7. Who stood in opposition to Moses?

PRAYER

O LORD, thank you for your Word and for all your loving promises, which encourage us in every difficulty. Help us, LORD, to turn to you in prayer at all times, especially when we are afraid. Help us always to hear your Word and obey your commands, however we feel, whatever the circumstances.

PSALMS TO SING

52B; 56; 140B; 143B . . . also 3; 5AB; 14ABC; 25D; 37AB; 43; 53; 54AB; 56; 58AB; 59AB; 68A; 70ABC; 77a (1); 120 (1); 129; 138AB; 140AB.

FIELD TRIP

Bricks are a part of man's life. They have been used as a building material for thousands of years. Go for a walk through any town and notice the red-brick and yellow-brick houses; notice the old brick streets or walls; notice the chimneys. If there is a brick factory in your vicinity, visit it. If a house is being built, watch the brick-layers at work. Remind the children that the ancient Egyptians made their bricks and built their cities with the slave labour of the Israelites.

(This student lesson starts on page 43.)

Two Kingdoms In Collision

Exodus 7:1–13

VISUAL AIDS

For this class you should bring photographs of the false idols and false worship from all around the world.

MEMORY WORK

"Dear friends, do not believe every spirit, but test the spirits to see whether they are from God, because many false prophets have gone out into the world . . . Dear children, you are from God and have overcome them, because the One who is in you is greater than the one who is in the world" (I John 4:1, 4).

CRAFT

You can put a brood of vipers on your classroom wall. Have the children draw snakes on large pieces of paper, paint them, add sequins or sparkles, cut them out, and display them.

REVIEW QUESTIONS

1. In those days, where could one find the true worship of the true God? In our days, where can one find the true worship of the true God?
2. What were some of the "gods" that the nations worshipped?
3. What was Satan's plan? What was God's plan? Whose plan seemed to be succeeding? Why?
4. God was going to show Egypt that He was the LORD. How?
5. What sign did Moses and Aaron perform to prove that they were sent from God?
6. Did Pharaoh believe this sign? Why not? What did he do?

7. By what power did Pharaoh's magicians and sorcerers turn their staffs into snakes? Why did God permit this?
8. In this miracle, how did God show that He was Almighty?
9. What warning did God give to Pharaoh?

PRAYER

LORD, God Almighty, we thank you for protecting us from all the powers of the Evil One. We thank you for giving us the great gift of the Holy Spirit, Who is greater than all the demonic spirits in this world. Please, LORD, grant us the wisdom to know your Word and your works. Let us discern false prophets and counterfeit signs. Lead us not into temptation, but deliver us from evil. By your grace, may we stand for you and fight for your kingdom in the name of our Lord, Jesus Christ.

PSALMS TO SING

68E; 96A . . . also 2; 16AB; 31E; 67AB; 79B; 86A; 95A; 97ABC; 115AC; 117AB; 135C.

FIELD TRIP

It is very sad to witness the false worship of false gods. Take your children to see some idols, gods of wood and stone and gold, before which people bow in worship. You could also take the children to some sort of snake exhibit.

(This student lesson starts on page 51.)

The Just Judgements of God: The Ten Plagues

This lesson is really ten lessons, one for each plague:

1. A river of blood (Exodus 7:14–24)
2. An army of frogs (Exodus 8:1–15)
3. Legions of lice (Exodus 8:16–19)
4. Swarms of flies (Exodus 8:20–32)
5. A deadly disease (Exodus 9:1–7)
6. An outbreak of boils (Exodus 9:8–12)
7. A hammering of hail (Exodus 9:13–35)
8. An invasion of insects (Exodus 10:1–20)
9. A dreadful darkness (Exodus 10:21–29)
10. A miracle at midnight (Exodus 11 & 12)

VISUAL AIDS

For each of the plagues find appropriate photographs from magazines or encyclopedias to show the children:

1. **A River of Blood**—Show them pictures of the great Nile River and how Egypt is dependent upon the Nile for fishing and farming, as well as for drinking water. Imagine what would happen to this nation if its prime source of water was changed into blood. You can also show them photos of contaminated bodies of water and the resulting devastation to marine life. Heaps of dead fish and birds are washed ashore in these environmental disasters.
2. **An Army of Frogs**—There are beautiful photos of frogs. There are whole calendars devoted to frogs. They are fascinating creatures, but devastating when God uses them as his soldiers.

3. **Legions of Lice**—Show the children a magnified picture of a louse, a horrible-looking creature that does terrible things.

4. **Swarms of Flies**—There are all kinds of winged creatures that we call "flies"—house flies, black flies, fruit flies, horse flies, flesh flies, etc. Most of them are tormentors that buzz and bite and carry diseases. You can show the children pictures of these various kinds of flies. Imagine swarms of them, from which there was no escape.

5. **A Deadly Disease**—Explain to the children that sometimes there is an outbreak of disease among farm animals, even in our day. Sometimes whole herds of cattle must be slaughtered—hundreds and thousands of animals—to check the disease. Not long ago there was the scare of "mad cow disease" in Britain. Perhaps you can find newspaper articles or magazine photographs about this event.

6. **An Outbreak of Boils**—Borrow a medical textbook or journal to show the children what a boil is. Let them see how awful these inflamed, festering sores on the skin can be.

7. **A Hammering of Hail**—You can find interesting entries about hailstones in encyclopedias, which show their size and shape, as well as tell fascinating facts. For example, the largest hailstone on record in the U.S.A. measured seventeen inches around and weighed one-and-a-half pounds. What a shame that no one weighed and measured the hailstones that fell in Egypt during the seventh plague. No doubt, those hailstones would hold the world record!

8. **An Invasion of Insects**—There are many interesting articles and photographs of locusts, but you must read to your children one fascinating account of such an invasion of insects. It is from a child's perspective, from the book *On the Banks of Plumb Creek* by Laura Ingalls Wilder. Read from the chapter entitled "Grasshoppers Walking," beginning "One day when Pa came in to dinner he said, 'The grasshoppers are hatching . . .'" (page 260). The children will love this true story from the 1800's of pioneer life in the U.S.A.

9. **A Dreadful Darkness**—A night picture, with a light shining from a window, would be useful for this lesson. The Egyptians had no such comforting sight during the plague of darkness.

10. **A Miracle at Midnight**—Photographs of grieving mourning people, who have lost loved ones, would be beneficial for this lesson. Also, your class

could study some articles about the deadly epidemics that have swept away millions of people, such as the bubonic plague or the black death. However, there has never been a plague like the one in Egypt, when only the first-born in each family was selected for death, while all Israel was spared. The LORD did this so that both Egypt and Israel—and the whole world—would know that this was not an ordinary plague, common to the natural diseases and disasters of man, but this was an awesome wonder, a miraculous judgement, executed by the God of all the earth to free His people from slavery.

MEMORY WORK

1. "O LORD, the hope of Israel, all who forsake You will be put to shame. Those who turn away from You will be written in the dust, because they have forsaken the LORD, the spring of living water" (Jeremiah 17:13).
2. "I will remember the deeds of the LORD; yes I will remember your miracles of long ago. I will meditate on all your works and consider all your mighty deeds" (Psalm 77:11, 12).
3. "Look to the LORD and His strength. Seek His face always   Remember the wonders He has done, His miracles, and the judgements He pronounced" (Psalm 105:4, 5).
4. "Whoever believes in the Son has eternal life, but whoever rejects the Son will not see life, for God's wrath remains on him" (John 3:36).
5. "Since we have been justified through faith, we have peace with God through our LORD Jesus Christ, through whom we have gained access by faith into this grace in which we now stand. And we rejoice in the hope of the glory of God" (Romans 5:1, 2).
5. "Heal me, O LORD, and I will be healed; save me and I will be saved, for you are the One I praise" (Jeremiah 17:14).
7. "He who dwells in the shelter of the Most High will rest in the shadow of the Almighty. I will say of the LORD, 'He is my refuge and my fortress, my God, in whom I trust" (Psalm 91:1, 2).
8. "Blessed is the man who always fears the LORD, but he who hardens his heart falls into trouble" (Proverbs 28:14).
9. Jesus said, "I am the light of the world. Whoever follows Me will never walk in darkness, but will have the light of life" (John 8:12).
10. "God demonstrates His own LOVE for us in this: While we were still sinners, Christ died for us. Since we have now been justified by His blood, how much more shall we be saved through His life" (Romans 5:8, 9).

CRAFT

Have your children make books of the ten plagues, to help them remember the deeds of the LORD. Have them illustrate each plague on a separate page. When I did this project with my classes, I had them draw each scene in plain pencil and then use a coloured pencil to accent the plague. For example, red was used for the first plague. Houses, pyramids, people, animals, etc. were all drawn in grey pencil, but the Nile River was coloured bright red, as were the ponds and pails, puddles and buckets, even bath-tubs. Next, green was used for the second plague. Once again, houses, pyramids, people, furniture, Pharaoh with his throne and his food and his bed, etc. were all drawn with plain pencil, but the frogs themselves were all coloured with bright green to emphasize that plague. Have the children sign their work, but you keep their pages until all ten drawings are completed. At the end, have the children illustrate a cover; then assemble the books for the children to take home. The finished projects are amazing. You will be surprised at how creative and artistic the children are and how much fun they have making these books. I was so impressed with their efforts, that I actually put their books on display for the whole church to admire.

REVIEW QUESTIONS

You can ask specific questions for each plague, but here are some general questions for all the plagues:

1. What command from God did Moses and Aaron bring to Pharaoh before this plague?
2. What was Pharaoh's response? What did he say? What did he do? What was happening to Pharaoh's heart?
3. How did God judge Egypt with this plague? How did this plague harm the country?
4. How did God show His mercy to Egypt during this plague?
5. How did God show His mercy to Israel during this plague?
6. Was some false "god" in Egypt destroyed by this plague?
7. Why did God display all these signs and wonders and miracles in Egypt? What great purpose did God have?

PRAYERS:

1. LORD, we thank you for many blessings, one of which is pure, clean, drinking water. It is a daily gift You give us, so simple, yet so vital. Thank

you for water for drinking, cooking, bathing, cleaning. Thank you for the lakes, rivers and ponds for boating, fishing and swimming. Most of all, we thank you for Jesus Christ, who is the spring of living water unto eternal life. Jesus said, "If anyone is thirsty, let him come to Me and drink" (John 7:37). LORD, may each child here believe in Jesus Christ, and so live forever.

2. LORD, we worship you because you have created and commanded all creatures. Even the frogs do your will. We thank you for this mighty miracle, which you performed so long ago—to the praise of your glorious name. O LORD, you are an awesome God! May we fear you and worship you, love you and obey you, all our days.

3. Our Father, we praise you for you are good and just; you are righteous and holy in all your judgements. Thank you for displaying your awesome deeds and strange wonders, so that all the world might know that you alone are God. Thank you for your Word, which informs us about the great things you have done. Help us to fear you and love you as we should. May we never harden our hearts against you, O LORD. Deliver us from evil, even this day.

4. LORD, you have provided a way for us to escape your wrath which is through faith in your Son, Jesus Christ. We thank you for Jesus and for the sacrifice of Himself on the cross for our sins, that we might have peace, mercy and forgiveness. Peace with God—for this gracious gift to us, to all who believe in the Son of God, we thank you, O LORD.

5. LORD, we thank you for protecting us from deadly diseases and for rescuing us from death itself. We thank you for the health and strength and life with which you have blessed us. We thank you for the faith and hope and peace we have in Jesus Christ.

6. O LORD, may our hearts now and forever be turned towards you in love and faith and hope. May our hearts be softened and opened to your Word. Deliver us, we pray, from the sins which so easily ensnares us. Deliver us especially from hardness of heart. We thank you for the Bible, which instructs us, and for your Spirit, who convicts us, that we might not sin against you.

7. LORD, we thank you for being our shelter and refuge in all the storms and trials of this life. May we never forget, LORD, that we must flee to you for protection and salvation.

8. LORD, God of Armies, we worship you because you create and command all beings. Sometimes you send forth an army of angels; at other times you send forth an army of insects. We love you, LORD, and praise you, for this awesome display of your power.

9. LORD, we thank you for giving this world the gift of light. We thank you for sunlight, moonlight and starlight. We thank you for dawn and dusk and the mysterious northern lights. We thank you for the light of flickering candles and blazing fires. We thank you for flashlights and searchlights and all kinds of electric lights from the tiniest twinkles to grandest shimmering chandeliers. LORD, they are all a comfort and delight for us.

10. LORD, we thank you for that great miracle at midnight, when you freed your people from the bondage of their slavery in Egypt. LORD, we thank you for the greatest miracle of all, for your Son shedding His blood and dying on the cross to save us from our bondage to sin and our slavery to Satan. We thank you for freeing us from sin and death, that we might love and serve you, that we might adore and worship you, all the days of our lives here on earth and forever in heaven. LORD, we praise your holy name for such grace and LOVE toward us.

PSALMS TO SING

105D; 91AC . . . also 2; 72C (11, 12); 77B; 78E; 98A; 105A; 135AB; 136AB (1–6); 148.

FIELD TRIP

People are "plagued" with all kinds of pests. It is not uncommon for us to experience annual "invasions" of insects. For example, where I live in Canada, the window screens hum . . . mmm loudly all night in the month of June, as millions of mosquitoes try to enter our rooms to take our blood. It's a terrible sound, but at least there are screens to keep this "plague" away from us! Sometimes there are unusual arrivals of insects. Once, when I was a small child, there was a "plague" of caterpillars. These pests dropped from the trees, covered the sidewalks, crawled on people. They were everywhere! If there is not some devastating plague you can show your children, perhaps you can observe one of the minor common varieties. Also, you can point out to the children ways that people try to protect themselves from such difficulties: We have screens on the windows, lightening rods on the roof, storm warnings on the radio, vaccinations for diseases, poisons and pesticides, etc.

(This student lesson starts on page 55.)

Do This In Remembrance of Me

Exodus 12:1–13:16

VISUAL AIDS

Show your children a "Jewish" calendar, which marks and names their months, both civil and sacred, differently than our calendars. Note also the special holidays, particularly Passover night and the week-long Feast of Unleavened Bread. Bring to your class photos of Jewish families celebrating the Passover meal. Buy a package of Passover Matzos for your class and also bring a fluffy role of leavened bread to compare with the flat piece of unleavened bread. You may also wish to bring a container of yeast. Let the children see it, touch it, taste it, smell it, and watch how the yeast works: Mix it with warm sweet water and it will froth and foam and ferment.

MEMORY WORK

"Christ our passover lamb has been sacrificed. Therefore, let us keep the [Feast,] not with the old yeast, the yeast of malice and wickedness, but with bread without yeast, the bread of sincerity and truth" (I Corinthians 5:7, 8).

CRAFT

Perhaps you could bake some rolls, one batch of dough made with yeast and the other batch made without yeast. Instruct the children: "Don't you know that a little yeast works through the whole batch of dough? Get rid of the old yeast, that you may be a new batch without yeast . . ." (I Corinthians 5:6, 7). We must get rid of even the smallest sins, for like a tiny grain of yeast, sin grows. It foams and froths inside our hearts and starts to affect our entire lives. We must be very careful to rid our lives of sin. A simpler craft might be to have the children make special Passover plates. Give each child a white paper plate to decorate with a gold rim, blue Jewish stars, etc. Do the children know what food would be put on their Passover plate?

REVIEW QUESTIONS

1. Could the Israelites ever forget the exodus? What three ceremonies did God give the Israelites to help them remember?
2. What must the Israelites do to celebrate the Passover?
3. God gave the Israelites the Passover ceremony so that they would remember and never forget their deliverance from Egypt. There was another very important reason why God gave them this ceremony   What was it?
4. Why is Jesus called our Passover Lamb?
5. We too must find refuge under the sprinkled blood of thePassover Lamb. How? How can we be safe? Where can we find shelter, so that death will pass over us?
6. Jesus changed the Passover meal into the Lord's Supper. What did He say about the bread? What did He say about the wine? What did He say we are to remember?
7. We were bought with a price. God redeemed us; He bought us back. What price did God pay for us?

PRAYER

LORD, we thank you for showing us so clearly the Lamb of God, who takes away the sin of the world. LORD, help us to believe in Jesus, our Passover Lamb. Help us to believe in the way of salvation, that you ordained for us from the beginning. LORD, help us to trust in the Lamb's sprinkled blood, to save us from sin and death. Oh LORD, let us never forget the night of our deliverance. Let us always remember what you did to deliver us from the slavery of our sins and the terror of death and the power of the devil: you sent your Son to die on the cross for us. His body was broken for us; His blood was poured out for us that death might pass over us, that we might live for ever and ever. Oh God, we thank you, for His death. Thank you for sending the Passover Lamb to us. Thank you for giving us life in Him.

PSALMS TO SING

116C & 118C ... as well as all the other Passover Songs: Psalms 113–118. It was one of these "hymns" that Jesus sang with the disciples at the Passover supper, the last song He sang before the cross. (See Mark 14:26.)

FIELD TRIP

If you could take your children to observe a Passover Seder at a Jewish home or elsewhere, this would be very educational for them. Also, it would be very instructive for them to observe the Lord's Supper in your church. (Children should always be part of the Lord's Supper, at least to observe it and ask questions about it.)

(This student lesson starts on page 90.)

Please turn the page for the guide to lesson 12.

God With Us
Day and Night

Exodus 13:17–22

VISUAL AIDS

Alas! There are no photographs of that amazing pillar of cloud that the Israelites saw in the day or pillar of fire that they saw in the night. Perhaps you could show the children a picture of the enormous mushroom-shaped cloud from an atom bomb. If a man-made cloud inspires such awe, we can only imagine the splendour of God's "appearance" to Israel.

MEMORY WORK

"The LORD will keep you from all harm. He will watch over your life. The LORD will watch over your coming and going both now and forevermore" (Psalm 121:7, 8).

CRAFT

The children could draw two pictures of Israel's camp, one a night scene on black paper and the other a day scene on white paper. Paint, pastels, gelpens and coloured pencils all work well on black construction paper.

REVIEW QUESTIONS

1. How many Israelite slaves marched out of Egypt as free people?
2. What did the Israelites take with them on their journey?
3. What did they eat at their first campsite?
4. Why did God not lead them straight to the Promised Land?
5. How did the Israelites know which way to go and where to camp?
6. How did God show the Israelites that He was with them?
7. How did the pillar of cloud help the Israelites during the day? How did the pillar of fire help them at night?

PRAYER

LORD, we thank you for the wonderful way you took care of the Israelites in the wilderness and we thank you for taking care of us too. Thank you for guiding us and guarding us and giving us everything that we need. LORD, help us to trust in you at all times and for all things.

PSALMS TO SING

121B & 139A . . . also 23ABCD; 91AC; 105E.

FIELD TRIP

Huddle around a campfire on a cold dark night and imagine how comforting it would be if a pillar of friendly fire was there to give you warmth and light, to scare away prowlers and predators, to shield and shelter you from winds and storms.

(This student lesson starts on page 100.)

Through the Red Sea... By Faith

Exodus 14:1–15:21

VISUAL AIDS

Show your class of children pictures of horses and chariots, especially those used in ancient Egypt. There are also interesting photos of the chariot wheels that archaeologists have found at the bottom of the Red Sea.

MEMORY WORK

"The LORD is my strength and my song. He has become my salvation. He is my God, and I will praise Him, my father's God, and I will exalt Him" (Exodus 15:2).

CRAFT

God's path led through the sea, though His footprints were not seen (Psalm 77:19). The LORD does not leave footprints, but people and animals do. In the sea bed that night, there were many millions of footprints left by the Israelites. There are several ways the children could make prints of their feet:

1. Ink the soles of their feet, as they do for newborn babies in a hospital; then have them stand on a white sheet of paper.
2. Photocopy their feet.
3. Have them make impressions of their feet in the sand. Then make plaster-of-paris molds of their footprints.

REVIEW QUESTIONS

1. How did God set a trap for Pharaoh and his soldiers?
2. Why did the Egyptians think it would be easy to capture their runaway slaves?
3. The Israelites appeared to be trapped, with the sea in front of them and their foes behind them. How did they rebel against God in this situation?

4. How did God protect His people from enemy attack throughout the night?
5. How did the LORD make a path for His people through the sea?
6. What must the Israelites do by faith?
7. How were the Israelites baptized into Moses?

PRAYER

LORD, you did gain glory for yourself by this miraculous deliverance of your people and we also praise you, exalt you and glorify you for parting the waters of the sea and saving all the children of Israel. But LORD, you have demonstrated your LOVE for us by an even greater deliverance; we thank you for saving us from the fires of hell through the death of your beloved Son, Jesus Christ. To Him be the glory forever and ever.

PSALMS TO SING

20AB; 66A; 77C; 106B . . . 46ABC; 57B; 74B; 76AB; 78B (4–7); 93A; 104A; 136A (1, 2,7, 8); 147A (1, 4,7).

FIELD TRIP

Horses and chariots have been out of style for quite a few centuries, so there is no longer anywhere to view a horse and chariot race. However, you could take the children to see for themselves what powerful creatures horses are. Fall fairs often have horse shows. In Canada you can view the Royal Canadian Mounted Police and, on Canada Day in the capital, you can watch the famous RCMP Musical Ride.

(This student lesson starts on page 104.)

Bitterness to Blessedness

Exodus 15:22–27

VISUAL AIDS

Make sure to follow Israel's route on a map. Photos of this desert region or any other harsh, dry, wasteland should be shown in contrast to an oasis, that is, a watered area with palm trees.

You could also bring two glasses of water: one with pure, clear, fresh water and the other with murky, muddy, smelly water. One brings life; the other brings death. Impress upon the children how blessed we are to have good drinking water.

MEMORY WORK

1. "I am the LORD, Who heals you" (Exodus 15:26).
2. "Praise the LORD, O my soul; all my inmost being, praise his holy name. Praise the LORD, O my soul, and forget not all His benefits—who forgives all your sins and heals all your diseases, who redeems your life from the pit and crowns you with LOVE and compassion, who satisfies your desires with good things, so that your youth is renewed like the eagle's" (Psalm 103:1–5).

CRAFT

Your children could make cards for a sick person, with a portion of God's Word to refresh and comfort them.

REVIEW QUESTIONS

1. After the Israelites left the Red Sea, through what sort of region did they travel?
2. What serious problem did they face in this desert region?

3. When the Israelites finally found water, they were very disappointed. Why? Did they handle their disappointment in a godly way? What should they have done instead of complaining and rebelling against God?
4. In this crisis, what did Moses do?
5. How did God answer Moses' prayer?
6. What great promise did God give to the Israelites there?
7. Where did God lead the Israelites next? Why was this new place a good place for the Israelites to camp?

PRAYER

Our loving heavenly Father, help us to always trust in you, no matter what difficulties we face. Forgive us when we fail. We thank you, LORD, for loving us and never failing us.

PSALMS TO SING

103A . . . also 6; 23ABCD; 30AB; 32C; 42A; 46ABC; 63B; 78EF; 107E.

FIELD TRIP

Rushing rivers, flowing streams, bubbling springs, gushing geysers—are all sources of refreshment from the LORD. Enjoy them. Thank God for them.

(This student lesson starts on page 110.)

The Bread of Angels

Exodus 16

VISUAL AIDS

Show the children pictures of quail, the kind of bird that God sent to the Israelites for meat. There are no pictures of manna, but it looked like flakes of white frost on the ground, and there are many beautiful photos of frost that you can show the children.

MEMORY WORK

Jesus said, "I tell you the truth: He who believes has everlasting life. I am the bread of life. Your forefathers ate the manna in the desert, yet they died. But here is the bread that comes down from heaven, which a man may eat and not die. I am the Living bread that came down from heaven. If anyone eats of this bread, he will live forever. This bread is my flesh, which I will give for the life of the world" (John 6:47–51).

CRAFT

Perhaps your children could make thin white wafers, sweetened with honey, flavoured with almonds, delicious and nutritious, like the manna cakes the Israelites made in the wilderness.

REVIEW QUESTIONS

1. God tested the Israelites. What was this third test? Did they pass the test?
2. The people were lying, complaining and unbelieving in the face of this trial. How should they have responded?
3. How did God provide meat for all those people? How did God provide bread for them?

4. What was this "bread" called? What did the word mean?
5. What directions did God give for the gathering of the manna?
6. What happened to the people who disobeyed God's commands?
7. Why is Jesus called the bread of life?

PRAYER

Our Father, who art in heaven . . . Give us this day our daily bread. LORD, help us trust you, that you will provide everything that we need. LORD, we thank you for all your blessings to us, for the food we eat each day and for the bread of life, even Jesus Christ, Who commanded us to believe in Him that we might live forever. LORD, we thank you for the eternal life that we have through faith in the Son of God.

PSALMS TO SING

78C (9–12) & 105E . . . also 22H; 34AC; 37ACD; 85B; 107A; 111A; 145C; 146AB.

FIELD TRIP

I remember visiting a large bread factory when I was a small child. I found the trip fascinating. If your community doesn't have a large factory, even a visit to a small bakery would be interesting for the children. This is the ordinary way in which God provides bread for people, but remind the children of the extraordinary way God provided bread for the Israelites in the wilderness. The manna was called "grain of heaven" and "bread of angels" (Psalm 78:24, 25). The manna was a daily miracle for God's people.

(This student lesson starts on page 113.)

The Lord Is My Rock

Exodus 17:1–7

VISUAL AIDS

Find photographs of the world's great rocks and the fortresses built upon them, such as the Rock of Gibraltar, which is the largest monolith in the world.

MEMORY WORK

1. "My soul finds rest in God alone. My salvation comes from Him. He alone is my rock and my salvation. He is my fortress; I will never be shaken" (Psalm 62:1, 2).
2. "Come; let us sing for joy to the LORD. Let us shout aloud to the Rock of our salvation" (Psalm 95:1).

CRAFT

In the Bible we are commanded to "shout aloud to the Rock of our salvation." To help the children do this, to magnify their voices, you could make simple megaphones by folding semi-circles of thin cardboard into cone-shaped speakers. The children can decorate these half-circles with bright colours or sparkles before you tape them into megaphones. What should they shout? Praise and thanks to the LORD! Be sure to tell the children that God hears us, even when we whisper, even when we speak to Him silently in our hearts.

REVIEW QUESTIONS

1. Moses led the Israelites into a mountainous region. What problem did the people face there? Was it a serious problem?
2. How should the people have faced this problem? What did they do instead? What did they say?

3. How was Moses almost killed in this crisis?
4. How did God provide water for the people?
5. Why did God lead them to a place without water?
6. How does a person receive the living water that Christ offers?
7. God demonstrated His LOVE for the Israelites by providing water for them in the wilderness. How has God demonstrated His great LOVE for us?

PRAYER

LORD, we thank you for providing for us, not only daily food and daily drink to keep us alive, but spiritual food and spiritual drink, that we might live forever. Thank you for Jesus Christ, the Rock of our salvation.

PSALMS TO SING

62A (1, 4,5) & 95C . . . also 18A (1); 31AE; 40ABE; 61 (1, 2); 62B (1, 2); 71A (1, 2); 78B; 92C; 95AB; 105E.

FIELD TRIP

One summer vacation, our family stayed at a beach house on the coast of Oregon. Three miles off-shore a mighty monolith rose out of the ocean, called Haystack Rock, supposedly the third largest rock in the world. We became fixated on this rock, watching it shrouded in the morning mist or sparkling in the noonday sun or backlit by the glowing sunset. We even awoke in the night and stared out at the rock in the moonlight. One day we took a fishing boat and toured all around the rock and discovered that it was covered with life. The low tide revealed hundreds of multi-coloured starfish clinging to its base and above the high-tide mark were the nests and the songs and the flights of thousands of sea birds. This was an amazing rock! One as spectacular as this would be hard to find, but I am sure every community has some enormous rock, on which you can climb and sit and eat a picnic lunch. Show the children some special rock in your area, perhaps even a rock with a spring of water flowing from it.

(This student lesson starts on page 120.)

The Lord Is My Banner

Exodus 17:8–16

VISUAL AIDS

For this lesson you will need pictures of the nations' flags. It is under these flags that the different countries march to war, or compete in the olympic games or stand at attention for their national anthem.

MEMORY WORK

"The LORD is my banner" (Exodus 17:15).

CRAFT

Have the children make colourful banners. "We will lift up our banners in the name of our God" (Psalm 20:5).

REVIEW QUESTIONS

1. What new crisis did the Israelites face?
2. Which Israelites did the Amalekites attack?
3. Who did Moses choose to lead Israel's army into war? What kind of man was he?
4. How did Moses fight?
5. Who won the war? Why?
6. What did Moses build after Israel's victory? What did he name this altar? Why?
7. The Bible says that the LORD "will raise a banner for the nations" (Isaiah 11:12). Who is the One who stands like a banner to rally the peoples to Himself?

PRAYER

LORD, we thank you for making Jesus Christ our banner, for lifting Him up on the cross and for drawing us to yourself through Him. May we always identify with the crucified Christ and may we always glorify the risen Saviour.

PSALMS TO SING

20AB; 54AB; 56 . . . also 3; 5AB; 7AB; 9A; 10AB; 13; 18; 27AD; 28AB; 31F; 35AB; 37B; 41B; 44A; 59AB; 60A (4, 5); 64A; 70ABC; 83ABC; 92ABC; 98A; 138AB; 142; 143B; 144AC; 149.

FIELD TRIP

Go for a walk and count the number of flags you find fluttering in the wind. Make a special trip to a place where flags fly from many different countries or regions. For example, at Parliament Hill in the capital city of Canada, you can see the flags of all the provinces, as well as the national, red-and-white, maple-leaf flag on the pinnacle of the parliament buildings. Moses said "The LORD is my banner!" God was the highly exalted banner, under whom Moses marched.

(This student lesson starts on page 124.)

The Voice of God

Exodus 19

VISUAL AIDS

There have been other mountains in the world that have blazed with fire and billowed with smoke; there have been other mountains that have had tremors and quakes. You could find pictures of some these active volcanos, such as the recent terrifying volcanic explosion of Mount Saint Helen's in U.S.A. What made Mount Sinai unique in all human history was the fact that this mountain was blazing and smoking and shaking, not because it was a volcano, but because the LORD descended upon it!

MEMORY WORK

"Today, if you hear His voice, do not harden your hearts . . . See to it that none of you has a sinful, unbelieving heart that turns away from the living God . . . See to it that you do not refuse Him who speaks" (Hebrews 3:15; 3:12; 12:25).

CRAFT

The children could draw/paint pictures of Mount Sinai on that day when the LORD descended upon it in bright flames of fire and black clouds of smoke.

REVIEW QUESTIONS

1. Three months after the Israelites left Egypt, they arrived at a very special place, where they would camp for almost a year. What was that place? Why was it special?
2. Why did God bring them to this isolated mountain? What were they going to do here?
3. At Mount Sinai God would make a covenant with Israel. What covenant promises did God make to Israel?

4. What covenant promise did the Israelites make to God?
5. On the morning of the third day, when God came to speak to Israel, what did the people see? What did the people hear?
6. How did the people experience the sound of God's Voice? Was it comforting, or was it terrifying?
7. What did God speak from Mount Sinai?

PRAYER

LORD, thank you for speaking to Israel, for causing them to hear the sound of your voice and to know the words of your Law. LORD, thank you for causing your Word to be written in the Bible for us, that we too may "hear" your voice and know your Law. Help us, LORD, to believe and obey your Holy Word. LORD, we thank you also for giving us voices and for hearing our voices, even if we speak to you in only a whisper. LORD, help us to use our voices to glorify you in everything that we say.

PSALMS TO SING

29AB & 68E . . . also 68B (5, 6); 97A; 104E.

FIELD TRIP

Today God "speaks" to us in our hearts and minds through the sacred Scriptures by His Holy Spirit. There is no mountain you can visit to hear with your ears the sound of the voice of God. However, the LORD's voice is described in the Bible and compared to sounds we have heard. It is "a loud voice, like a trumpet" (Revelation 1:10). God's voice is often compared to thunder: "Listen! Listen to the *roar* of His voice, to the rumbling that comes from His mouth. He unleashes His lightning beneath the whole heaven and sends it to the ends of the earth. After that comes the sound of His *roar*. He thunders with His majestic voice. When His voice resounds, he holds nothing back. God's voice thunders in marvellous ways" (Job 37:2–5). "The LORD thundered from heaven; the voice of the Most High resounded" (Psalm 18:13). God's voice is also likened to the sound of many waters: "His voice was like the sound of rushing waters" (Revelation 1:15). I love to sit beside rushing river rapids or roaring waterfalls or crashing ocean waves; I love to listen to the sound of many waters and think about the sound of the voice of the LORD. This is an experience you can share with your children.

(This student lesson starts on page 127.)

The Ten Commandments

Exodus 20:1–17

VISUAL AIDS

Jewish artifacts, such as tefillin, mezuzahs and a tallit, would be interesting for the children to see. (Ask a Jewish friend if you can borrow these things). Tefillin are the black leather boxes containing God's Word, which pious Jews bind to their foreheads and arms, in a literal obedience to God's instruction: "Fix these words on mine [God's Laws] in your hearts and minds; tie them as symbols on your hands and bind them on your foreheads" (Deuteronomy 6:8 & 11:18). Mezuzahs are little scrolls with Biblical passages on them housed in small cases of metal or wood, some of them elaborately carved. These are attached to the doorways of Jewish homes, because God instructed the Israelites: "Write [God's Commandments] on the doorframes of your houses and on your gates" (Deuteronomy 6:9 & 11:20). A Tallit is a Jewish prayer shawl with fringes (tzitzit) attached to the corners, to fulfil God's requirement: "You are to make tassels on the corners of your garments . . . You will have these tassels to look at and so you will remember all the commands of the LORD that you may obey them . . ." (Numbers 15:38, 39).

MEMORY WORK

1. The children should memorize the Ten Commandments.
2. "Love the LORD your God with all your heart and with all your soul and with all your mind. This is the first and greatest commandment. And the second is like it: Love your neighbour as yourself. All the Law and the Prophets hang on these two commandments" (Matthew 22:36–40).

CRAFT

For each of the Ten Commandments you could make a collage of newspaper clippings and magazine photos of people breaking that commandment. For example, for the sixth commandment, cut out the many reports of various and hideous murders, clue them to a cardboard backing, then in big red letters attach God's Law against this crime.

REVIEW QUESTIONS

1. Where did God speak to Israel the Ten Commandments?
2. What is the first [second, third, etc.] commandment and what does it mean?
3. Why must all people obey God's Law?
4. What did Jesus say was the first and foremost commandment?
5. What commandment is called "the royal law," which sums up the whole law?
6. If we love God, what will we do?
7. Can a person be saved by keeping God's Law? How then are people saved?
8. How does God's Law benefit us?
9. What do you think is the greatest benefit of God's Law to us?
10. What should be our response to God's Law?
11. Which command of God leads to eternal life?
12. Do you believe in the Lord Jesus, the Son of God?

PRAYER

O LORD, open our eyes that we may see the wonderful things in your Law. Turn our hearts to your commandments, that we may love them and keep them all our lives. Let us treasure your Word in our hearts, that we might not sin against you. O LORD, forgive us and preserve us, in your great LOVE. Thank you for the salvation that we have through faith in Jesus Christ.

PSALMS TO SING

19BD; 78A; 119M . . . also 1AB; 37E; 40E; 99C; 119.

FIELD TRIP

You can sometimes see the Ten Commandments ornately carved or stitched or drawn on plaques or banners or pictures, hanging in churches, courthouses or synagogues. The ones in synagogues are particularly interesting, because the "Ten Words" are written in Hebrew letters. Perhaps you could ask a local rabbi if your children might see the Ten Commandments, wherever they are written in his synagogue.

(This student lesson starts on page 132.)

Worship the Lord Your God

Exodus 20, 23

VISUAL AIDS

You can show the children pictures of people worshipping other gods and bowing down to idols.

MEMORY WORK

"Worship the LORD your God and serve Him only" (Matthew 4:10).

CRAFT

Show the children examples of ornate lettering from medieval texts. Now they can try it, working together on a large mural for your classroom or on their own on individual sheets of paper. Use the memory work verse as the text for their decorative endeavour.

REVIEW QUESTIONS

1. Why did God terrify the Israelites with the sound of His voice?
2. The Israelites heard God's voice, but saw no form. They must not make anything in the form of God; they must not make any idol in the form of anything. However, the Israelites must make something for worshipping the LORD. What was it? How was it used in the worship?
3. What did God promise the people He would do, if they worshipped the LORD according to His commands?
4. Whom did God promise to send ahead of the Israelites, to guard them on the way and bring them into the Promised Land?
5. The Promised Land was a good land, flowing with milk and honey, but there were ugly and evil things filling that land. What were they?

6. What must the Israelites do with the idols in the land?

7. Why is it important that we worship the LORD?

PRAYER

LORD, help us to love you and praise you, worship you and obey you, magnify you and glorify you—always! Blessed be the name of the LORD forever and ever!

PSALMS TO SING

34A; 138AB (1) . . . also 29AB (1); 31G; 33C (9, 10); 66A (1–3, 7); 66C (1); 81B; 85B; 95A; 95B (5, 6); 95C (1–3); 96AB; 99C; 115AC; 118C (17); 135C.

FIELD TRIP

As you walk or drive through city streets, point out places of worship. In some of these places the LORD is worshipped; in some of the places false gods and idols are worshipped.

(This student lesson starts on page 139.)

The Blood
of the Covenant

Exodus 24

VISUAL AIDS

The leaders of Israel saw under God's feet "something like a pavement made of sapphire, clear as the sky itself" (Exodus 24:10). We also read that "a rainbow, resembling an emerald" encircles God's throne in heaven (Revelation 4:3). These are human attempts to describe the divine glory. Show the children pictures (or samples) of these jewels.

MEMORY WORK

1. Jesus said, "This is My blood of the covenant, poured out for many for the forgiveness of sins" (Matthew 26:28).
2. "God demonstrates His own LOVE for us in this: While we were still sinners, Christ died for us. Since we have now been justified by His blood, how much more shall we be saved from God's wrath through Him" (Romans 5:8, 9).

CRAFT

Have your children ever made "splatter pictures"? For each child you will need a sheet of white construction paper, a cardboard cross that fits inside the paper, red paint and an old toothbrush. Put rolled tape on the back of the cross and fix it on the paper so it does not move. Then dip the brush in the red paint and, rubbing your thumb across the bristles, splatter or sprinkle spots of paint all over the page. When the paint is dry, remove the cross. Add the memory work to the bottom of the page.

REVIEW QUESTIONS

1. What did Moses build at the foot of the mountain? Why?
2. What did Moses sprinkle with the blood of the sacrifice? Why?
3. What did Moses read to the people?
4. What is a covenant? What promise did the people make three times? What promise did God make? How were these promises sealed?
5. What did the blood of these animal sacrifices in the Old Covenant foreshadow in the future, in the New Covenant?
6. How are we cleansed from our sins?
7. What did the leaders of Israel see on the mountain?

PRAYERS

O LORD, we thank you for the blood of Jesus, poured out for us for the forgiveness of our sins. Thank you that in Him we have eternal life. LORD, we look forward to the day when we will stand in your majestic presence and behold your radiant glory. LORD, keep our faith firm until the end.

PSALMS TO SING

51AD; 113A (1–3) . . . also 72D; 89D; 96A; 99C; 104E; 105A; 108A; 145A.

FIELD TRIP

Where can the children behold the glory of the LORD? "The heavens declare the glory of God" (Psalm 19:1); His glory is exalted above the heavens (Psalm 113:4)! More glorious than the most glorious sunset or sunrise sky, more glorious than a night sky glowing with the moon, twinkling with the stars and pulsating with northern lights is the glory of the LORD. We catch only a glimmer of it in the glorious things that He has made.

(This student lesson starts on page 144.)

Moses On the Mountain

Exodus 24:12–18

VISUAL AIDS

An architectural blueprint would be interesting for the children to see, especially if they could also view the actual building constructed from that pattern. On the mountain Moses was given the pattern for the God's Tabernacle.

MEMORY WORK

"The time is coming, declares the LORD, when I will make a new covenant with the house of Israel . . . I will put my laws in their minds and write them on their hearts. I will be their God and they will be my people" (Jeremiah 31:31, 33).

CRAFT

At that time in the Old Covenant, the Law was written on tablets of stone by the finger of God. Our fingers cannot write in stone, unless we have a hard tool to carve the letters. For this lesson the children could try "rock-writing." You will need a stone and a nail for each child to write/scratch/carve his/her names into a rock. You can also put ink into the scratches to make the writing more visible and legible. Their names written in rock will last longer than their names written on paper.

REVIEW QUESTIONS

1. What two ways did God give His Law to Israel?
2. The laws of men are sometimes good, sometimes bad. How would you describe God's Law?
3. Where did Moses receive the two stone tablets?

4. How long was Moses on the mountain? What did he eat and drink during that time? How then did he stay alive?
5. What else did God give to Moses during that time on the mountain, besides the Ten Commandments written in stone?
6. Why was God's tabernacle called the "Tent of Meeting"?
7. God showed His LOVE for Israel by living in a tent among them, but thousands of years later there was a greater demonstration of God's LOVE? What was it? How did God draw even closer to His people?

PRAYER

Lord Jesus, eternal Son of God, we thank you for humbling yourself by becoming a man and dying on the cross to save us from our sins and to bring us close to God. We praise you for your great LOVE for us. Help us to live faithful lives in obedience to your commands.

PSALMS TO SING

27BE; 84AB . . . also 15; 65A; 96A; 100ABC; 134AB.

FIELD TRIP

If you walk with your children through any graveyard, you will see many tablets of hard stone—marble and granite—all inscribed, not by the finger of God, but by the tools of men. Have the children try to "write" on the stones with just their fingers. Of course, it can't be done. Only the finger of God can write on tablets of stone.

(This student lesson starts on page 147.)

Israel Makes An Idol

Exodus 32:1–10

VISUAL AIDS

Show the children pictures of idols, both modern and ancient, from all around the world. People actually worship these false gods. There is no picture to show the children of the one true God.

MEMORY WORK

"Dear children, keep yourselves from idols" (I John 5:21).

CRAFT

Sorry! I can't think of one.

REVIEW QUESTIONS

1. How had God demonstrated to Israel that He was with them and that He loved them?
2. How had God and Moses impressed upon Israel the Ten Commandments?
3. The Israelites exchanged the truth of God for a lie. They exchanged the glory of God for—what?
4. Although it would have been evil anywhere, why was it particularly wicked that the Israelites engaged in idolatry at the foot of this mountain?
5. How did Aaron participate in this sin? What could Aaron have done to try and stop this evil rebellion against the LORD?
6. Which of the Ten Commandments did the Israelites break?
7. God saw and heard what the people were doing. How did God respond? What did He threaten to do to Israel?

PRAYER

LORD, have mercy upon us! Please, keep us from idols. Spare us from anything that would come before you. Teach us to worship you in spirit and in truth. Help us to love you more than anything, more than anyone. LORD, thank you for guarding our hearts and our minds in Christ Jesus.

PSALMS TO SING

115C; 135C . . . also 16AB; 31E; 44C; 86A; 96A; 97ABC; 106C (11–13, 15–17).

FIELD TRIP

Is it wrong to view an idol or to visit a place of idolatry? When I was in Japan, I saw people bowing down and praying to statues of Buddha in the many temples and shrines throughout the country. It broke my heart that these people were so lost and utterly without hope in the world. They had a false hope in a false god . . . and it was sorrowful to see.

(This student lesson starts on page 151.)

Preserved By the Power of Prayer

Exodus 32:10–35

VISUAL AIDS

Show the children photographs of people earnestly praying.

MEMORY WORK

"The prayer of a righteous man is powerful and effective" (James 5:16).

"Be joyful always; pray continually; give thanks in all circumstances, for this is God's will for you in Christ Jesus" (I Thessalonians 5:16–18).

"Christ Jesus, who died—more than that, who was raised to life—is at the right hand of God and is also interceding for us" (Romans 8:34).

CRAFT

The children could make prayer calendars or prayer booklets (blank pages with attractive covers), where they can list certain needs for prayer. Remind the children to write in the date when each prayer was answered.

REVIEW QUESTIONS

1. Why did God's anger burn against Israel?
2. God said to Moses, "Let Me alone, so that I may destroy them." Did Moses leave God alone? What did Moses do?
3. What three appeals did Moses make to God to save Israel?
4. How was Israel preserved?
5. What does this account teach us about God? What does this account teach us about prayer?

6. We have an advocate greater than Moses, who intercedes for us   Who is the One who ever lives and prays for us?
7. How do you feel, knowing that Jesus Christ is praying for you?

PRAYER

LORD, we thank you that we may talk to you at any time, that we may bring all our cares and concerns to you. Thank you for listening to us and answering us. LORD, help us to be fervent and constant in prayer.

PSALMS TO SING

86A; 130AB . . . also 4AB; 5AB (1); 6; 17B (5–7); 20AB; 27BE; 28AB; 32AC; 34AC; 38D; 39B; 54AB; 55AC (1); 61; 65A; 66B (12–14); 69C (11, 12); 77A; 88A (1); 102A (1); 116A; 118A; 141A; 142; 143ABC; 145C (10–13).

FIELD TRIP

You don't have to go on an excursion anywhere to pray to God, although you may choose to withdraw to a quiet place to pray, as Jesus did. You may wish to take your children to a hillside or a garden or a forest and there pray together to God. My first prayer of faith was when I was all alone in an orchard in the Netherlands. A lonely place is a good place to be with God, because there are no distractions or interruptions.

(This student lesson starts on page 156.)

Seven Sorrows From Israel's Sin

Exodus 32:15–35

VISUAL AIDS

Many are the sorrows in this world because of man's sin. There are wars, famines, massacres, epidemics—often a result of sin. Show the children some of the sorrowful sights that are a direct result of man's breaking God's Laws.

MEMORY WORK

"Many are the woes of the wicked, but the LORD's unfailing LOVE surrounds the man who trusts in Him" (Psalm 32:10).

CRAFT

Have each of the children make two masks: one joyful and one woeful (similar to the drama masks for comedy and tragedy). These can be cut very simply out of paper plates or cardboard and then decorated. The children have a choice: a life filled with the joy of the LORD or a life filled with the many woes of sin. You could display these masks on your classroom wall, the sad faces under the heading: "MANY ARE THE WOES OF THE WICKED," the glad faces under the rest of their memory-work verse: "THE LORD'S UNFAILING LOVE SURROUNDS THE MAN WHO TRUSTS IN HIM."

REVIEW QUESTIONS

What were the seven sorrows that resulted from Israel's sin?

1. Why were the stone tablets that Moses smashed so valuable?
2. What did Moses do to the golden "god" that Israel worshipped?
3. What did Aaron do and say that disgraced himself?
4. How were the leaders of the rebellion put to death?

5. Who were blotted out of God's Book of Life?
6. How did the hand of God execute the rebels, who escaped execution by the hands of men?
7. What caused the people to mourn and grieve over their sin?

PRAYER

LORD, help us to live righteous lives, that we may be spared from the many sorrows that sin brings. LORD, help us not to stumble; forgive us when we fall. LORD, deliver us, we pray, from every harm and every sin, for the sake of your Son Jesus Christ. LORD, we thank you for your LOVE and mercy and compassion toward us. May we ever love you and praise you for your Grace.

PSALMS TO SING

1AB; 104E . . . also 5AB; 6; 7AB; 9AB; 16AB; 28AB; 34BD; 36B; 37ABCDEF; 94B (8); 97ABC; 99C; 101; 145C (10–13).

FIELD TRIP

People also have laws that, if broken, are punished. Drive by a prison and show the children how we punish criminals who break our nation's laws. They lose their freedom. They must live behind bars and walls for many years. In some countries, they may even lose their lives. Our actions have consequences, even in this life.

(This student lesson starts on page 160.)

All God's Goodness

Exodus 33, 34

VISUAL AIDS

Do the children know what a "cleft" in a rock is? Show them pictures of cracks and crevices in rocks, some large enough for a man to stand or hide inside them. Mountain climbers sometimes find shelter in cave-like clefts on their expeditions. Also, show the children a dark veil or make a simple one for each child, and let them wear it. It hides the face, but one can still see through it! In some cultures women are forced to wear veils to hide their beauty. You could also show the children photos of the world's veiled women.

MEMORY WORK

"The LORD, the LORD, the compassionate and gracious God, slow to anger, abounding in LOVE and faithfulness, maintaining LOVE to thousands, and forgiving wickedness, rebellion and sin. Yet He does not leave the guilty unpunished" (Exodus 34:6, 7).

CRAFT

Moses put a veil over his face, so the Israelites would not see the fading glory. In some cultures (e.g., Japan) fans were used to hide the face, and fans are an easy craft project for the children to make. Have them draw or paint on sheets of paper, add a Bible verse in black letters, then fold the paper into fans.

REVIEW QUESTIONS

1. Moses pitched a tent outside the camp where he could meet with God. What did he call this tent? What did he do in this tent? When he was in this tent,

what did the people do? How did they know that God really was meeting with Moses?

2. Moses did not communicate with God the way we do. What was amazing about the way Moses talked with God?

3. Why did Moses urgently want to speak with God this time? Why was Moses grieving? Why were the Israelites grieving?

4. What was Moses' request in prayer? What was God's answer?

5. Moses said to God, "Now show me Your glory." What was God's answer?

6. Why did Moses put a veil over his face?

7. What seven ways was God good to Israel, even after their sin of idolatry?

PRAYER

O God, forgive our sin and forsake us not. LORD, we too wish to behold your glory and see you face to face. Help us to overcome the unbelief that is within us and all around us; help us to live by faith, trusting in you and believing your Word—now and until the end of our lives, that we may be with you forever in heaven. We ask this in the Name of our Saviour, Jesus Christ, through whom we have access to you by believing in Him. We know we must believe in Jesus to have eternal life.

PSALMS TO SING

1. *God's face*—89D . . . also 4B; 11 (6); 17C (13); 27E; 31C (11); 67A; 80B (1, 2); 84B; 105A; 119R; 143C.

2. *god's goodness*—100ABC . . . also 25ABC; 34AC; 118A (1); 107A; 109B (9); 136AB (1, 2).

3. *God's love, mercy & compassion*—86A; 103A; 108A; 145B . . . also 25ABC; 31D; 32D; 40CDF; 42C (1, 4,5); 44CF; 51AD (1); 52B (3); 55C; 57B; 69C (11, 12); 77B; 86B; 106A; 111A; 115C (1); 117A; 118A; 119F (1); 119J (3); 135ABC (1); 136A (1, 2).

FIELD TRIP

Do you know where there is a cleft in a rock, large enough for a child to stand inside it? You could visit such a place. I remember as a child hiking with my parents along a rocky ridge which was filled with large cracks and crevices. A child could hide in a vertical crack, but he/she could fall into a horizontal one, so we had to be very careful. I found this place of frightening fissures fascinating and remember it to this day. Many years later on a family vacation, I took my own children to Arches National Park in Utah, U.S.A., where they found shelter from the hot sun in the red sandstone formations of this famous place. There were all kinds of caves and clefts, arches and bridges, holes and hollows and hiding places—all naturally formed in the rocks. Remember that God put Moses in a cleft in the rock and covered him with His hand, when He caused all His goodness to pass in front of Moses.

(This student lesson starts on page 166.)

Please turn the page for the guide to lesson 27.

The Surpassing Glory

II Corinthians 3:7–18

VISUAL AIDS

In this lesson we are dealing with the *superlative* ministry of Christ. The dictionary defines superlative as "the highest degree of excellence," that which is "superior to all others." It is important that the children understand this type of comparison. They must grasp the difference, not between good and bad, but between good, better and best. The Old Covenant was good, but the New Covenant is better. Moses was a good prophet (indeed, a great prophet), but Jesus is the One who is better and greater than Moses. Jesus Christ is the superlative Man, the One who is superior to all others. This idea can be easily demonstrated: Show the children a perfect apple, one that is round and rosy, firm and shiny, one that is without any spot or bruise or blemish. This is a good apple, but it is possible to show them a better apple, a superlative apple, one that is breath-takingly beautiful, one that is bigger, rounder and redder, one that has the highest degree of excellence!

MEMORY WORK

"We, who with unveiled faces all reflect the Lord's glory, are being transformed into His likeness with ever-increasing glory, which comes from the Lord, who is the Spirit" (II Corinthians 3:18).

CRAFT

Have each child draw a good-better-best picture. Divide a sheet of drawing paper into three equal vertical sections. Then have the children draw the same thing three times, each time trying to improve on their original good drawing.

REVIEW QUESTIONS

1. Although the Israelites heard the Voice of God speak to them the Ten Commandments and although they promised to obey them, very quickly they broke God's Holy Law. What does this show us about the human heart? What does this show us about the Old Covenant?
2. If the Law of God could not make anyone perfect, what then was the real purpose of the Law?
3. In the Old Covenant God wrote His Law on tablets of stone   Where would God write His Law in the New Covenant?
4. Tell three ways in which Jesus is a superior high priest.
5. Explain how Jesus was a superior prophet to Moses.
6. How do we know that the sacrifices of the Old Covenant were insufficient? How was Jesus' sacrifice of Himself superior in every way?
7. What must we do to be saved?

PRAYER

Our heavenly Father, we thank you for the surpassing glory of the New Covenant and for the excellency and supremacy of Jesus Christ, through whose sacrifice on the cross we can be made perfect forever. We thank you and praise you for your LOVE, in giving us so great a salvation!

PSALM TO SING

57B; 113A (1–3) . . . also 29A (1); 66A (1–3); 72CD; 96A; 108A; 111A; 145AB; 150AB.

FIELD TRIP

Where can you see God's surpassing glory? The Bible says: "The heavens declare the glory of God" (Psalm 19:1) and "His glory is above the heavens" (Psalm 113:4). Take your children to see the most glorious display of heavenly splendour and then tell them that God's glory far surpasses anything we can see on earth.

(This student lesson starts on page 172.)

The Tabernacle

Exodus 25–40

VISUAL AIDS

Reference books such as *The World Book Encyclopedia* have drawings of the Tabernacle, which you could show your children. Also, you could bring samples of the materials used to make the Tabernacle. You probably have articles of fine linen or shiny brass, but you may have difficulty finding the hide of a sea cow!

MEMORY WORK

God promised: "I will make a covenant of peace with them; it will be an everlasting covenant. I will establish them and increase their numbers, and I will put My sanctuary among them forever. My dwelling place [Tabernacle] will be with them. I will be their God and they will be My people. Then the nations will know that I the LORD make Israel holy, when My sanctuary is among them forever" (Ezekiel 37:26–28).

"You are no longer foreigners and aliens, but fellow citizens with God's people and members of God's household, built on the foundation of the apostles and prophets, with Christ Jesus Himself as the chief cornerstone. In Him the whole building is joined together and rises to become a holy temple in the Lord. And in Him you too are being built together to become a dwelling in which God lives by His Spirit"

(Ephesians 2:19–22).

CRAFT

It would be a great project for the children to make a model of the Tabernacle. However, if you would prefer a less ambitious undertaking, each child could make for him/herself a high priest's breastpiece. (Bring pictures of the twelve different gemstones, so the children can colour their "stones" appropriately).

REVIEW QUESTIONS

1. What did Moses bring back from Mount Sinai?
2. What holy work did God permit His people to do for Him? When did they do this work?
3. Where in the desert could they find all the valuable materials from which God commanded them to make the Tabernacle?
4. Name the different things that had to be made and the different work that had to be done.
5. Describe how God's Tabernacle was durable. Describe how it was beautiful. Describe how it was spiritual.
6. Name the three sections of the Tabernacle and what was done in each place.
7. How did the Old Testament Tabernacle foreshadow a greater Tabernacle in the New Testament?

PRAYER

Heavenly Father, we thank you for your LOVE by choosing to dwell among us and within us. Help us to live holy lives, remembering that our bodies are the temple of your Spirit.

PSALMS TO SING

27ABDE; 65A; 84ABC; 100ABC; 134AB . . . also 5AB; 15; 20AB; 23ABCD; 24AB; 26B; 42A; 43; 46ABC; 48B; 63B (1); 66C; 76B; 96AB; 116C; 122AB; 138AB; 150AB.

The psalms are filled with references to God's dwelling place on earth—His tabernacle, His Temple, His tent, the courts and gates of His house, His sanctuary, the most holy place, etc. The psalms show us a faithful Israelite's attitude towards God's Tabernacle. It was the place where they worshipped the LORD with awe and joy, with thanks and praise! "O LORD . . . I, by Your great mercy, will come into your house; in reverence will I bow down toward your holy temple" (Psalm 5:7). "I love the house where you live, O LORD, the place where your glory dwells" (Psalm 26:8). "One thing I ask of the LORD; this is what I seek: that I may dwell in the house of the LORD all the days of my life, to gaze upon the beauty of the LORD and to seek Him in His temple. For in the day of trouble He will keep me safe in His dwelling; He will hide me in the shelter of His tabernacle and set me high upon a rock. Then my head will be exalted above the enemies who surround me. At His tabernacle will I sacrifice with shouts of joy. I will sing and make music to the LORD" (Psalm 27:4–6). "O

God . . . send forth Your light and Your truth. Let them guide me; let them bring me to your holy mountain, to the place where you dwell. Then will I go to the altar of God, to God, my joy and my delight . . ." (Psalm 43:3, 4). "Within your temple, O God, we meditate on your unfailing LOVE" (Psalm 48:9). "O God, you are my God. Earnestly I seek you. My soul thirsts for you; my body longs for you . . . I have seen you in the sanctuary and beheld your power and your glory. Because your LOVE is better than life, my lips will glorify you. I will praise you as long as I live, and in your name I will lift up my hands" (Psalm 63:1–4). "Blessed are those you choose and bring near to live in your courts! We are filled with the good things of your house, of your holy temple" (Psalm 65:4). "How lovely is your dwelling place, O LORD Almighty! My soul yearns, even faints, for the courts of the LORD. My heart and my flesh cry out for the living God . . . Blessed are those who dwell in your house. They are ever praising you" (Psalm 84:1–4). "Worship the LORD with gladness; come before Him with joyful songs . . . Enter His gates with thanksgiving and His courts with praise. Give thanks to Him and praise His name. For the LORD is good and His LOVE endures forever. His faithfulness continues through all generations" (Psalm 100:2, 4,5). "I rejoiced with those who said to me, 'Let us go to the house of the LORD' " (Psalm 122:1). "Praise the LORD, all you servants of the LORD, who minister by night in the house of the LORD. Lift up your hands in the sanctuary and praise the LORD" (Psalm 134:1, 2). "I will praise you, O LORD, with all my heart . . . I will bow down toward your holy temple and will praise your Name for Your LOVE and your faithfulness" (Psalm 138:1, 2). "Praise the LORD, Praise God in His sanctuary . . ." (Psalm 150:1).

FIELD TRIP

Although God in this age is building His temple with living stones, with the people who believe in the Lord Jesus Christ, still men continue to construct magnificent cathedrals and temples to worship God. You could visit some of these beautiful buildings. Also, many skilled craftsmen and women were needed to make God's tabernacle in the wilderness. Perhaps you could watch some skilled people work at their crafts.

(This student lesson starts on page 178.)